The American Pageant

Twelfth Edition

Guidebook

A Manual for Students
Volume II: Since 1865

Mel Piehl

Valparaiso University

Houghton Mifflin Company   Boston   New York

Sponsoring Editor: Colleen Shanley Kyle
Senior Manufacturing Coordinator: Marie Barnes
Senior Marketing Manager: Sandra McGuire
Editorial Associate: Michael Kerns

Copyright © 2002 by Houghton Mifflin Company. All rights reserved.

No part of this work may be reproduced or transmitted in any form or by any means, electronic or mechanical, including photocopying and recording, or by any information storage or retrieval system without the prior written permission of Houghton Mifflin Company unless such copying is expressly permitted by federal copyright law. Address inquiries to College Permissions, Houghton Mifflin Company, 222 Berkeley Street, Boston, MA 02116-3764.

Printed in the U.S.A.

ISBN: 0-618-10357-0

6789-VGI-07 06 05

Contents

	To the Student v	
22.	The Ordeal of Reconstruction, 1865–1877	217
23.	Politics in the Gilded Age, 1869–1896	227
24.	Industry Comes of Age, 1865–1900	237
25.	America Moves to the City, 1865–1900	247
26.	The Great West and the Agricultural Revolution, 1865–1896	257
27.	The Path of Empire, 1890–1899	267
28.	America on the World Stage, 1899–1909	277
29.	Progressivism and the Republican Roosevelt, 1901–1912	285
30.	Wilsonian Progressivism at Home and Abroad, 1912–1916	295
31.	The War to End War, 1917–1918	305
32.	American Life in the "Roaring Twenties," 1919–1929	315
33.	The Politics of Boom and Bust, 1920–1932	325
34.	The Great Depression and the New Deal, 1933–1938	333
35.	Franklin D. Roosevelt and the Shadow of War, 1933–1941	343
36.	America in World War II, 1941–1945	353
37.	The Cold War Begins, 1945–1952	363
38.	The Eisenhower Era, 1952–1960	373
39.	The Stormy Sixties, 1960–1968	383
40.	The Stalemated Seventies, 1968–1980	393
41.	The Resurgence of Conservatism, 1981–1992	403
42.	The American People Face a New Century	413
	Answers to Chapters 22–42 A 1	

To the Student

This revised *Guidebook* is intended to assist you in comprehending American history as presented in *The American Pageant*, Twelfth Edition, by David M. Kennedy, Lizabeth Cohen, and Thomas A. Bailey,. The *Guidebook* focuses attention on the central themes and major historical developments of each chapter while presenting a variety of exercises and other material designed to reinforce your comprehension of the text. Factual knowledge of history is important, and some of the exercises will help you to review facts and recall their significance. But the *Guidebook* attempts to demonstrate that facts are best learned when they are understood in relation to key historical events and issues.

The forty-two chapters of the *Guidebook* correspond with those of *The American Pageant* and are best used in close association with the text. Each chapter of the *Guidebook* contains the same sequence of material and exercises, except for the Map Discrimination section, which is omitted from some chapters.

The **Checklist of Learning Objectives** in Part I ("Reviewing the Chapter") of each *Guidebook* chapter provides a summary of the essential chapter themes and underscores the major historical developments to be learned. The **Glossary** defines basic social-science terms and shows their usage in the text. Learning this vocabulary will not only reinforce your understanding of *The American Pageant* but also familiarize you with terms often encountered in the study of politics, economics, geography, military science, and law, as well as history.

The various exercises in Part II ("Checking Your Progress") will assist in your careful reading of the text as well as foster your comprehension and spotlight the essential facts and concepts. **True-False**, **Multiple Choice**, and **Identification** exercises stress reading for understanding of important ideas and terms. **Matching People, Places, and Events** checks your knowledge of key historical figures, locations, and events. **Putting Things in Order** (which is specifically tied to the Chronology section at the end of each chapter of *The American Pageant*) and **Matching Cause and Effect** develop two essential principles of historical understanding: chronological sequence, and the causal relation between events. **Developing Historical Skills** is designed to hone your ability to use the diverse techniques employed in the study of history, including the interpretation of charts, maps, and visual evidence. **Map Mastery** includes Map Discrimination—specific questions focused on map reading—and Map Challenge, which asks you to use maps to discuss a historical issue or problem in a brief essay.

Completion of the exercises in Part II should enable you to handle successfully the crucial questions in Part III ("Applying What You Have Learned"). Your instructor may suggest that you use these questions as guides to study and review or may assign them as essay questions to be answered following your reading of the chapter. The last question is an especially challenging one that often draws on earlier chapters of *The American Pageant* and asks you to make historical comparisons, draw conclusions, or consider broad historical issues.

You and your instructor hence may utilize the *Guidebook* in a variety of ways, to suit a variety of needs. It can be used for class preparation and assignments, for guidance in your reading of the text, or for independent review of course contents. The answers to all the exercises, except for the questions in Part III, may be found in the back of this *Guidebook* or by your careful rereading of the pertinent sections of *The American Pageant*. May your exploration of American history be stimulating and enriching.

M. P.

Name_____ Section_____ _____ Date_____

22

The Ordeal of Reconstruction, 1865–1877

PART I: Reviewing the Chapter

A. Checklist of Learning Objectives

After mastering this chapter, you should be able to

1. define the major problems facing the South and the nation after the Civil War.
2. describe the responses of both whites and African-Americans to the end of slavery.
3. analyze the differences between the presidential and congressional approaches to Reconstruction.
4. explain how the blunders of President Johnson and the white South opened the door to more radical congressional Reconstruction policies.
5. describe the actual effects of congressional Reconstruction in the South.
6. indicate how militant white opposition gradually undermined the Republican attempt to empower Southern blacks.
7. explain why the radical Republicans impeached Johnson but failed to convict him.
8. explain the legacy of Reconstruction, and assess its successes and failures.

B. Glossary

To build your social science vocabulary, familiarize yourself with the following terms.

1. **treason** The crime of betrayal of one's country, involving some overt act violating an oath of allegiance or providing illegal aid to a foreign state. In the United States, treason is the only crime specified in the Constitution. "What should be done with the captured Confederate ringleaders, all of whom were liable to charges of treason?" (p. 477)
2. **civil disabilities** Legally imposed restrictions of a person's civil rights or liberties. "But Congress did not remove all remaining civil disabilities until thirty years later. . . ." (p. 478)
3. **legalistically** In accord with the exact letter of the law, sometimes with the intention of thwarting its broad intent. "Some planters resisted emancipation more legalistically. . . ." (p. 479)
4. **mutual aid societies** Nonprofit organizations designed to provide their members with financial and social benefits, often including medical aid, life insurance, funeral costs, and disaster relief. "These churches . . . gave rise to other benevolent, fraternal, and mutual aid societies." (p. 480)
5. **confiscation (confiscated)** Legal government seizure of private property without compensation. ". . . the bureau was authorized to settle former slaves on forty-acre tracts confiscated from the Confederates. . . ." (p. 481)
6. **pocket veto** The presidential act of blocking a Congressionally passed law not by direct veto but by simply refusing to sign it at the end of a session. (A president can pocket-veto a bill within ten days of a session's end or after.) "Lincoln 'pocket-vetoed' this bill by refusing to sign it after Congress had adjourned." (p. 483)
7. **lease** To enter into a contract by which one party gives another use of land, buildings, or other property for a fixed time and fee. ". . . some [codes] even barred blacks from renting or leasing land." (p. 484)

8. **chain gang** A group of prisoners chained together while engaged in forced labor. "A black could be punished for 'idleness' by being sentenced to work on a chain gang." (p. 484)
9. **sharecrop** An agricultural system in which a tenant receives land, tools, and seed on credit and pledges in return a share of the crop to the creditor. "... former slaves slipped into the status of sharecropper farmers...." (p. 484)
10. **peonage** A system in which debtors are held in servitude, to labor for their creditors. "Luckless sharecroppers gradually sank into a morass of virtual peonage...." (p. 484)
11. **scalawag** A white Southerner who supported Republican Reconstruction after the Civil War. "The so-called scalawags were Southerners, often former Unionists and Whigs." (p. 492)
12. **carpetbagger** A Northern politician who came south to exploit the unsettled conditions after the Civil War; hence, any politician who relocates for political advantage. "The carpet-baggers, on the other hand, were supposedly sleazy Northerners...." (p. 492)
13. **felony** A major crime for which severe penalties are exacted under the law. "The crimes of the Reconstruction governments were no more outrageous than the scams and felonies being perpetrated in the North at the same time...." (p. 493)
14. **terror (terrorist)** Using violence or the threat of violence in order to create intense fear in the attempt to promote some political policy or objectives. "Such tomfoolery and terror proved partially effective." (p. 493)
15. **president pro tempore** In the United States Senate, the officer who presides in the absence of the vice president. "Under existing law, the president pro tempore of the Senate ... would then become president." (p. 495)

PART II: Checking Your Progress

A. True-False

Where the statement is true, mark **T**. Where it is false, mark **F**, and correct it in the space immediately below.

____ 1. The South was economically devastated by the Civil War.

____ 2. Military defeat in the Civil War brought white Southerners to accept the reality of Northern political domination.

____ 3. The newly freed slaves often used their liberty to travel or seek lost loved ones.

____ 4. The focus of black community life after emancipation became the black church.

____ 5. Lincoln's "10 percent" Reconstruction plan was designed to return the Southern states to the Union quickly and with few restrictions.

____ 6. Southerners at first feared Andrew Johnson because he had been one of the few elite planters who backed Lincoln.

____ 7. The cause of black education was greatly advanced by white Northern female teachers who came South after the Civil War.

____ 8. The enactment of the Black Codes in the south strengthened those who supported a moderate approach to Reconstruction.

____ 9. Congressional Republicans demanded that the Southern states ratify the Fourteenth Amendment in order to be readmitted to the Union.

___ 10. Radical Republicans succeeded in their goal of redistributing land to the former slaves.

___ 11. During Reconstruction, blacks controlled most of the Southern state legislatures.

___ 12. The Republican Reconstruction legislature enacted educational and other reforms in Southern state government.

___ 13. The Ku Klux Klan largely failed in its goal of intimidating blacks and preventing them from voting.

___ 14. Johnson's impeachment was essentially an act of political vindictiveness by radical Republicans.

___ 15. The moderate Republican plan for Reconstruction might have succeeded if the Ku Klux Klan had been suppressed.

B. Multiple Choice

Select the best answer and write the proper letter in the space provided.

___ 1. After emancipation, many blacks traveled in order to
   a. return to Africa or the West Indies.
   b. seek a better life in Northern cities.
   c. find lost family members or seek new economic opportunities.
   d. track down and punish cruel overseers.

___ 2. The Freedmen's Bureau was originally established to provide
   a. land and supplies for black farmers.
   b. labor registration.
   c. food, clothes, and education for emancipated slaves.
   d. political training in citizenship for black voters.

___ 3. Lincoln's original plan for Reconstruction in 1863 was that a state could be re-integrated into the Union when
   a. it repealed its original secession act and took its soldiers out of the Confederate Army.
   b. 10 percent of its voters took an oath of allegiance to the Union and pledged to abide by emancipation.
   c. it formally adopted a plan guaranteeing black political and economic rights.
   d. it ratified the Fourteenth and Fifteenth Amendments to the Constitution.

___ 4. The Black Codes passed by many of the Southern state governments in 1865 aimed to
   a. provide economic assistance to get former slaves started as sharecroppers.
   b. ensure a stable and subservient labor force under white control.
   c. permit blacks to vote if they met certain educational or economic standards.
   d. gradually force blacks to leave the South.

___ 5. The congressional elections of 1866 resulted in

  a. a victory for Johnson and his pro-Southern Reconstruction plan.
  b. a further political stalemate between the Republicans in Congress and Johnson.
  c. a decisive defeat for Johnson and a veto-proof Republican Congress.
  d. a gain for Northern Democrats and their moderate compromise plan for Reconstruction.

___ 6. In contrast to radical Republicans, moderate Republicans generally

  a. favored states' rights and opposed direct federal involvement in individuals' lives.
  b. favored the use of federal power to alter the Southern economic system.
  c. favored emancipation but opposed the Fourteenth Amendment.
  d. favored returning the Southern states to the Union without significant Reconstruction.

___ 7. Besides putting the South under the rule of federal soldiers, the Military Reconstruction Act of 1867 required that

  a. Southern states give blacks the vote as a condition of readmittance to the Union.
  b. blacks and carpetbaggers be given control of Southern legislatures.
  c. former slaves be given land and education at federal expense.
  d. former Confederate officials and military officers be tried for treason.

___ 8. The Fourteenth amendment provided for

  a. an end to slavery.
  b. permanent disfranchisement of all Confederate officials.
  c. full citizenship and civil rights for former slaves.
  d. voting rights for women.

___ 9. The Fifteenth Amendment provided for

  a. readmitting Southern states to the Union.
  b. full citizenship and civil rights for former slaves.
  c. voting rights for former slaves.
  d. voting rights for women.

___ 10. Women's-rights leaders opposed the Fourteenth and Fifteenth Amendments because

  a. they objected to racial integration in the women's movement.
  b. the amendments granted citizenship and voting rights to black and white men but not to women.
  c. they favored passage of the Equal Rights Amendment first.
  d. most of them were Democrats who would be hurt by the amendments.

___ 11. The right to vote encouraged southern black men to

  a. form a third political party as an alternative to the Democrats and Republicans.
  b. seek an apology and reparations for slavery.
  c. organize the Union League as a vehicle for political empowerment and self-defense.
  d. organize large-scale migrations out of the South to the West.

___ 12. The radical Reconstruction regimes in the Southern states

  a. took away white Southerners' civil rights and voting rights.
  b. consisted almost entirely of blacks.
  c. included white Northerners, white Southerners, and blacks.
  d. eliminated the public education systems in most Southern states.

Name_____ Section_____ Date_____

____ 13. Most of the Northern "carpetbaggers" were actually
   a. former Union soldiers, businessmen, or professionals.
   b. undercover agents of the federal government.
   c. former Southern Whigs and Unionists who had opposed the Confederacy.
   d. Northern teachers and missionaries who wanted to aid the freedmen.

____ 14. The radical Republicans' impeachment of President Andrew Johnson resulted in
   a. Johnson's acceptance of the radicals' Reconstruction plan.
   b. a failure to convict and remove Johnson by a margin of only one vote.
   c. Johnson's conviction on the charge of violating the Tenure of Office Act.
   d. Johnson's resignation and appointment of Ulysses Grant as his successor.

____ 15. The skeptical public finally accepted Seward's purchase of Alaska because
   a. there were rumors of extensive oil deposits in the territory.
   b. it was considered strategically vital to American defense.
   c. it would provide a new frontier safety valve after the settling of the West.
   d. Russia had been the only great power friendly to the Union during the Civil War.

C. Identification

Supply the correct identification for each numbered description.

_____ 1. Common term for the blacks newly liberated from slavery

_____ 2. Federal agency that greatly assisted blacks educationally but failed in other aid efforts

_____ 3. The largest African-American denomination (church) after slavery

_____ 4. Lincoln's 1863 program for a rapid Reconstruction of the South

_____ 5. The constitutional amendment freeing all slaves

_____ 6. The harsh Southern state laws of 1865 that limited black rights and imposed restrictions to ensure a stable black labor supply

_____ 7. The constitutional amendment granting civil rights to freed slaves and barring former Confederates from office

_____ 8. Republican Reconstructionists who favored a more rapid restoration of Southern state governments and opposed radical plans for drastic economic transformation of the South

_____ 9. Republican Reconstructionists who favored keeping the South out of the federal government until a complete social and economic revolution was accomplished in the region

_____ 10. The black political organization that promoted self-help and defense of political rights

_____ 11. Supreme Court ruling that military tribunals could not try civilians when the civil courts were open

_____ 12. Derogatory term for white Southerners who cooperated with the Republican Reconstruction governments

_____ 13. Derogatory term for Northerners who came to the South during Reconstruction and sometimes took part in Republican state governments

_____ 14. Constitutional amendment guaranteeing blacks the right to vote

_____ 15. "Seward's Folly," acquired in 1867 from Russia

D. Matching People, Places, and Events

Match the person, place, or event in the left column with the proper description in the right column by inserting the correct letter on the blank line.

___ 1. Exodusters
___ 2. Oliver O. Howard
___ 3. Andrew Johnson
___ 4. Abraham Lincoln
___ 5. Civil Rights Bill of 1866
___ 6. Charles Sumner
___ 7. Thaddeus Stevens
___ 8. Military Reconstruction Act of 1867
___ 9. Hiram Revels
___ 10. Ku Klux Klan
___ 11. Force Acts of 1870 and 1871
___ 12. Tenure of Office Act
___ 13. Union League
___ 14. Benjamin Wade
___ 15. William Seward

A. A constitutionally questionable law whose violation by President Johnson formed the basis for his impeachment
B. The first congressional attempt to guarantee black rights in the South, passed over Johnson's veto
C. Born a poor white southerner, he became the white South's champion against radical Reconstruction
D. Secretary of state who arranged an initially unpopular but valuable land deal in 1867
E. Laws designed to stamp out Ku Klux Klan terrorism in the South
F. Black Republican senator from Mississippi during Reconstruction
G. Secret organization that intimidated blacks and worked to restore white supremacy
H. Blacks who left the South for Kansas and elsewhere during Reconstruction
I. Congressional law that imposed military rule on the South and demanded harsh conditions for readmission of the seceded states
J. Beaten in the Senate chamber before the Civil War, he became the leader of Senate Republican radicals during Reconstruction
K. Problack general who led an agency that tried to assist the freedmen
L. Leading Black political organization during Reconstruction
M. Author of the moderate "10 percent" Reconstruction plan that ran into congressional opposition
N. The president pro tempore of the Senate who hoped to become president of the United States after Johnson's impeachment conviction.
O. Leader of radical Republicans in the House of Representatives

E. Putting Things in Order

Put the following events in correct order by numbering them from 1 to 5.

___ Constitution is amended to guarantee former slaves the right to vote.

___ Lincoln announces a plan to rapidly restore southern states to the Union.

___ Northern troops are finally withdrawn from the South, and Southern state governments are reconstituted without federal constraint.

___ An unpopular antiradical president escapes conviction and removal from office by one vote.

___ Johnson's attempt to restore the South to the Union is overturned because of congressional hostility to ex-Confederates and southern passage of the Black Codes.

F. Matching Cause and Effect

Match the historical cause in the left column with the proper effect in the right column by writing the correct letter on the blank line.

Cause

___ 1. The South's military defeat in the Civil War

___ 2. The Freedmen's Bureau

___ 3. The Black Codes of 1865

___ 4. The election of ex-Confederates to Congress in 1865

___ 5. Johnson's "swing around the circle" in the election of 1866

___ 6. Military Reconstruction and the Fourteenth and Fifteenth Amendments

___ 7. The "radical" Southern state Reconstruction governments

___ 8. The Ku Klux Klan

___ 9. The radical Republicans' hatred of Johnson

___ 10. The whole Reconstruction era

Effect

A. Provoked a politically motivated trial to remove the president from office

B. Intimidated black voters and tried to keep blacks "in their place"

C. Prompted Republicans to refuse to seat Southern delegations in Congress

D. Destroyed the southern economy but strengthened Southern hatred of "yankees"

E. Successfully educated former slaves but failed to provide much other assistance to them

F. Forced all the Southern states to establish governments that upheld black voting and other civil rights

G. Embittered white Southerners while doing little to really help blacks

H. Engaged in some corruption but also enacted many valuable social reforms

I. Weakened support for mild Reconstruction policies and helped elect overwhelming Republican majorities to Congress

J. Imposed slaverylike restrictions on blacks and angered the North

G. Developing Historical Skills

Interpreting Photographs and Drawings

Answer the following questions about the photographs and drawings in this chapter.

1. *The Faculty of a Freedmen's Bureau School near Norfolk, Virginia* (p. 481)

    What is the ratio of black to white teachers on the freedmen's school staff? Who appears to be the principal of the school? Where are the black teachers positioned in the photograph? Might this suggest anything about the relations between white and black teachers in the school?

2. *A Family of Sharecroppers at the End of the Civil War* (photograph, p. 485)

    What physical details suggest the poverty of these former slaves? How would you characterize the attitudes of the people in the photograph?

3. *Freedmen Voting, Richmond, Virginia, 1871* (drawing, p. 482)

    What appears to be the economic status of the new black voters portrayed here? How does their condition differ from that of the voting officials, black and white? What does the drawing suggest about the power of the newly enfranchised freedmen?

Name_____ Section_____ Date_____

Part III: Applying What You Have Learned

1. What were the major problems facing the South and the nation after the Civil War? How did Reconstruction address them, or fail to do so?
2. How did freed blacks react to the end of slavery? How did both Southern and Northern whites react?
3. How did the white South's intransigence and President Johnson's political bungling open the way for the congressional Republican program of military Reconstruction?
4. What was the purpose of congressional Reconstruction, and what were its actual effects in the South?
5. What did the attempt at black political empowerment achieve? Why did it finally fail? Could it have succeeded with a stronger Northern political will behind it?
6. Why did Reconstruction apparently fail so badly? Was the failure primarily one of immediate political circumstances, or was it more deeply rooted in the history of American sectional and race relations?

23

Politics in the Gilded Age, 1869–1896

PART I: Reviewing the Chapter

A. Checklist of Learning Objectives

After mastering this chapter, you should be able to

1. describe the political corruption of the Grant administration and the various efforts to clean up politics in the Gilded Age.
2. describe the economic slump of the 1870s and the growing conflict between "hard-money" and "soft-money" advocates.
3. explain the intense political activity of the Gilded age, despite the low quality of political leadership and the agreement of the two parties on most issues.
4. indicate how the disputed Hayes-Tilden election of 1876 led to the Compromise of 1877 and the end of Reconstruction.
5. describe how the end of Reconstruction led to the loss of black rights and the imposition of the Jim Crow system of segregation in the South.
6. explain the growth of class and ethnic conflict during the 1870s and after.
7. describe the sharp personal and partisan clashes between Grover Cleveland and his Republican opponents.
8. show how the rise of the Populists and the depression of the 1890s stirred growing social protests and class conflict.

B. Glossary

To build your social science vocabulary, familiarize yourself with the following terms.

1. **coalition** A temporary alliance of political factions or parties for some specific purpose. "The Republicans, now freed from the Union party coalition of war days, enthusiastically nominated Grant...." (p. 503)
2. **corner** To gain exclusive control of a commodity in order to fix its price. "The crafty pair concocted a plot in 1869 to corner the gold market." (p. 503)
3. **censure** An official statement of condemnation passed by a legislative body against one of its members or some other official of government. While severe, a censure itself stops short of penalties or **expulsion**, which is removal from office. "A newspaper exposé and congressional investigation led to formal censure of two congressmen...." (p. 504)
4. **amnesty** A general pardon for offenses or crimes against a government. "The Republican Congress in 1872 passed a general amnesty act...." (p. 506)
5. **civil service** Referring to regular employment by government according to a standardized system of job descriptions, merit qualifications, pay, and promotion, as distinct from **political appointees** who receive positions based on affiliation and party loyalty. "Congress also moved to reduce high Civil War tariffs and to fumigate the Grant administration with mild civil service reform." (p. 506)

6. **unsecured loans** Money loaned without identification of collateral (existing assets) to be forfeited in case the borrower defaults on the loan. "The Freedman's Savings and Trust Company had made unsecured loans to several companies that went under." (p. 506)
7. **contraction** In finance, reducing the available supply of money, thus tending to raise interest rates and lower prices. "Coupled with the reduction of greenbacks, this policy was called 'contraction.'" (p. 507)
8. **deflation (ary)** An increase in the value of money in relation to available goods, causing prices to fall. **Inflation**, a decrease in the value of money in relation to goods, causes prices to rise. "It had a noticeable deflationary effect—the amount of money per capita in circulation actually *decreased*...." (p. 507)
9. **fraternal organization** A society of men drawn together for social purposes and sometimes to pursue other common goals. "... the Grand Army of the Republic [was] a politically potent fraternal organization of several hundred thousand Union veterans of the Civil War." (p. 507)
10. **consensus** Common or unanimous opinion. "How can this apparent paradox of political consensus and partisan fervor be explained?" (p. 507)
11. **kickback** The return of a portion of the money received in a sale or contract, often secretly or illegally, in exchange for favors. "The lifeblood of both parties was patronage—disbursing jobs by the bucketful in return for votes, kickbacks, and party service." (p. 507)
12. **lien** A legal claim by a lender or another party on a borrower's property as a guarantee against repayment, and prohibiting any sale of the property. "... storekeepers extended credit to small farmers for food and supplies and in return took a lien on their harvest." (p. 510)
13. **assassination** Politically motivated murder of a public figure. "... he asked all those who had benefited politically by the assassination to contribute to his defense fund." (p. 514)
14. **laissez-faire** The doctrine of noninterference, especially by the government, in matters of economics or business (literally, "leave alone"). "[The new president was] a staunch apostle of the hands-off creed of laissez-faire...." (p. 518)
15. **pork barrel** In American politics, government appropriations for political purposes, especially projects designed to please a legislator's local constituency. "One [way to reduce the surplus] was to squander it on pensions and 'pork-barrel' bills...." (p. 519)

PART II: Checking Your Progress

A. True-False

Where the statement is true, mark **T**. Where it is false, mark **F**, and correct it in the space immediately below.

____ 1. Ulysses Grant's status as a military hero enabled him to become a successful president who stood above partisan politics.

____ 2. The scandals of the Grant administration included bribes and corrupt dealings reaching to the cabinet and the vice president of the United States.

____ 3. The Liberal Republican movement's political skilled enabled it to clean up the corruption of the Grant administration.

____ 4. The severe economic downturn of the 1870s caused business failures, labor conflict, and battles over currency.

____ 5. The close, fiercely contested elections of the Gilded Age reflected the deep divisions between Republicans and Democrats over national issues.

____ 6. The battles between the "Stalwart" and "Half-Breed" Republican factions were mainly over who would get patronage and spoils.

____ 7. The disputed Hayes-Tilden election was settled by a political deal in which Democrats got the presidency and Republicans got economic and political concessions.

____ 8. The Compromise of 1877 purchased political peace between North and South by sacrificing southern blacks and removing federal troops in the South.

____ 9. The sharecropping and tenant farming systems forced many Southern blacks into permanent economic debt and dependency.

____ 10. Western hostility to Chinese immigrants arose in part because the Chinese provided a source of cheap labor that competed with white workers.

____ 11. By reducing politicians' use of patronage, the new civil-service system inadvertently made them more dependent on big campaign contributors.

____ 12. The Cleveland-Blaine campaign of 1884 was conducted primarily as a debate about the issues of taxes and the tariff.

____ 13. The Republican party in the post–Civil War era relied heavily on the political support of veterans' groups, to which it gave substantial pension benefits in return.

____ 14. The Populist party's attempt to form a coalition of farmers and workers failed partly because of the racial division between poor whites and blacks in the South.

____ 15. Cleveland effectively addressed the depression of the 1890s by compromising with pro-silver money advocates.

B. Multiple Choice

Select the best answer and write the proper letter in the space provided.

____ 1. Financiers Jim Fisk and Jay Gould tried to involve the Grant administration in a corrupt scheme to
   a. skim funds from the Bureau of Indian Affairs.
   b. sell "watered" railroad stock at high prices.
   c. corner the gold market.
   d. bribe congressmen in exchange for federal land grants.

____ 2. Boss Tweed's widespread corruption was finally brought to a halt by
   a. federal prosecutors who uncovered the theft.
   b. outraged citizens who rebelled against the waste of public money.
   c. the journalistic exposés of *The New York Times* and cartoonist Thomas Nast.
   d. Tweed's political opponents in New York City.

3. The Credit Mobilier scandal involved
    a. the abuse of federal credit intended for urban development.
    b. railroad corporation fraud and the subsequent bribery of congressmen.
    c. Secretary of War Belknap's fraudulent sale of contracts to supply Indian reservations.
    d. the attempt of insiders to gain control of New York's gold and stock markets.

4. Grant's greatest failing in the scandals that plagued his administration was
    a. his refusal to turn over evidence to congressional investigators.
    b. his toleration of corruption and his loyalty to crooked friends.
    c. his acceptance of behind-the-scenes payments for performing his duties as president.
    d. his use of large amounts of "dirty" money in his political campaigns.

5. The depression of the 1870s led to increasing demands for
    a. inflation of the money supply by issuing more paper or silver currency.
    b. federal programs to create jobs for the unemployed.
    c. restoration of sound money by backing all paper currency with gold.
    d. stronger regulation of the banking system.

6. The political system of the "Gilded Age" was generally characterized by
    a. "split-ticket" voting, low voter turnout, and single-issue special-interest groups.
    b. strong party loyalties, low voter turnout, and deep ideological differences.
    c. "third-party" movements, high voter turnout and strong disagreement on foreign-policy issues.
    d. strong party loyalties, high voter turnout, and few disagreements on national issues.

7. The primary goal for which all factions in both political parties contended during the Gilded Age was
    a. racial justice.
    b. a sound financial and banking system.
    c. patronage.
    d. a more assertive American foreign policy.

8. The key tradeoff featured in the Compromise of 1877,
    a. Republicans got the presidency in exchange for the final removal of federal troops from the South.
    b. Democrats got the presidency in exchange for federal guarantees of black civil rights.
    c. Republicans got the presidency in exchange for Democratic control of the cabinet.
    d. Democrats got the presidency in exchange for increased immigration quotas from Ireland.

9. Which of the following was *not* among the changes that affected African-Americans in the South after federal troops were withdrawn in the Compromise of 1877?
    a. the forced relocation of black farmers to the Kansas and Oklahoma "dust bowl."
    b. the imposition of literacy requirements and poll taxes to prevent black voting.
    c. the development of the tenant farming and share-cropping systems.
    d. the introduction of legal systems of racial segregation.

___ 10. The Supreme Court's ruling in *Plessy* v. *Ferguson* upholding "separate but equal" public facilities in effect legalized
   a. southern blacks' loss of voting rights.
   b. the system of unequal segregation between the races.
   c. the program of separate black and white economic development endorsed by Booker T. Washington.
   d. the rights to "equal protection of the law" guaranteed by the Fourteenth Amendment.

___ 11. The great railroad strike of 1877 revealed
   a. the growing strength of American labor unions.
   b. the refusal of the U.S. federal government to intervene in private labor disputes.
   c. the ability of American workers to cooperate across ethnic and racial lines.
   d. the growing threat of class warfare in response to the economic depression of the mid-1870s.

___ 12. The final result of the widespread anti-Chinese agitation in the West was
   a. a program to encourage Chinese students to enroll in American colleges and universities.
   b. a Congressional law to prohibit any further Chinese immigration.
   c. the stripping of citizenship even from native-born Chinese-Americans.
   d. legal segregation of all Chinese into "Chinatown" districts in San Francisco and elsewhere.

___ 13. President James Garfield was assassinated by
   a. a fanatically anti-Republican Confederate veteran.
   b. a mentally unstable disappointed office seeker.
   c. an anticapitalist immigrant anarchist.
   d. a corrupt gangster under federal criminal indictment.

___ 14. In its first years, the Populist Party advocated, among other things
   a. free silver, a graduated income tax, and government ownership of the railroads, telegraph, and telephone.
   b. higher tariffs and federally sponsored unemployment insurance and pensions.
   c. tighter restriction on black economic, social, and political rights.
   d. a Homestead Act to permit farmers and unemployed workers to obtain free federal land in the West.

___ 15. Grover Cleveland stirred a furious storm of protest when, in response to the extreme financial crisis of the 1890s, he
   a. lowered tariffs to permit an influx of cheaper foreign goods into the country.
   b. signed a bill introducing a federal income tax that cut into workers' wages.
   c. pushed the Federal Reserve Board into sharply raising interest rates.
   d. borrowed $65 million dollars from J.P. Morgan and other bankers in order to save the monetary gold standard.

C. Identification

Supply the correct identification for each numbered description.

_____ 1. The symbol of the Republican political tactic of attacking Democrats with reminders of the Civil War

_____ 2. Corrupt construction company whose bribes and payoffs to congressmen and others created a major Grant administration scandal

_____ 3. Short-lived third party of 1872 that attempted to curb Grant administration corruption

_____ 4. Precious metal that "soft-money" advocates demanded be coined again to compensate for the "Crime of '73"

_____ 5. "Soft-money" third party that polled over a million votes and elected fourteen congressmen in 1878 by advocating inflation

_____ 6. Mark Twain's sarcastic name for the post–Civil War era, which emphasized its atmosphere of greed and corruption

_____ 7. Civil War Union veterans' organization that became a potent political bulwark of the Republican party in the late nineteenth century

_____ 8. Republican party faction led by Senator Roscoe Conkling that opposed all attempts at civil-service reform

_____ 9. Republican party faction led by Senator James G. Blaine that paid lip service to government reform while still battling for patronage and spoils

_____ 10. The complex political agreement between Republicans and Democrats that resolved the bitterly disputed election of 1876

_____ 11. Asian immigrant group that experienced discrimination on the West Coast

_____ 12. System of choosing federal employees on the basis of merit rather than patronage introduced by the Pendleton Act of 1883

_____ 13. Sky-high Republican tariff of 1890 that caused widespread anger among farmers in the Midwest and the South.

_____ 14. Insurgent political party that gained widespread support among farmers in the 1890s

_____ 15. Notorious clause in southern voting laws that exempted from literacy tests and poll taxes anyone whose ancestors had voted in 1860, thereby excluding blacks

D. Matching People, Places, and Events

Match the person, place, or event in the left column with the proper description in the right column by inserting the correct letter on the blank line.

___ 1. Ulysses S. Grant
___ 2. Jim Fisk
___ 3. Boss Tweed
___ 4. Horace Greeley

A. Heavyweight New York political boss whose widespread fraud landed him in jail in 1871
B. Bold and unprincipled financier whose plot to corner the U.S. gold market nearly succeeded in 1869
C. Winner of the contested 1876 election who presided over the end of Reconstruction and a sharp economic downturn
D. Great military leader whose presidency foundered in corruption and political ineptitude

___ 5. Jay Cooke
___ 6. Denis Kearney
___ 7. Tom Watson
___ 8. Roscoe Conkling
___ 9. James G. Blaine
___ 10. Rutherford B. Hayes
___ 11. James Garfield
___ 12. Jim Crow
___ 13. Grover Cleveland
___ 14. William Jennings Bryan
___ 15. J. P. Morgan

E. Term for the racial segregation laws imposed in the 1890s
F. Eloquent young Congressman from Nebraska who became the most prominent advocate of "free silver" in the early 1890s.
G. President whose assassination after only a few months in office spurred the passage of a civil-service law
H. Irish-born leader of the anti-Chinese movement in California
I. Radical Populist leader whose early success turned sour, and who then became a vicious racist
J. Wealthy New York financier whose bank collapse in 1873 set off an economic depression
K. Imperious New York senator and leader of the "Stalwart" faction of Republicans
L. First Democratic president since the Civil War; defender of *laissez-faire* economics and low tariffs
M. Enormously wealthy banker whose secret bailout of the federal government in 1895 aroused fierce public anger
N. Colorful, eccentric newspaper editor who carried the Liberal Republican and Democratic banners against Grant in 1872
O. Charming but corrupt "Half-Breed" Republican senator and presidential nominee in 1884

E. **Putting Things in Order**

Put the following events in correct order by numbering them from 1 to 5.

___ A bitterly disputed presidential election is resolved by a complex political deal that ends Reconstruction in the South.

___ Two unscrupulous financiers use corrupt means to manipulate New York gold markets and the U.S. Treasury.

___ A major economic depression causes widespread social unrest and the rise of the Populist Party as a vehicle of protest.

___ Grant administration scandals split the Republican party, but Grant overcomes the inept opposition to win reelection.

___ Monetary deflation and the high McKinley Tariff lead to growing agitation for "free silver" by Congressman William Jennings Bryan and others.

F. **Matching Cause and Effect**

Match the historical cause in the left column with the proper effect in the right column by writing the correct letter on the blank line.

	Cause		Effect
___	1. Favor-seeking businesspeople and corrupt politicians	A.	Created fierce partisan competition and high voter turnouts, even though the parties agreed on most national issues
___	2. *The New York Times* and cartoonist Thomas Nast	B.	Caused anti-Chinese violence and restrictions against Chinese immigration

Chapter 23 *Politics in the Gilded Age, 1869–1896* 233

___ 3. Upright Republicans' disgust with Grant administration scandals

___ 4. The economic crash of the mid-1870s

___ 5. Local cultural, moral, and religious differences

___ 6. The Compromise of 1877 that settled the disputed Hayes-Tilden election

___ 7. White workers' resentment of Chinese labor competition

___ 8. Public shock at Garfield's assassination by Guiteau

___ 9. The 1890s depression and the drain of gold from the federal treasury

___ 10. The inability of Populist leaders to overcome divisions between white and black farmers

C. Led to the formation of the Liberal Republican party in 1872
D. Induced Grover Cleveland to negotiate a secret loan from J. P. Morgan's banking syndicate
E. Forced Boss Tweed out of power and into jail
F. Helped ensure passage of the Pendleton Act
G. Caused numerous scandals during President Grant's administration
H. Led to failure of the third party revolt in the South and a growing racial backlash
I. Caused unemployment, railroad strikes, and a demand for "cheap money"
J. Led to the withdrawal of troops from the South and the virtual end of federal efforts to protect black rights there

G. Developing Historical Skills

Historical Fact and Historical Explanation

Historians uncover a great deal of information about the past, but often that information takes on significance only when it is analyzed and interpreted. In this chapter, many facts about the presidents and elections of the Gilded Age are presented: for example, the very close elections in 1876, 1884, 1888, and 1892; the large voter turnouts; and the lack of significant issues in most elections.

These facts take on larger meaning, however, when we examine the *reasons* for them. Reread the section "Pallid Politics in the Gilded Age" (pp. 507–508) and answer each of the following questions in a sentence or two.

1. What *fundamental* difference between the two parties made partisan politics so fiercely contested in the Glided Age?

2. Why did this underlying difference *not* lead to differences over issues at the national level?

3. Why were so many of the elections extremely close, no matter who the candidates were?

Name_____ Section_____ Date_____

4. Why was winning each election so very important to both parties, even though there was little disagreement on issues?

H. Map Mastery

Map Discrimination

Using the maps and charts in Chapter 23, answer the following questions.

1. *Hayes-Tilden Disputed Election of 1876*: In the controversial Hayes-Tilden election of 1876, how many *undisputed* electoral votes did Republican Hayes win in the former Confederate states?

2. *Hayes-Tilden Disputed Election of 1876*: Democrat Tilden carried four states in the North—states that did not have slavery before 1865. Which were they?

3. *Growth of Classified Civil Service*: The *percentage* of offices classified under civil service was approximately how many times greater under President McKinley than under President Arthur: two, three, four, five, or ten?

4. *Presidential Election of 1884*: Which of the following states gained the most electoral votes between 1876 and 1884: New York, Indiana, Missouri, or Texas?

5. *Presidential Election of 1884*: How many states that were carried by Republican Hayes in 1876 were carried by Democrat Cleveland in 1884?

Map Challenge

Using the election map on p. 508 and the account of the Compromise of 1877 in the text (pp. 508–509), discuss the election of 1876 in relation to both Reconstruction and the political balance of the Gilded Age. Include some analysis of the reasons why this was the last time for nearly a century that the states in the Deep South voted Republican.

PART III: Applying What You Have Learned

1. What made politics in the Gilded Age extremely popular—with over 80 percent voter participation—yet so often corrupt and unconcerned with issues?
2. What caused the end of the Reconstruction? What did the North and South each gain from the Compromise of 1877?
3. What were the results of the Compromise of 1877 for race relations? How were the political, economic, and social conditions of southern African-Americans interrelated?
4. What caused the rise of the "money issue" in American politics? What were the backers of "greenback" and silver money trying to achieve?
5. What were the causes and political results of the rise of agrarian protest in the 1880s and 1890s? Why were the Populists' attempts to form a coalition of white and black farmers and industrial workers ultimately unsuccessful?
6. In what ways did the political conflicts of the Gilded Age still reflect the aftermath of the Civil War and Reconstruction? (See Chapter 22.) To what extent did the political leaders of the time address issues of race and sectional conflict, and to what extent did they merely shove them under the rug?

24

Industry Comes of Age, 1865–1900

PART I: Reviewing the Chapter

A. Checklist of Learning Objectives

After mastering this chapter, you should be able to

1. explain how the transcontinental railroad network provided the basis for the great post–Civil War industrial transformation.
2. identify the abuses in the railroad industry and discuss how these led to the first efforts at industrial regulation by the federal government.
3. describe how the economy came to be dominated by giant "trusts," such as those headed by Carnegie and Rockefeller in the steel and oil industries.
4. discuss the growing class conflict caused by industrial growth and combination, and the early efforts to alleviate it.
5. explain why the South was generally excluded from industrial development and fell into a "third world" economic dependency.
6. analyze the social changes brought by industrialization, particularly the altered position of working men and women.
7. explain the failures of the Knights of Labor and the modest success of the American Federation of Labor.

B. Glossary

To build your social science vocabulary, familiarize yourself with the following terms.

1. **pool** In business, an agreement to divide a given market in order to avoid competition. "The earliest form of combination was the 'pool'. . . ." (p. 535)
2. **rebate** A return of a portion of the amount paid for goods or services. "Other rail barons granted secret rebates. . . ." (p. 535)
3. **free enterprise** An economic system that permits unrestricted entrepreneurial business activity; capitalism. "Dedicated to free enterprise . . . , they cherished a traditionally keen pride in progress." (p. 535)
4. **regulatory commission** In American government, any of the agencies established to control a special sphere of business or other activity; members are usually appointed by the president and confirmed by Congress. "It heralded the arrival of a series of independent regulatory commissions in the next century. . . ." (p. 536)
5. **trust** A combination of corporations, usually in the same industry, in which stockholders trade their stock to a central board in exchange for trust certificates. (By extension, the term cam to be applied to any large, semi-monopolistic business.) "He perfected a device for controlling bothersome rivals—the 'trust.' " (p. 538)

6. **syndicate** An association of financiers organized to carry out projects requiring very large amounts of capital. "His prescribed remedy was to . . . ensure future harmony by placing officers of his own banking syndicate on their various boards of directors." (p. 538)
7. **patrician** Characterized by noble or high social standing. "An arrogant class of 'new rich' was now elbowing aside the patrician families. . . ." (p. 542)
8. **plutocracy** Government by the wealthy. "Plutocracy . . . took its stand firmly on the Constitution." (p. 542)
9. **Third World** Term developed during the Cold War for the non-Western (first world) and noncommunist (second world) nations of the world, most of them formerly under colonial rule and still economically poor and dependent. "The net effect was to keep the South in a kind of 'Third World' servitude to the Northeast. . . ." (p. 544)
10. **socialist (socialism)** Political belief in promoting social and economic equality through the ownership and control of the major means of production by the whole community rather than by individuals or corporations. "Some of it was envious, but much of it rose from the small and increasingly vocal group of socialists. . . ." (p. 548)
11. **radical** One who believes in fundamental change in the political, economic, or social system. ". . . much of [this criticism] rose from . . . socialists and other radicals, many of whom were recent European immigrants." (p. 548)
12. **lockout** The refusal by an employer to allow employees to work unless they agree to his or her terms. "Employers could lock their doors against rebellious workers—a process called the 'lockout'. . . ." (p. 549)
13. **yellow dog contract** A labor contract in which an employee must agree not to join a union as a condition of holding the job. "[Employers] could compel them to sign 'ironclad oaths' or 'yellow dog contracts'. . . ." (p. 549)
14. **cooperative** An organization for producing, marketing, or consuming goods in which the members share the benefits. ". . . they campaigned for . . . producers' cooperatives. . . ."
15. **anarchist (anarchism)** Political belief that all organized, coercive government is wrong in principle, and that society should be organized solely on the basis of free cooperation. (Some anarchists practiced violence against the state, while others were nonviolent pacifists.) "Eight anarchists were rounded up, although nobody proved that they had anything to do directly with the bomb." (p. 551)

PART II: Checking Your Progress

A. True-False

Where the statement is true, mark **T**. Where it is false, mark **F**, and correct it in the space immediately below.

___ 1. Private railroad companies built the transcontinental rail lines by raising their own capital funds without the assistance of the federal government.

___ 2. The rapid expansion of the railroad industry was often accompanied by rapid mergers, bankruptcies, and reorganizations.

___ 3. The railroads created an integrated national market, stimulated the growth in cities, and encouraged European immigration.

___ 4. Railroad owners were generally fair and honest in their dealings with shippers, the government, and the public.

___ 5. The early, weak federal efforts at railroad regulation did bring some order and stability to industrial competition.

___ 6. The Rockefeller oil company technique of "horizontal integration" involved combining into one organization all the phases of manufacturing from the raw material to the customer.

___ 7. Rockefeller, Morgan, and others organized monopolistic trusts and "interlocking directorates" in order to consolidate business and eliminate cutthroat competition.

___ 8. Corporations effectively used the Fourteenth Amendment and sympathetic court rulings to prevent much effective government regulations of their activities.

___ 9. The pro-industry ideology of the "New South" enabled that region to make rapid economic gains by 1900.

___ 10. Two new inventions that brought large numbers of women into the workplace were the typewriter and the telephone.

___ 11. Industrialization generally gave the industrial wage earner greater status and control over his or her own life.

___ 12. The impact of new machines and mass immigration held down wages and gave employers advantages in their dealings with labor.

___ 13. The Knights of Labor organized skilled and unskilled workers, blacks and whites, women and men.

___ 14. The Knights of Labor were severely hurt by the Haymarket Square episode, even though they had no connection with the bombing.

___ 15. The American Federation of Labor tried hard but failed to organize unskilled workers, women, and blacks.

B. Multiple Choice

Select the best answer and write the proper letter in the space provided.

___ 1. The federal government contributed to the building of the national rail network by
   a. importing substantial numbers of Chinese immigrants to build the railroads.
   b. providing free grants of federal land to the railroad companies.
   c. building and operating the first transcontinental rail lines.
   d. transporting the mail and other federal shipments over the rail lines.

___ 2. The most efficient and public-minded of the early railroad-building industrialists was
   a. Collis P. Huntington.
   b. Leland Stanford.
   c. Cornelius Vanderbilt.
   d. James J. Hill.

3. The railroad most significantly stimulated American industrialization by
   a. opening up the West to settlement.
   b. creating a single national market for raw materials and consumer goods.
   c. eliminating the inefficient canal system.
   d. inspiring greater federal investment in technical research and development.

4. The railroad barons aroused considerable public opposition by practices such as
   a. forcing Indians off their traditional hunting grounds.
   b. refusing to pay their employees decent wages.
   c. refusing to build railroad lines in less settled areas.
   d. stock watering and bribery of public officials.

5. The railroads affected even the organization of time in the United States by
   a. introducing regularly scheduled departures and arrivals on railroad timetables.
   b. introducing the concept of daylight savings time.
   c. introducing four standard time zones across the country.
   d. turning travel that had once taken days into a matter of hours.

6. The first important federal law aimed at regulating American industry was
   a. the Federal Communications Act.
   b. the Pure Food and Drug Act.
   c. the Interstate Commerce Act.
   d. the Federal Trade Commission.

7. Financier J. P. Morgan exercised his economic power most effectively by
   a. developing "horizontal integration" in the oil industry.
   b. lending money to the federal government.
   c. consolidating rival industries through "interlocking directorates."
   d. serving as the middleman between American industrialists and foreign governments.

8. Two late-nineteenth-century technological inventions that especially drew women out of the home and into the workforce were
   a. the railroad and the telegraph.
   b. the electric light and the phonograph.
   c. the cash register and the stock ticker.
   d. the typewriter and the telephone.

9. Andrew Carnegie's industrial system of "vertical integration" involved
   a. the construction of large, vertical steel factories in Pittsburgh and elsewhere.
   b. the cooperation between manufacturers like Andrew Carnegie and financiers like J. P. Morgan.
   c. the integration of diverse immigrant ethnic groups into the steel industry labor force.
   d. the combination of all phases of the steel industry from mining to manufacturing into a single organization.

____ 10. The large trusts like Standard Oil and Swift and Armour justified their economic domination of their industries by claiming that
   a. they were fundamentally concerned with serving the public interest over private profit.
   b. only large-scale methods of production and distribution could provide superior products at low prices.
   c. competition among many small firms was contrary to the law of economics.
   d. only large American corporations could compete with huge British and German international companies.

____ 11. The oil industry first thrived in the late 1880s by producing
   a. natural gas and heating oil for home heating purposes.
   b. kerosene for oil lamps.
   c. gasoline for automobiles.
   d. heavy-duty diesel fuel for the railroads and industry.

____ 12. Andrew Carnegie's "Gospel of Wealth" proclaimed his belief that
   a. wealth was God's reward for hard work, while poverty resulted from laziness and immorality.
   b. churches needed to take a stronger stand on the economic issues of the day.
   c. faith in capitalism and progress should take the place once reserved for religion.
   d. those who acquired great wealth were morally responsible to use it for the public good.

____ 13. The attempt to create an industrialized "New South" in the late nineteenth century generally failed because
   a. the South was discriminated against and held down as a supplier of raw materials to northern industry.
   b. southerners were too bitter at the Union to pursue national goals.
   c. continued political violence made the South an unattractive place for investment.
   d. there was little demand for southern products like textiles and cigarettes.

____ 14. For American workers, industrialization generally meant
   a. a steady, long-term decline in wages and the standard of living.
   b. an opportunity to create small businesses that might eventually produce large profits.
   c. a long-term rise in the standard of living but a loss of independence and control of work.
   d. a stronger sense of identification with their jobs and employers.

____ 15. In contrast to the Knights of Labor, the American Federation of Labor advocated
   a. uniting both skilled and unskilled workers into a single large union.
   b. concentrating on improving wages and hours and avoiding general social reform.
   c. working for black and female labor interests as well as those of white men.
   d. using secrecy and violence against employers.

C. Identification

Supply the correct identification for each numbered description.

_____ 1. Federally owned acreage granted to the railroad companies in order to encourage the building of rail lines

_____ 2. The original transcontinental railroad, commissioned by Congress, which built its rail line west from Omaha

_____ 3. The California-based railroad company, headed by Leland Stanford, that employed Chinese laborers in building lines across the mountains

_____ 4. The northernmost of the transcontinental railroad lines, organized by economically wise and public-spirited industrialist James J. Hill

_____ 5. Dishonest device by which railroad promoters artificially inflated the price of their stocks and bonds

_____ 6. Supreme Court case of 1886 that prevented states from regulating railroads or other forms of interstate commerce

_____ 7. Federal regulatory agency often used by rail companies to stabilize the industry and prevent ruinous competition

_____ 8. Late-nineteenth-century invention that revolutionized communication and created a large new industry that relied heavily on female workers

_____ 9. First of the great industrial trusts, organized through a principle of "horizontal integration" that ruthlessly incorporated or destroyed competitors

_____ 10. The first billion-dollar American corporation, organized when J. P. Morgan bought out Andrew Carnegie

_____ 11. Term that identified southern promoters' belief in a technologically advanced industrial South

_____ 12. Black labor organization that briefly flourished in the late 1860s

_____ 13. Secret, ritualistic labor organization that enrolled many skilled and unskilled workers but collapsed suddenly after the Haymarket Square bombing

_____ 14. Skilled labor organizations, such as those of carpenters and printers, that were most successful in conducting strikes and raising wages

_____ 15. The conservative labor group that successfully organized a minority of American workers but left others out

D. Matching People, Places, and Events

Match the person, place, or event in the left column with the proper description in the right column by inserting the correct letter on the blank line.

___ 1. Leland Stanford   A. Inventive genius of industrialization who worked on devices such as the electric light, the phonograph, and the motion picture

___ 2. Russell Conwell

___ 3. James J. Hill   B. The only businessperson in America wealthy enough to buy out Andrew Carnegie and organize the United States Steel Corporation

___ 4. Cornelius Vanderbilt
___ 5. Charles Dana Gibson
___ 6. Alexander Graham Bell
___ 7. Thomas Edison
___ 8. Andrew Carnegie
___ 9. John D. Rockefeller
___ 10. J. Pierpont Morgan
___ 11. Henry Grady
___ 12. Terence V. Powderly
___ 13. Haymarket Square
___ 14. John P. Altgeld
___ 15. Samuel Gompers

C. Illinois governor who pardoned the Haymarket anarchists
D. Southern newspaper editor who tirelessly promoted industrialization as the salvation of the economically backward South
E. Aggressive energy-industry monopolist who used tough means to build a trust based on "horizontal integration"
F. Magazine illustrator who created a romantic image of the new, independent woman
G. Aggressive eastern railroad builder and consolidator who scorned the law as an obstacle to his enterprise
H. Pro-business clergyman whose "Acres of Diamonds" speeches criticized the poor
I. Scottish immigrant who organized a vast new industry on the principle of "vertical integration"
J. Former California governor and organizer of the Central Pacific Railroad
K. Organizer of a conservative craft-union group and advocate of "more" wages for skilled workers
L. Eloquent leader of a secretive labor organization that made substantial gains in the 1880s before it suddenly collapsed
M. Public-spirited railroad builder who assisted farmers in the northern areas served by his rail lines
N. Site of a bombing, during a labor demonstration, that aroused public hysteria against strikes
O. Former teacher of the deaf whose invention created an entire new industry

E. Putting Things in Order

Put the following events in correct order by numbering them from 1 to 5.

___ J. P. Morgan buys out Andrew Carnegie to form the first billion-dollar U.S. corporation.

___ The first federal law regulating railroads is passed.

___ The killing of policemen during a labor demonstration results in the execution of radical anarchists and the decline of the Knights of Labor.

___ A teacher of the deaf invents a machine that greatly eases communication across distance.

___ A golden spike is driven, fulfilling the dream of linking the nation by rail.

F. Matching Cause and Effect

Match the historical cause in the left column with the proper effect in the right column by writing the correct letter on the blank line.

Cause

___ 1. Federal land grants and subsidies

___ 2. The building of a transcontinental rail network

Effect

A. Eliminated competition and created monopolistic "trusts" in many industries
B. Fostered growing class divisions and public demands for restraints on corporate trusts
C. Created a strong but narrowly based union organization

Chapter 24 *Industry Comes of Age, 1865–1900* 243

___ 3. Corrupt financial dealings and political manipulations by the railroads

___ 4. New developments in steel making, oil refining, and communication

___ 5. The ruthless competitive techniques of Rockefeller and other industrialists

___ 6. The growing concentration of wealth and power in the new corporate "plutocracy"

___ 7. The North's use of discriminatory price practices against the South

___ 8. The growing mechanization and depersonalization of factory work

___ 9. The Haymarket Square bombing

___ 10. The American Federation of Labor's concentration on skilled craft workers

D. Stimulated the growth of a huge unified national market for American manufactured goods
E. Created a public demand for railroad regulation, such as the Interstate Commerce Act
F. Often made laborers feel powerless and vulnerable to their well-off corporate employers
G. Helped destroy the Knights of Labor and increased public fear of labor agitation
H. Laid the technological basis for huge new industries and spectacular economic growth
I. Encouraged the railroads to build their lines across the North American continent
J. Kept the South in economic dependency as a poverty-stricken supplier of farm products and raw materials to the Northeast

G. Developing Historical Skills

Interpreting Historical Paintings and Photographs

Historical paintings, lithographs, and photographs not only convey substantive information; they can also tell us how an artist or photographer viewed and understood the society and events of his or her day. Examine the photographs and painting indicated below and answer the following questions about them.

1. Examine the working people in the images on pp. 542, 544, 546, and 547. What is the relationship of the workers in each image to their workplace? What is their relation to one another? What does each of the photos reveal about the nature of industrial labor?

2. Examine the painting of "The Strike" by Robert Koehler on p.550. Where is the scene taking place? What is the relationship between the place of work and the scene in the painting? What has likely happened to bring the workers to this scene?

Name_____ Section_____ Date_____

3. Analyze the clothing of all the figures in the Koehler painting. What does it tell you about the economic and social condition of the various people?

4. Two main conversations seem to be taking place in the foreground of the painting. What might each be about? What is the artist suggesting by presenting *both* conversations?

PART III: Applying What You Have Learned

1. What was the impact of the transcontinental rail system on the American economy and society in the late nineteenth century?
2. How did the huge industrial trusts develop in industries such as steel and oil, and what was their effect on the economy?
3. What early efforts were made to control the new corporate industrial giants, and how effective were these efforts?
4. What was the effect of the new industrial revolution on American laborers, and how did various labor organizations attempt to respond to the new conditions?
5. Compare the impact of the new industrialization on the North and the South. Why was the "New South" more a slogan than a reality?
6. William Graham Sumner said that the wealth and luxury enjoyed by millionaires was justifiable as a "good bargain for society." Based on the industrialists' role in the late 1800s, support or criticize Sumner's assertion.
7. How did the industrial transformation after the Civil War compare with the earlier phase of American economic development? (See Chapter 14.) Why were the economic developments of 1865–1900 often seen as a threat to American democracy, whereas those of 1815–1860 were not?

Name_____ Section_____ Date_____

25

America Moves to the City, 1865–1900

PART I: Reviewing the Chapter

A. Checklist of Learning Objectives

After mastering this chapter, you should be able to

1. describe the new industrial city and its impact on American society.
2. describe the "New Immigration" and explain why it aroused opposition from many native-born Americans.
3. discuss the efforts of social reformers and churches to aid the New Immigrants and alleviate urban problems.
4. analyze the changes in American religious life in the late nineteenth century.
5. explain the changes in American education from elementary to the college level.
6. describe the literary and cultural life of the period, including the widespread trend towards "realism."
7. explain the growing national debates about morality in the late nineteenth century, particularly in relation to the changing roles of women and the family.

B. Glossary

To build your social science vocabulary, familiarize yourself with the following terms.

1. **megalopolis** An extensive, heavily populated area, containing several dense urban centers. ". . . gave way to the immense and impersonal megalopolis. . . ." (p. 558)
2. **tenement** A multidwelling building, often poor or overcrowded. "The cities . . . harbored . . . towering skyscrapers and stinking tenements." (p. 560)
3. **affluence** An abundance of wealth. "These leafy 'bedroom communities' eventually ringed the brick-and-concrete cities with a greenbelt of affluence." (p. 560)
4. **despotism** Government by an absolute or tyrannical ruler. ". . . people had grown accustomed to cringing before despotism." (p. 561)
5. **parochial** Concerning a religious parish or small district. (By extension, the term is used, often negatively, to refer to narrow or local perspectives as distinct from broad or cosmopolitan outlooks.) "Catholics expanded their parochial-school system. . . ." (p. 565)
6. **sweatshop** A factory where employees are forced to work long hours under difficult conditions for meager wages. "The women of Hull House successfully lobbied in 1893 for an Illinois antisweatshop law that protected women workers. . . ." (p. 568)
7. **pauper** A poor person, often one who lives on tax-supported charity. "The first restrictive law . . . banged the gate in the faces of paupers. . . ." (p. 570)
8. **convert** A person who turns from one religion or set of beliefs to another. "A fertile field for converts was found in America's harried, nerve-racked, and urbanized civilization. . . ." (p. 572)

9. **Fundamentalist** A conservative Protestant who rejects religious modernism and adheres to a strict and literal interpretation of Christian doctrine and Scriptures. "Conservatives, or 'Fundamentalists,' stood firmly on the Scripture...." (p. 572)
10. **agnostic** One who believes that there can be no human knowledge of any God or gods. "The ... skeptic ... lectured widely on 'Some Mistakes of Moses' and 'Why I Am an Agnostic.'" (p. 573)
11. **behavioral psychology** The branch of psychology that examines human action, often considering it more important than mental or inward states. "His [work] helped to establish the modern discipline of behavioral psychology." (p. 576)
12. **syndicated** In journalism, material that is sold by an organization for publication in several newspapers. "Bare-knuckle editorials were, to an increasing degree, being supplanted by feature articles and non-controversial syndicated material." (p. 577)
13. **tycoon** A wealthy businessperson, especially one who openly displays power and position. "Two new journalistic tycoons emerged." (p. 577)
14. **feminist (feminism)** One who promotes complete political, social, and economic equality of opportunity for women. " ... in 1898 they heard the voice of a major feminist prophet." (p. 583)
15. **prohibition** Forbidding by law the manufacture, sale, or consumption of liquor. (**Temperance** is the voluntary abstention from liquor consumption.) "Statewide prohibition ... was sweeping new states into the 'dry' column." (p. 586)

PART II: Checking Your Progress

A. True-False

Where the statement is true, mark **T**. Where it is false, mark **F**, and correct it in the space immediately below.

____ 1. Rapid and uncontrolled growth made American cities places of both exciting opportunity and severe social problems.

____ 2. After 1880, most immigrants to America came from northern and western Europe.

____ 3. Most of the New Immigrants who arrived in America were escaping from the slums and poverty of European cities.

____ 4. Female social workers established settlement houses to aid struggling immigrants and promote social reform.

____ 5. Many native-born Americans considered the New Immigrants a threat to American democracy and Anglo-Saxon purity.

____ 6. Two religions that gained strength in the United States from the New Immigrants were Roman Catholicism and Judaism.

____ 7. The growth of Darwinian science contributed to the turn towards religious belief in the late nineteenth century.

____ 8. In the late nineteenth century, secondary (high school) education was increasingly carried on by private schools.

Name_____ Section_____ Date_____

_____ 9. Booker T. Washington believed that blacks should try to achieve social equality with whites but not economic equality.

_____ 10. American higher education depended on both public "land-grant" funding and private donations for its financial support.

_____ 11. Urban newspapers often promoted a sensational "yellow journalism" that emphasized sex and scandal rather that politics or social reform.

_____ 12. Post–Civil War writers like Mark Twain and William Dean Howells turned from social realism toward fantasy and science fiction in their novels.

_____ 13. There was growing tension in the late nineteenth century between women's traditionally defined "sphere" of family and home and the social and cultural changes of the era.

_____ 14. The new urban environment generally weakened the family but offered new opportunities for women to achieve social and economic independence.

_____ 15. Voices like Victoria Woodhull, Kate Chopin, and Charlotte Perkins Gilman signaled women's growing dissatisfaction with Victorian ideas about sex and gender roles.

B. Multiple Choice

Select the best answer and write the proper letter in the space provided.

_____ 1. The new cities' glittering consumer economy was symbolized especially by the rise of
   a. separate districts for retail merchants.
   b. fine restaurants and food shops.
   c. large, elegant department stores.
   d. large, carefully constructed urban parks.

_____ 2. One of the most difficult new problems generated by the rise of cities and the urban American life-style was
   a. dealing with horses and other animals in crowded urban settings.
   b. developing means of communication in densely populated city centers.
   c. disposing of large quantities of consumer-generated waste material.
   d. finding effective methods of high-rise construction for limited urban space.

_____ 3. Two new technical developments of the late nineteenth century that contributed to the spectacular growth of American cities were
   a. the telegraph and the railroads.
   b. the compressor and the internal combustion engine.
   c. the electric trolley and the skyscraper.
   d. the oil furnace and the air conditioner.

_____ 4. Countries from which many of the "New Immigrants" came included
   a. Sweden and Great Britain.
   b. Germany and Ireland.
   c. Poland and Italy.
   d. China and Japan.

5. Among the factors driving millions of European peasants from their homeland to America were
   a. American food imports and religious persecution.
   b. The rise of European nation-states and the decline of the Catholic Church.
   c. the rise of communist and fascist regimes.
   d. major international wars among the European great powers.

6. Besides providing direct services to immigrants, the reformers of Hull House worked for general goals like
   a. the secret ballot and direct election of senators.
   b. antisweatshop laws to protect women and child laborers.
   c. social security and unemployment compensation.
   d. conservation and federal aid to municipal governments.

7. The one immigrant group that was totally banned from America after 1882 as a result of nativist agitation was the
   a. Irish.
   b. Greeks.
   c. Africans.
   d. Chinese.

8. Two religious groups that grew most dramatically because of the "New Immigration" were
   a. Methodists and Baptists.
   b. Christian Scientists and the Salvation Army.
   c. Episcopalians and Unitarians.
   d. Jews and Roman Catholics.

9. The phrase "social Gospel" refers to
   a. the fact that many people were turning to God seeking solutions to social conflicts.
   b. the decline in traditional religious beliefs in the late nineteenth century.
   c. the efforts of some Christian reformers to apply their religious beliefs to new social problems.
   d. the conflict between socialists and traditional religious believers.

10. Besides aiding immigrants and promoting social reforms, settlement houses like Jane Addams's Hull House demonstrated that
    a. it was almost impossible to bring about real economic reform in the cities.
    b. the cities offered new challenges and opportunities for women.
    c. women could not bring about successful social change without the vote.
    d. labor was unsympathetic to middle-class reform efforts.

11. Traditional American Protestant religion received a substantial blow from
    a. the psychological ideas of William James.
    b. the theological ideas of the Fundamentalists.
    c. the chemical theories of Charles Eliot.
    d. the biological ideas of Charles Darwin.

12. Unlike Booker T. Washington, W. E. B. Du Bois advocated
    a. economic opportunity for blacks.
    b. integration and social equality for blacks.
    c. practical as well as theoretical education for blacks.
    d. that blacks remain in the South rather than move north.

13. In the late nineteenth century, American colleges and universities benefited especially from
    a. federal and state "land-grant" assistance and the private philanthropy of wealthy donors.
    b. the growing involvement of the churches in higher education.
    c. the fact that a college degree was becoming a prerequisite for employment in industry.
    d. the growth of federal grants and loans to college students.

14. American social reformers like Henry George and Edward Bellamy advocated
    a. utopian reforms to end poverty and eliminate class conflict.
    b. an end to racial prejudice and segregation.
    c. the resettlement of the urban poor on free western homesteads.
    d. a transformation of the traditional family through communal living arrangements.

15. Authors like Mark Twain, Stephen Crane, and Jack London turned American literature toward a greater concern with
    a. close observation and contemplation of nature.
    b. postmodernism and deconstruction of traditional narratives.
    c. fantasy and romance.
    d. social realism and contemporary problems.

C. Identification

Supply the correct identification for each numbered description.

1. High-rise urban buildings that provided barrackslike housing for urban slum dwellers
2. Term for the post-1880 newcomers who came to America primarily from southern and eastern Europe
3. Immigrants who came to America to earn money for a time and then returned to their native land
4. The religious doctrines preached by those who believed the churches should directly address economic and social problems
5. Settlement house in the Chicago slums that became a model for women's involvement in urban social reform
6. Profession established by Jane Addams and others that opened new opportunities for women while engaging urban problems
7. Nativist organization that attacked "New Immigrants" and Roman Catholicism in the 1880s and 1890s
8. The church that became the largest American religious group, mainly as a result of the "New Immigration"

_____ 9. Black educational institution founded by Booker T. Washington to provide training in agriculture and crafts

_____ 10. Organization founded by W. E. B. Du Bois and others to advance black social and economic equality

_____ 11. Henry George's best-selling book that advocated social reform through the imposition of a "single tax" on land

_____ 12. Federal law promoted by a self-appointed morality crusader and used to prosecute moral and sexual dissidents

_____ 13. Charlotte Perkins Gilman's book urging women to enter the work force and advocating cooperative kitchens and child-care centers

_____ 14. Organization formed by Elizabeth Cady Stanton and others to promote the vote for women

_____ 15. Women's organization founded by reformer Frances Willard and others to oppose alcohol consumption

D. Matching People, Places, and Events

Match the person, place, or event in the left column with the proper description in the right column by inserting the correct letter on the blank line.

___ 1. Louis Sullivan
___ 2. Walter Rauschenbusch
___ 3. Jane Addams
___ 4. Dwight L. Moody
___ 5. Mary Baker Eddy
___ 6. Booker T. Washington
___ 7. W. E. B. Du Bois
___ 8. William James
___ 9. Henry George
___ 10. Emily Dickinson
___ 11. Mark Twain
___ 12. Victoria Woodhull
___ 13. Anthony Comstock
___ 14. Charlotte Perkins Gilman

A. Controversial reformer whose book *Progress and Poverty* advocated solving problems of economic inequality by a tax on land

B. Midwestern-born writer and lecturer who created a new style of American literature based on social realism and humor

C. American painter whose sensitive portrayals made her one of the prominent new impressionists

D. Author and founder of a popular new religion based on principles of spiritual healing

E. Leading Protestant advocate of the "social gospel" who tried to make Christianity relevant to urban and industrial problems

F. Former slave who promoted industrial education and economic opportunity but not social equality for blacks

G. Harvard scholar who made original contributions to modern psychology and philosophy

H. Radical feminist propagandist whose eloquent attacks on conventional social morality shocked many Americans in the 1870s

I. Brilliant feminist writer who advocated cooperative cooking and child-care arrangements to promote women's economic independence and equality

J. Leading social reformer who lived with the poor in the slums and pioneered new forms of activism for women

K. Vigorous nineteenth-century crusader for sexual "purity" who used federal law to enforce his moral views

____ 15. Mary Cassatt

L. Harvard-educated scholar and advocate of full black social and economic equality through the leadership of a "talented tenth"

M. Chicago-based architect whose high-rise innovation allowed more people to crowd into limited urban space

N. Popular evangelical preacher who brought the tradition of old-time revivalism to the industrial city

O. Gifted but isolated New England poet, the bulk of whose works were not published until after her death

E. Putting Things in Order

Put the following events in correct order by numbering them from 1 to 5.

____ Well-educated young midwesterner moves to Chicago slums and creates a vital center of social reform and activism.

____ Introduction of a new form of high-rise slum housing drastically increases the overcrowding of the urban poor.

____ Nativist organization is formed to limit the "New Immigration" and attack Roman Catholicism.

____ The formation of a new national organization signals growing strength for the women's suffrage movement.

____ A western territory becomes the first U.S. government to grant full voting rights to women.

F. Matching Cause and Effect

Match the historical cause in the left column with the proper effect in the right column by writing the correct letter on the blank line.

Cause

____ 1. New industrial jobs and urban excitement

____ 2. Uncontrolled rapid growth and the "New Immigration" from Europe

____ 3. Cheap American grain exports to Europe

____ 4. The cultural strangeness and poverty of southern and eastern European immigrants

____ 5. Social gospel ministers and settlement-house workers

____ 6. Darwinian science and growing urban materialism

Effect

A. Encouraged the mass urban public's taste for scandal and sensation

B. Created intense poverty and other problems in the crowded urban slums

C. Weakened the religious influence in American society and created divisions within the churches

D. Led women and men to delay marriage and have fewer children

E. Helped uproot European peasants from their ancestral lands and sent them seeking new opportunities in America and elsewhere

F. Supported the substantial improvements in American undergraduate and graduate education in the late nineteenth century

___ 7. Government land grants and private philanthropy

___ 8. Popular newspapers and "yellow journalism"

___ 9. Changes in moral and sexual attitudes

___ 10. The difficulties of family life in the industrial city

G. Lured millions of rural Americans off the farms and into the cities

H. Assisted immigrants and other slum dwellers and pricked middle-class consciences about urban problems

I. Provoked sharp hostility from some native-born Americans and organized labor groups

J. Created sharp divisions about the "new morality" and issues such as divorce

G. Developing Historical Skills

Interpreting a Line Graph

A line graph is another visual way to convey information. It is often used to present notable historical changes occurring over substantial periods of time. Study the line graph on p.561 and answer the following questions.

1. There are five major "peaks" of immigration, and four major "valleys." What factors helped cause each of the periods of heavy immigration? What helped cause each of the sharp declines?

2. About how long did each of the first four periods of major immigration last? About how long did each of the four "valleys" last? How long has the current (to 1997) phase of rising or steady immigration lasted?

3. During what five-year period was there the sharpest rise in immigration? What five-year period saw the sharpest fall?

4. In about what *three* years did approximately 800,000 immigrants enter the United States? In about what *seven* years did approximately 200,000 immigrants enter the United States?

5. Approximately how many fewer immigrants came in 1920 than in 1914? About how many more immigrants came in 1990 than in 1950?

PART III: Applying What You Have Learned

1. What new opportunities did the cities create for Americans?
2. What new social problems did urbanization create? How did Americans respond to these problems?
3. How did the "New Immigration" differ from the "Old Immigration," and how did Americans respond to it?
4. How was American religion affected by the urban transformation, the New Immigration, and cultural and intellectual changes?
5. How did American social criticism, imaginative writing, and art all relate to the urban industrial changes of the late nineteenth century?
6. How and why did women assume a larger place in American society at this time? (Compare their status in this period with that of the pre–Civil War period described in Chapter 16.) How were changes in their condition related to changes in both the family and the larger social order?

Name_____ Section_____ _____ Date_____

26

The Great West and the Agricultural Revolution, 1865–1896

PART I: Reviewing the Chapter

A. Checklist of Learning Objectives

After mastering this chapter, you should be able to

1. describe the nature of the cultural conflicts and battles that accompanied the white American migration into the Great Plains and the Far West.
2. explain the development of federal policy towards Native Americans in the late nineteenth century.
3. analyze the brief flowering and decline of the cattle and mining frontiers.
4. explain the impact of the closing of the frontier, and the long-term significance of the frontier for American history.
5. describe the revolutionary changes in farming on the Great Plains.
6. describe the economic forces that drove farmers into debt, and describe how the Grange, the Farmers' Alliances, and the Populist Party organized to protest their oppression.

B. Glossary

To build your social science vocabulary, familiarize yourself with the following terms.

1. **nomadic (nomad)** A way of life characterized by frequent movement from place to place for economic sustenance. ". . . the Sioux transformed themselves from foot-traveling, crop-growing villagers to wide-ranging nomadic traders. . . ." (p. 591)
2. **immunity** Freedom or exemption from some imposition. ". . . [the] militia massacred . . . four hundred Indians who apparently thought they had been promised immunity." (p. 593)
3. **reservation** Public lands designated for use by Indians. "The vanquished Indians were finally ghettoized on reservations. . . ." (p. 595)
4. **ward** Someone considered incompetent to manage his or her own affairs and therefore placed under the legal guardianship of another person or group. ". . . there [they had] to eke out a sullen existence as wards of the government." (p. 595)
5. **probationary** Concerning a period of testing or trial, after which a decision is made based on performance. "The probationary period was later extended. . . ." (p. 597)
6. **folklore** The common traditions and stories of a people. "These bowlegged Knights of the Saddle . . . became part of American folklore." (p. 602)
7. **irrigation** Watering land artificially, through canals, pipes, or other means. ". . . irrigation projects . . . caused the 'Great American Desert' to bloom. . . ." (p. 604)
8. **meridian** In geography, any of the imaginary lines of longitude running north and south on the globe. ". . . settlers . . . rashly pushed . . . beyond the 100th meridian. . . ." (p. 604)

9. **contiguous** Joined together by common borders. "Only Oklahoma, New Mexico, and Arizona remained to be lifted into statehood from contiguous territory on the mainland of North America." (p. 606)
10. **safety valve** Anything, such as the American frontier, that allegedly serves as a necessary outlet for built-up pressure, energy, and so on. "But the 'safety-valve' theory does have some validity." (p. 607)
11. **loan shark** A person who lends money at an exorbitant or illegal rate of interest. "The [farmers] . . . cried out in despair against the loan sharks. . . ." (p. 610)
12. **serfdom** The feudal condition of being permanently bound to land owned by someone else. ". . . the farmers were about to sink into a status suggesting Old World serfdom." (p. 610)
13. **mumbo jumbo** Mysterious and unintelligible words or behavior. "Kelley, a Mason, even found farmers receptive to his mumbo jumbo of passwords and secret rituals. . . ." (p. 611)
14. **prophet** A person believed to speak with divine power or special gifts, sometimes including predicting the future (hence any specially talented or eloquent advocate of a cause). "Numerous fiery prophets leapt forward to trumpet the Populist cause." (p. 613)
15. **citadel** A fortress occupying a commanding height. " . . . join hands with urban workers, and mount a successful attack on the northeastern citadels of power." (p. 614)

PART II: Checking Your Progress

A. True-False

Where the statement is true, mark **T**. Where it is false, mark **F**, and correct it in the space immediately below.

_____ 1. Cultural conflicts and population loss to disease weakened the Plains Indians' ability to resist white encroachment onto their lands.

_____ 2. The Plains Indians were rather quickly and easily defeated by the U.S. Army.

_____ 3. A crucial factor in defeating the Indians was the destruction of the buffalo, a vital source of food and other supplies.

_____ 4. Humanitarian reformers respected the Indians' traditional culture and tried to preserve their tribal way of life.

_____ 5. Individual gold and silver miners proved unable to compete with large mining corporations and trained engineers.

_____ 6. During the peak years of the Long Drive, the cattlemen's prosperity depended on driving large beef herds great distances to railroad terminal points.

_____ 7. More families acquired land under the Homestead Act than from the states and private owners.

_____ 8. Although very few city dwellers ever migrated west to take up farming, the frontier "safety valve" did have some positive effects on eastern workers.

_____ 9. The farmers who settled the Great Plains were usually single-crop producers dependent on unstable distant markets for their livelihoods.

____ 10. The greatest problem facing the farmers was inflation in the prices of machinery and supplies they had to buy.

____ 11. A fundamental problem of the Farmers' Alliance was their inability to overcome the racial division between white and black farmers in the South.

____ 12. The economic crisis of the 1890s strengthened the Populists' belief that farmers and industrial workers should form an alliance against economic and political oppression.

____ 13. Republican political manager Mark Hanna struggled to raise enough funds to combat William Jennings Bryan's pro-silver campaign.

____ 14. Bryan's populist campaign failed partly because he was unable to persuade enough urban workers to join his essentially rural-based cause.

____ 15. McKinley's victory in 1896 ushered in an era marked by Republican domination, weakened party organization, and the fading of the money issue in American politics.

B. Multiple Choice

Select the best answer and write the proper letter in the space provided.

____ 1. Western Indians offered strong resistance to white expansion through their effective use of
   a. artillery and infantry tactics.
   b. their alliance with remaining Mexican resisters in the West.
   c. nighttime and winter campaigning.
   d. repeating rifles and horses.

____ 2. Intertribal warfare among Plains Indians increased in the late nineteenth century because of
   a. the attempt of the Chippewas to gain dominance over all other groups.
   b. the confining of several different groups within a single reservation.
   c. growing competition for the rapidly dwindling hunting grounds.
   d. the rise of the "Ghost Dance" among some Indian groups.

____ 3. The federal government's attempt to confine Indians to certain areas through formal treaties was largely ineffective because
   a. the nomadic Plains Indians largely rejected the idea of formal authority and defined territory.
   b. Congress refused to ratify treaties signed with the Indians.
   c. the treaties made no effective provisions for enforcement.
   d. the largest tribe, the Sioux, refused to sign any treaties with the whites.

____ 4. The warfare that led up to the Battle of the Little Big Horn was set off by
   a. white intrusion into the previously reserved Indian territory of Oklahoma.
   b. Indian attacks on the transcontinental railroad construction crews.
   c. white intrusions after the discovery of gold in the sacred Black Hills.
   d. a conflict over the interpretation of the second Treaty of Fort Laramie.

5. Indian resistance was finally subdued because
    a. most of the effective Indian leadership was bought off.
    b. the coming of the railroad led to the destruction of the buffalo and the Indians' way of life.
    c. most Indians lost the will to resist.
    d. the army developed effective techniques of guerrilla warfare.

6. The federal government attempted to force Indians away from their traditional values and customs by
    a. instructing them in white farming methods.
    b. creating a network of children's boarding schools and white "field matrons."
    c. establishing scholarships for Indian students at white colleges.
    d. developing programs of bilingual education in reservation schools.

7. Both the mining and cattle frontiers saw
    a. an increase of ethnic and class conflict.
    b. a loss of economic viability after an initial boom.
    c. a turn from large-scale investment to the individual entrepreneur.
    d. a movement from individual operations to large-scale corporate businesses.

8. The problem of developing agriculture in the arid West was solved most successfully through
    a. concentrating agriculture in the more fertile mountain valleys.
    b. the use of small-scale family farms rather than large "bonanza" farms.
    c. the use of irrigation from dammed western rivers.
    d. the turn to desert crops like olives and dates.

9. The "safety valve" theory of the frontier holds that
    a. Americans were able to divert the most violent elements of the population to the West.
    b. the conflict between farmers and ranchers was relieved by the Homestead Act.
    c. unemployed city dwellers could move west and thus relieve labor conflict in the East.
    d. political movements such as the Populists provided relief for the most serious grievances of western farmers.

10. Which one of these factors did *not* make the trans-Mississippi West a unique part of the America frontier experience?
    a. the large numbers of Indians, Hispanics, and Asian-Americans in the region
    b. the problem of applying new technologies in a hostile wilderness
    c. the scale and severity of environmental challenges in an arid environment
    d. the large role of the federal government in economic and social development

11. By the 1880s, most western farmers faced hard times because
    a. free land was no longer available under the Homestead Act.
    b. they were unable to increase grain production to keep up with demand.
    c. they were being strangled by excessive federal regulation of agriculture.
    d. they were forced to sell their grain at low prices in a depressed world market.

Name_____ Section_____ Date_____

____ 12. Which of the following was *not* among the political goals advocated by the Populist Party in the 1890s?

   a. nationalizing the railroad, telegraph, and telephone
   b. creation of a national system of unemployment insurance and old-age pensions
   c. a graduated income tax
   d. free and unlimited coinage of silver money

____ 13. The U.S. government's response to the Pullman strike aroused great anger from organized labor because

   a. it seemed to represent "government by injunction" designed to destroy labor unions.
   b. it broke apart the growing alliance between urban workers and farmers.
   c. it undermined efforts to organize federal workers like those in the postal service.
   d. it turned their most effective leader, Eugene V. Debs, into a cautious conservative.

____ 14. William Jennings Bryan gained the Democratic nomination in 1896 because he strongly advocated

   a. unlimited coinage of silver in order to inflate currency.
   b. higher tariffs in order to protect the American farmer.
   c. government ownership of the railroads and the telegraph system.
   d. a coalition between white and black farmers in the South and Midwest.

____ 15. McKinley defeated Bryan primarily because he was able to win the support of

   a. white southern farmers.
   b. eastern wage earners and city dwellers.
   c. urban and rural blacks.
   d. former Populists and Greenback Laborites.

C. Identification

Supply the correct identification for each numbered description.

_____ 1. Major northern Plains Indian nation that fought and eventually lost a bitter war against the U.S. Army, 1876–1877

_____ 2. Southwestern Indian tribe led by Geronimo that carried out some of the last fighting against white conquest

_____ 3. Generally poor areas where vanquished Indians were eventually confined under federal control

_____ 4. Indian religious movement, originating out of the sacred Sun Dance that the federal government attempted to stamp out in 1890

_____ 5. Federal law that attempted to dissolve tribal landholding and establish Indians as individual farmers

_____ 6. Huge silver and gold deposit that brought wealth and statehood to Nevada

_____ 7. General term for the herding of cattle from the grassy plains to the railroad terminals of Kansas, Nebraska, and Wyoming

_____ 8. Federal law that offered generous land opportunities to poorer farmers but also provided the unscrupulous with opportunities for hoaxes and fraud

_____ 9. Improved type of fencing that enabled farmers to enclose land on the treeless plains

_____ 10. Former "Indian Territory" where "sooners" tried to get the jump on "boomers" when it was opened for settlement in 1889

_____ 11. Third political party that emerged in the 1890s to express rural grievances and mount major attacks on the Democrats and Republicans

_____ 12. Popular pamphlet written by William Hope Harvey that portrayed pro-silver arguments triumphing over the traditional views of bankers and economics professors.

_____ 13. Bitter labor conflict in Chicago that brought federal intervention and the jailing of union leader Eugene V. Debs

_____ 14. Spectacular convention speech by a young pro-silver advocate that brought him the Democratic presidential nomination in 1896

_____ 15. Popular term for those who favored the "status quo" in metal money and opposed the pro-silver Bryanites in 1896

D. Matching People, Places, and Events

Match the person, place, or event in the left column with the proper description in the right column by inserting the correct letter on the blank line.

___ 1. Sand Creek, Colorado
___ 2. Little Big Horn
___ 3. Sitting Bull
___ 4. Chief Joseph
___ 5. Geronimo
___ 6. Helen Hunt Jackson
___ 7. John Wesley Powell
___ 8. William Hope Harvey
___ 9. Eugene V. Debs
___ 10. James B. Weaver
___ 11. Mary E. Lease
___ 12. Mark Hanna

A. Ohio industrialist and organizer of McKinley's victory over Bryan in the election of 1896
B. Leader of the Nez Percé tribe who conducted a brilliant but unsuccessful military campaign in 1877
C. Author of the popular pro-silver pamphlet "Coin's Financial School"
D. Former Civil War general and Granger who ran as the Greenback Labor party candidate for president in 1880
E. Leader of the Sioux during wars of 1876–1877
F. Explorer and geologist who warned that traditional agriculture could not succeed west of the 100th meridian
G. Leader of the Apaches of Arizona in their warfare with the whites
H. Site of Indian massacre by militia forces in 1864
I. Massachusetts writer whose books aroused sympathy for the plight of the Native Americans
J. Site of major U.S. Army defeat in the Sioux War of 1876–1877
K. Railway union leader who converted to socialism while serving jail time during the Pullman strike
L. Eloquent Kansas Populist who urged farmers to "raise less corn and more hell"

E. Putting Things in Order

Put the following events in correct order by numbering them from 1 to 5.

____ A sharp economic depression leads to a major railroad strike and the intervention of federal troops in Chicago.

____ The violation of agreements with the Dakota Sioux leads to a major Indian war and a military disaster for the U.S. cavalry.

____ A federal law grants 160 acres of land to farmers at token prices, thus encouraging the rapid settlement of the Great West.

____ The U.S. Census Bureau declares that there is no longer a clear line of frontier settlement, ending a formative chapter of American history.

____ Despite a fervent campaign by their charismatic young champion, pro-silver Democrats lose a pivotal election to "Gold Bug" Republicans.

F. Matching Cause and Effect

Match the historical cause in the left column with the proper effect in the right column by writing the correct letter on the blank line.

Cause

____ 1. The encroachment of white settlement and the violation of treaties with Indians

____ 2. Railroad building, disease, and the destruction of the buffalo

____ 3. Reformers' attempts to make Native Americans conform to white ways

____ 4. The coming of big-business mining and stock-raising to the West

____ 5. "Dry farming," barbed wire, and irrigation

____ 6. The passing of the frontier of 1890

____ 7. The growing economic specialization of western farmers

____ 8. The rise of the Populist Party in the early 1890s

____ 9. The economic depression that began in 1893

____ 10. The return of prosperity after 1897 and new gold discoveries in Alaska, South Africa, and elsewhere

Effect

A. Caused widespread protests and strikes like the one against the Pullman Company in Chicago

B. Threatened the two-party domination of American politics by the Republicans and Democrats

C. Created new psychological and economic problems for a nation accustomed to a boundlessly open West

D. Ended the romantic, colorful era of the miners' and the cattlemen's frontier

E. Decimated Indian populations and hastened their defeat at the hands of advancing whites

F. Effectively ended the free-silver agitation and the domination of the money question in American politics

G. Made settlers vulnerable to vast industrial and market forces beyond their control

H. Made it possible to farm the dry, treeless areas of the Great Plains and the West

I. Further undermined Native Americans' traditional tribal culture and morale

J. Led to nearly constant warfare with Plains Indians from 1868 to about 1890

G. Developing Historical Skills

Comparing Election Maps

Comparing maps of two consecutive elections enables you to see what political changes have occurred in a relatively brief historical period. The election map on p. 628 shows the vote by county; the one on p. 637 shows the vote by state. Keep that difference in mind as you answer the following questions.

1. Six western states had significant votes for the Populist Weaver in 1892. Who carried them in 1896?

2. List six states where Democrat Cleveland had strong support in 1892 that turned around and voted Republican in 1896. In which region were most such states located?

3. List five states that stayed solidly Republican in both 1892 and 1896, and five states that stayed solidly Democratic. In which regions were each of these groups of "solid" states located?

4. In 1892, nine midwestern and western states had substantial concentrations of Populist voters. In the election of 1896, how many of those nine states went Democratic, and how many went Republican?

H. Map Mastery

Map Discrimination

Using the maps and charts in Chapter 26, answer the following questions.

1. In the election of 1892, which three western states had no counties that backed the Populist party?

2. Which four southern states had the most Populist support in the election of 1892 (that is, at least three counties that went Populist)?

3. In the election of 1896, how many electoral votes did McKinley win from states west of the Mississippi River?

4. How many electoral votes did McKinley win in the southern states of the old Confederacy?

Name_____ Section_____ Date_____

Map Challenge

Using the maps of *American Agriculture in 1900* (p. 609) and *Presidential Election of 1896* (p. 620), discuss why the relationship between the Populist and pro-silver movements and the patterns of American agriculture. Include in your analysis some analysis of those Midwestern agricultural states that did may have been influenced by Populism but did not vote for Bryan in 1896.

PART III: Applying What You Have Learned

1. How did whites finally overcome resistance of the Plains Indians, and what happened to the Indians after their resistance ceased?
2. What social, ethnic, environmental, and economic factors made the trans-Mississippi West a unique region among the successive American frontiers?
3. What were the actual effects of the frontier on American society at different stages of its development? What was valuable in Frederick Jackson Turner's "frontier thesis," despite its being discredited by subsequent historians?
4. How did the forces of economic class conflict and race figure into the farmer and labor revolt of the 1880s and 1890s? Was there ever any chance that a bi-racial coalition of farmers could have succeeded not only in economic change but in overcoming the South's racial divisions?
   Were race relations actually worse after the Populist revolt failed?
5. Were the Populist and pro-silver movements of the 1880s and 1890s essentially backward-looking protests by a passing rural America, or were they, despite their immediate political failure, genuine prophetic voices raising central critical questions about democracy and economic justice in the new corporate industrial America?
6. What were the major issues in the crucial campaign of 1896? Why did McKinley win, and what were the long-term effects of his victory?
7. Some historians have seen Bryan as the political heir of Jefferson and Jackson, and McKinley as the political heir of Hamilton and the Whigs. Are such connections valid? Why or why not? (See Chapters 10, 12, and 13.)

27

The Path of Empire, 1890–1899

PART I: Reviewing the Chapter

A. Checklist of Learning Objectives

After mastering this chapter, you should be able to

1. explain why the United States suddenly abandoned its isolationism and turned outward at the end of the nineteenth century.
2. indicate how the Venezuelan and Hawaiian affairs expressed the new American assertiveness as well as American ambivalence about foreign involvements.
3. describe how America became involved with Cuba and explain why a reluctant President McKinley was forced to go to war with Spain.
4. state the unintended consequences of Dewey's victory at Manila Bay.
5. describe the easy American military conquest of Cuba and Puerto Rico.
6. explain McKinley's decision to keep the Philippines and list the opposing arguments in the debate about imperialism.
7. analyze the long-term consequences and significance of the Spanish-American War.

B. Glossary

To build your social science vocabulary, familiarize yourself with the following terms.

1. **concession** A privilege granted by a government to another government, private company, or individual. ". . . Japan, Germany, and Russia all extorted concessions from the anemic Chinese Empire." (p. 624)
2. **nation-state** The modern form of political organization in which the government coincides exactly with a single national territory and population having a distinctive culture, language, history, and so on. "If America was to survive in the competition of modern nation-states, perhaps it, too, would have to become an imperial power." (p. 624)
3. **reciprocity** An exchange of equal privileges between two governments. "America's grip was further tightened in 1875 by a commercial reciprocity agreement. . . ." (p. 627)
4. **scorched-earth policy** The policy of burning and destroying all the property in a given area so as to deny it to an enemy. "Driven to desperation, the insurgents now adopted a scorched-earth policy." (p. 628)
5. **reconcentration** The policy of forcibly removing a population to confined areas in order to deny support to enemy forces. " He undertook to crush the rebellion by herding many civilians into barbed-wire reconcentration camps." (p. 629)
6. **jingoist** Aggressively patriotic and warlike. ". . . Cleveland—an antijingoist and anti-imperialist—refused to budge." (p. 629)
7. **atrocity** A specific act of extreme cruelty. "Where atrocity stories did not exist, they were invented." (p. 629)

8. **proviso** An article or clause in a statute, treaty, or contract establishing a particular stipulation or condition affecting the whole document. "This proviso proclaimed . . . that when the United States had overthrown Spanish misrule, it would give the Cubans their freedom. . . ." (p. 631)
9. **archipelago** A large group of islands within a limited area. "An impression spread that America needed the archipelago. . . ." (p. 633)
10. **hostage** A person or thing forcibly held in order to obtain certain goals or agreements. "Hereafter these distant islands were to be . . . a kind of indefensible hostage given to Japan." (p. 642)

PART II: Checking Your Progress

A. True-False

Where the statement is true, mark **T**. Where it is false, mark **F**, and correct it in the space immediately below.

_____ 1. The American government was deeply involved in the key international developments of the 1870s and 1880s.

_____ 2. Alfred T. Mahan argued in his book that the conquest of colonies necessary to provide raw materials and markets was the key to world history.

_____ 3. The South American boundary dispute over Guyana in 1895–1896 nearly resulted in a U.S. war with Venezuela.

_____ 4. The Venezuelan boundary dispute was resolved when the United States backed away because of its growing conflict with Germany.

_____ 5. President Cleveland refused to annex Hawaii because he believed that the white America planters there had unjustly deposed Hawaii's Queen Liliuokalani.

_____ 6. Americans first became involved in Cuba because they sympathized with the Cubans' revolt against imperialist Spain.

_____ 7. The Hearst press worked to promote a peaceful, negotiated settlement involving Cuban self-government under Spanish rule.

_____ 8. President McKinley tried to resist the pressure for war with Spain coming from business-people and Wall Street financiers.

_____ 9. Admiral Dewey's squadron attacked Spanish forces in the Philippines because of secret orders give by Assistant Navy Secretary Theodore Roosevelt.

_____ 10. American forces received assistance in capturing Manila by native Filipinos who were rebelling against Spain.

_____ 11. The American military conquest of Cuba was efficient but very costly in battlefield casualties.

_____ 12. President McKinley declared that religion played a role in his decision to keep the Philippines.

_____ 13. The treaty to annex the Philippines was approved by a wide margin in the Senate.

___ 14. The Supreme Court decided in the insular cases that American constitutional law and the bill of rights applied to the people under American rule in Puerto Rico and the Philippines.

___ 15. The Spanish-American War made the United States a full-fledged power in East Asia.

B. Multiple Choice

Select the best answer and write the proper letter in the space provided.

___ 1. Alfred Thayer Mahan promoted American overseas expansion by
   a. developing a lurid "yellow press" that stimulated popular excitement.
   b. arguing that sea power was the key to world domination.
   c. provoking naval incidents with Germany and Britain in the Pacific.
   d. arguing that the Monroe Doctrine implied American control of Latin America.

___ 2. Which of the following was *not* among the factors propelling America toward overseas expansion in the 1890s?
   a. the desire to expand overseas agricultural and manufacturing exports
   b. the "yellow press" of Joseph Pulitzer and William Randolph Hearst
   c. the need to find new African and Asian sources of raw materials for American industry
   d. the ideologies of Anglo-Saxon superiority and social Darwinism

___ 3. The final result of the Venezuela-Guiana crisis with Britain was
   a. a series of battles between British and American naval forces.
   b. the intervention of the German kaiser in Latin America.
   c. American colonial control of Guiana.
   d. British retreat and growing American-British friendship.

___ 4. President Grover Cleveland refused to annex Hawaii because
   a. white planters had illegally overthrown Queen Liliuokalani against the wishes of most native Hawaiians.
   b. there was no precedent for the United States to acquire territory except by purchase.
   c. the Germans and the British threatened possible war.
   d. he knew the public disapproved and the Senate would not ratify a treaty of annexation.

___ 5. Americans first became concerned with the situation in Cuba because
   a. Spanish control of Cuba violated the Monroe Doctrine.
   b. imperialists and business leaders were looking to acquire colonial territory for the United States.
   c. Americans sympathized with Cuban rebels in their fight for freedom from Spanish rule.
   d. the Battleship *Maine* exploded in Havana harbor.

___ 6. Even before the sinking of the Maine, the American public's indignation at Spain had been whipped into a frenzy by
   a. Spanish Catholics' persecution of the Protestant minority in Cuba.
   b. Spain's aggressive battleship-building program.
   c. William Randolph Hearst's sensational newspaper accounts of Spanish atrocities in Cuba.
   d. the Spanish government's brutal treatment of American sailors on leave in Havana.

_____ 7. Even after the *Maine* exploded, the United States was slow to declare war on Cuba because
   a. the public was reluctant to get into a war.
   b. President McKinley was reluctant to get into a war.
   c. the Cubans did not want Americans to intervene in their affairs.
   d. there was no clear evidence that the Spanish had really blown up the *Maine*.

_____ 8. As soon as the U.S. declared war on Spain, Commodore George Dewey sailed to the Philippine Islands because
   a. that was the best place to strike a blow for a free Cuba.
   b. he had been ordered to do so by Assistant Navy Secretary Theodore Roosevelt.
   c. the American navy happened to be on a tour of East Asian ports.
   d. he was invited to do so by Philippine nationalists.

_____ 9. Emilio Aguinaldo was
   a. the leader of Cuban insurgents against Spanish rule.
   b. the leader of Filipino insurgents against Spanish rule.
   c. the commander of the Spanish navy in the Battle of Manila Bay.
   d. the first native Hawaiian to become governor of the islands after the American takeover.

_____ 10. The largest cause of American deaths in Cuba was
   a. the direct-charge tactics of Theodore Roosevelt's Rough Riders.
   b. the effective artillery bombardments of the Spanish navy.
   c. armed clashes with Cuban rebels and civilians.
   d. bad food, disease, and unsanitary conditions.

_____ 11. In addition to Cuba, American forces successfully seized the Spanish-owned Caribbean colony of
   a. Puerto Rico.
   b. the Virgin Islands.
   c. the Dominican Republic.
   d. Guam.

_____ 12. President William McKinley based his decision to make the Philippines an American colony on
   a. the belief in white Anglo-Saxon superiority to the Asian Filipinos.
   b. a combination of religious piety and material economic interests.
   c. the belief that the Philippines would be the first step toward an American empire in China.
   d. the strong agitation for empire coming from the Hearst and Pulitzer yellow press.

_____ 13. Among prominent Americans who opposed annexation of the Philippines were
   a. Leonard Wood and Walter Reed.
   b. William Randolph Hearst and Theodore Roosevelt.
   c. Mark Twain and William James.
   d. Mark Hanna and "Czar" Thomas Reed.

____ 14. Pro-imperialist Americans argued that the Philippines should be seized because of
   a. patriotism and economic opportunities.
   b. the Monroe Doctrine and national security.
   c. the Declaration of Independence and the wishes of the Philippine people.
   d. overpopulation and the need to acquire new land for American settlers.

____ 15. The Platt Amendment provided that
   a. the people of Puerto Rico were citizens of the United States.
   b. the United States would eventually grant independence to the Philippines and Puerto Rico.
   c. no European power could establish new bases or colonies in the Pacific.
   d. the United States had the right to intervene with troops and maintain military bases in Cuba.

C. Identification

Supply the correct identification for each numbered description.

_____ 1. Book written by a Protestant minister that proclaimed the superiority of Anglo-Saxon civilization

_____ 2. Remote Pacific site of a naval clash between the United States and Germany in 1889

_____ 3. South American nation that nearly came to blows with the United States in 1892 over an incident involving the deaths of American sailors

_____ 4. The principle of American foreign policy invoked by Secretary of State Olney to justify American intervention in the Venezuelan boundary dispute

_____ 5. Valuable naval base acquired by the United States from the Hawaiian government in 1887

_____ 6. Term for the sensationalistic and jingoistic prowar journalism practiced by W. R. Hearst and Joseph Pulitzer

_____ 7. American battleship sent on a "friendly" visit to Cuba that ended in disaster and war

_____ 8. Amendment to the declaration of war with Spain that stated the United States would grant Cubans their independence after the war

_____ 9. Site of the dramatic American naval victory that led to U.S. acquisition of rich, Spanish-owned Pacific islands

_____ 10. Colorful volunteer regiment of the Spanish-American War led by a militarily inexperienced but politically influential colonel

_____ 11. The Caribbean island conquered from Spain in 1898 that became an important American colony

_____ 12. Group that battled against American colonization of the Philippines, which included such influential citizens as Mark Twain and Andrew Carnegie

_____ 13. Supreme Court cases of 1901 that determined that the U.S. Constitution and bill of rights did not apply in colonial territories under the American flag

14. American-imposed restriction written into the constitution of Cuba that guaranteed American naval bases on the island and declared that the United States had the right to intervene in Cuba

15. Deadly tropical disease conquered during the Spanish-American War by Dr. Walter Reed and other American medical researchers

D. Matching People, Places, and Events

Match the person, place, or event in the left column with the proper description in the right column by inserting the correct letter on the blank line.

1. Josiah Strong
2. Alfred Thayer Mahan
3. Richard Olney
4. Queen Liliuokalani
5. Grover Cleveland
6. "Butcher" Weyler
7. William R. Hearst
8. William McKinley
9. George E. Dewey
10. Theodore Roosevelt
11. Emilio Aguinaldo
12. Leonard Wood
13. William James
14. William Jennings Bryan
15. Walter Reed

A. Imperialist advocate, aggressive assistant navy secretary, Rough Rider
B. Harvard philosopher and one of the leading anti-imperialists opposing U.S. acquisition of the Philippines
C. Spanish general whose brutal tactics against Cuban rebels outraged American public opinion
D. Native Hawaiian ruler overthrown in a revolution led by white planters and aided by U.S. troops
E. Commander in Spanish-American War who organized the efficient American military government of Cuba
F. American naval officer who wrote influential books emphasizing sea power and advocating a big navy
G. Naval commander whose spectacular May Day victory in 1898 opened the doors to American imperialism in Asia
H. Vigorous promoter of sensationalistic anti-Spanish propaganda and eager advocate of imperialistic war
I. American doctor who led the medical efforts to conquer yellow fever during U.S. occupation of Cuba
J. American clergyman who preached Anglo-Saxon superiority and called for stronger U.S. missionary effort overseas
K. Belligerent U.S. secretary of state who used the Monroe Doctrine to pressure Britain in the Venezuelan boundary crisis
L. President who initially opposed war with Spain but eventually supported U.S. acquisition of the Philippines
M. Leading Democratic politician whose intervention narrowly tipped the Senate vote in favor of acquiring the Philippines in 1899
N. American president who refused to annex Hawaii on the grounds that the native ruler had been unjustly deposed
O. Leader of the Filipino insurgents who aided Americans in defeating Spain and taking Manila

E. Putting Things in Order

Put the following events in correct order by numbering them from 1 to 5.

___ American rebels in Hawaii seek annexation by the United States, but the American president turns them down.

___ A battleship explosion arouses fury in America and leads the nation into a "splendid little war" with Spain.

___ A South American boundary dispute leads to aggressive American assertion of the Monroe Doctrine against Britain.

___ Americans grant Cuba self-government but retain naval bases and the right to intervene.

___ The U.S. Senate narrowly approves a treaty giving the United States a major colony off the coast of Asia.

F. Matching Cause and Effect

Match the historical cause in the left column with the proper effect in the right column by writing the correct letter on the blank line.

Cause

___ 1. Economic expansion, the yellow press, and competition with other powers

___ 2. The Venezuelan boundary dispute

___ 3. The white planter revolt against Queen Liliuokalani

___ 4. The Cuban revolt against Spain

___ 5. The *Maine* explosion

___ 6. Theodore Roosevelt's secret orders to Commodore Dewey

___ 7. The confusion and weakness of Spain's army and navy

___ 8. McKinley's decision to keep the Philippines

___ 9. W. J. Bryan's last-minute support for the treaty acquiring the Philippines

___ 10. The Spanish-American War

Effect

A. Enabled America's unprepared military forces to gain quick and easy victories

B. Created an emotional and irresistible public demand for war with Spain

C. Strengthened the Monroe Doctrine and made Britain more willing to accommodate U.S. interests

D. Led to the surprising U.S. victory over Spain at Manila Bay

E. Set off the first debate about the wisdom and rightness of American overseas imperialism

F. Turned America away from isolationism and toward international involvements in the 1890s

G. Aroused strong sympathy from most Americans

H. Enhanced American national pride and made the United States an international power in East Asia

I. Set off a bitter debate about imperialism in the Senate and the country

J. Tipped a narrow Senate vote in favor of imperialist acquisition of the Philippines

G. Map Mastery

Map Discrimination

Using the maps and charts in Chapter 27, answer the following questions.

1. *The Venezuela-British Guiana Boundary Dispute*: In the Venezuelan boundary conflict, which nation—Britain or Venezuela—gained more of the disputed territory in the final settlement?

2. *The Pacific*: What two prime naval harbors did the United States acquire in (a) Samoa and (b) Hawaii?

3. *Dewey's Route in the Philippines, 1898*: Manila Bay lies off the coast of which island of the Philippine archipelago?

4. *The Cuban Campaign, 1898*: Which of the two battles fought by Rough Riders—San Juan Hill and El Caney—occurred nearer Santiago Harbor?

5. *The Cuban Campaign, 1898*: Which of the two Spanish-owned Caribbean islands conquered by the United States in 1898 was farthest from Florida?

Map Challenge

Using the map of *The Pacific* on p. 627, discuss the exact geographical relation of each of America's new Pacific colonies—Samoa, Hawaii, the Philippines—to (a) the United States mainland and (b) China and Japan. Which of the colonies was most strategically important to America's position in the Pacific, which least, and which was most vulnerable? Why?

PART III: Applying What You Have Learned

1. What were the causes and signs of America's sudden turn toward international involvement at the end of the nineteenth century?
2. How did the United States get into the Spanish-American War over the initial objections of President McKinley?
3. What role did the press and public opinion play in the origin, conduct, and results of the Spanish-American War?
4. What were the key arguments for and against U. S. imperialism?
5. What were some of the short-term and long-term results of American acquisition of the Philippines and Puerto Rico?
6. How was U. S. overseas imperialism in 1898 similar to and different from earlier American expansion across North America, or "Manifest Destiny"? (See especially Chapter 13.) Was this "new imperialism" a fundamental departure from America's traditions, or simply a further extension of "westward migration"?

28

America on the World Stage, 1899–1909

PART I: Reviewing the Chapter

A. Checklist of Learning Objectives

After mastering this chapter, you should be able to

1. describe the Filipino rebellion against U.S. rule and the war to suppress it.
2. explain the U.S. "Open Door" policy in China.
3. discuss the significance of the "proimperialist" Republican victory in 1900 and the rise of Theodore Roosevelt as a strong advocate of American power in international affairs.
4. describe the aggressive steps Roosevelt took to build a canal in Panama and explain why his "corollary" to the Monroe Doctrine aroused such controversy.
5. discuss Roosevelt's other diplomatic achievements, particularly in relation to Japan.

B. Glossary

To build your social science vocabulary, familiarize yourself with the following terms.

1. **Americanization** The process of assimilating American character, manner, ideals, culture, and so on. "The Filipinos, who hated compulsory Americanization, preferred liberty." (p. 648)
2. **sphere of influence** In international affairs, the territory where a powerful state exercises the dominant control over weaker states or territories. ". . . they began to tear away valuable leaseholds and economic spheres of influence from the Manchu government." (p. 648)
3. **partition** In politics, the act of dividing a weaker territory or government among several more powerful states. "Defenseless China was spared partition during these troubled years." (p. 649)
4. **blue blood** Person descended from nobility or aristocracy. "What manner of man was Theodore Roosevelt, the red-blooded blue blood?" (p. 653)
5. **bellicose** Disposed to fight or go to war. "Incurably boyish and bellicose, Roosevelt loved to fight. . . ." (p. 654)
6. **preparedness** The accumulation of sufficient armed forces and matériel to go to war. "[Roosevelt was] an ardent champion of military and naval preparedness. . . ." (p. 654)
7. **corollary** A secondary inference or deduction from a main proposition that is taken as established or proven. "Roosevelt therefore devised a devious policy of 'preventive intervention,' better known as the Roosevelt Corollary of the Monroe Doctrine." (p. 657)
8. **dictum** An authoritative edict or assertion. "Roosevelt's corollary . . . bore only a strained relation to the original dictum of 1823." (p. 657)
9. **preemptive** The prior appropriation of land or other goods, in order to prevent their appropriation by others. "Yet in its own right the corollary had considerable merit as a preemptive stroke." (p. 658)
10. **indemnity** A payment assessed to compensate for an injury or unwarranted action. "The Japanese presented stern demands for a huge indemnity." (p. 659)

PART II: Checking Your Progress

A. True-False

Where the statement is true, mark **T**. Where it is false, mark **F**, and correct it in the space immediately below.

____ 1. The Filipino insurrection against U.S. rule was larger and more costly in lives than the Spanish-American War.

____ 2. John Hay's Open Door notes effectively saved China from foreign intervention and partition.

____ 3. The McKinley-Roosevelt victory in 1900 over the anti-imperialist campaign of William Jennings Bryan was interpreted as a public mandate for American imperialism.

____ 4. Theodore Roosevelt believed that America and its president should exercise restraint in international involvements.

____ 5. Roosevelt encouraged and assisted the Panamanian revolution against Colombia in 1903.

____ 6. Roosevelt took strong action to acquire canal rights in Panama because there was no alternative route for a Central American canal.

____ 7. The Roosevelt corollary to the Monroe Doctrine stated that only the United States had the right to intervene in Latin American nations' affairs.

____ 8. Roosevelt's negotiation to bring about a peace treaty between Russia and Japan earned the United States the gratitude of both nations.

____ 9. The Japanese crisis of 1906 forced President Roosevelt to intervene in the policies of the San Francisco School Board.

____ 10. The "Gentlemen's Agreement" and the Root-Takahira agreement demonstrated Roosevelt's eagerness to avoid a major conflict with Japan.

B. Multiple Choice

Select the best answer and write the proper letter in the space provided.

____ 1. The most immediate consequence of American acquisition of the Philippines was
   a. the establishment of Manila as a crucial American defense post in East Asia.
   b. an agreement between Americans and Filipinos to move toward Philippine independence.
   c. a guerrilla war between the United States and Filipino rebels.
   d. threats by Japan to seize the Philippines from American control.

____ 2. In the Open Door notes, Secretary of State John Hay called on all the imperial powers to
   a. guarantee American control of the Philippines.
   b. reduce the arms race in China and the Pacific.
   c. respect Chinese rights and permit economic competition in their spheres of influence.
   d. grant the United States an equal share in the colonization of China.

Name_____ Section_____ Date_____

___ 3. The Boxer Rebellion marked a sharp departure for American foreign policy because
   a. the United States had previously backed anti-imperialist nationalist forces in China.
   b. the United States had never before sent military forces to intervene on the East Asian mainland.
   c. it involved the United States in military cooperation with Japan.
   d. it contradicted the policies spelled out in Secretary Hay's Open Door notes.

___ 4. Theodore Roosevelt was nominated as President McKinley's vice-presidential running mate in 1900 because
   a. his exploits in the Spanish-American War had made him a national hero.
   b. the midwestern McKinley needed an easterner to balance the ticket.
   c. McKinley wanted to take advantage of Roosevelt's military experience in the Spanish-American War.
   d. local political bosses in New York wanted to get Roosevelt out of the state.

___ 5. In the election of 1900, Democrat William Jennings Bryan declared that the key issue was
   a. American imperialism in the Philippines.
   b. Republican mismanagement of the economy.
   c. American foreign policy toward China.
   d. social reform in both cities and agricultural areas.

___ 6. As president, Theodore Roosevelt gained political strength especially through
   a. his careful use of traditional diplomacy.
   b. his willingness to follow Congress's lead in domestic policy.
   c. his personal popularity with the public and his belief in direct action.
   d. his ability to subordinate his own personality to that of his cabinet.

___ 7. Besides Panama, the primary alternative site for a Central American canal was
   a. Cuba.
   b. Nicaragua.
   c. Mexico.
   d. Colombia.

___ 8. Roosevelt overcame Colombia's refusal to approve a canal treaty by
   a. increasing the amount of money the United States was willing to pay for a canal zone.
   b. encouraging Panamanian rebels to revolt and declare independence from Colombia.
   c. looking for another canal site elsewhere in Central America.
   d. seeking mediation of the dispute by other Latin American nations.

___ 9. The Roosevelt corollary to the Monroe Doctrine declared that
   a. no European powers could intervene in or colonize Latin America.
   b. the United States had a right to build, maintain, and defend the Panama Canal.
   c. the United States would take no more colonial territory in Latin America.
   d. the United States had the right to intervene in Latin American countries to maintain financial and political order.

___ 10. Roosevelt's policies in Panama and elsewhere in Latin America led to
   a. a Good Neighbor policy between the United States and its "little brothers" in Latin America.
   b. resentment and hostility toward American intervention in Latin America.
   c. growing tension between the United States and Germany over influence in the region.
   d. anti-Roosevelt feeling among the Hispanic population in the United States.

___ 11. Theodore Roosevelt's slogan that stated his essential foreign policy principle was
   a. "Open covenants openly arrived at."
   b. "Millions for defense but not one cent for tribute."
   c. "Speak softly and carry a big stick."
   d. "Democracy and Liberty in a New World Order."

___ 12. Roosevelt mediated the Portsmouth Treaty to settle the war between
   a. Britain and Japan.
   b. Russia and Japan.
   c. China and Japan.
   d. Spain and North Africa.

___ 13. The diplomatic crisis between the United States and Japan in 1906 was caused by
   a. confrontations between the American and Japan navies.
   b. American refusal to recognize Japanese spheres of influence in China.
   c. the San Francisco School Board's segregation of Japanese immigrant children.
   d. American prohibition of all immigration from Japan.

___ 14. The Gentlemen's Agreement" between the United States and Japan provided that
   a. the Americans and Japanese would each guarantee the other's rights in China.
   b. the San Francisco schools would integrated in exchange for Japan putting and end to Japanese immigration to America.
   c. Japan would recognize American control of the Philippines in exchange for American acceptance of Japan's domination of Manchuria and Korea.
   d. Japanese immigrants would be able to work in the United States but not become citizens.

___ 15. Roosevelt's "Great White Fleet" essentially served as
   a. a support force for the Roosevelt corollary to the Monroe Doctrine.
   b. a demonstration of American naval power in East Asia.
   c. a sign that America would intervene in China if necessary.
   d. a means of providing relief shipment of food to famine victims in Latin America and Asia.

C. Identification

Supply the correct identification for each numbered description.

_____ 1. John Hay's clever diplomatic efforts to preserve Chinese territorial integrity and maintain American access to China

_____ 2. Antiforeign Chinese revolt of 1900 that brought military intervention by Western troops, including Americans

_____ 3. Proverbial symbol of Roosevelt's belief that presidents should engage in diplomacy but also maintain a strong military readiness to back up their policy

_____ 4. Diplomatic agreement of 1901 that permitted the United States to build and fortify a Central American canal alone, without British involvement

_____ 5. Nation whose senate in 1902 refused to ratify a treaty permitting the United States to build a canal across its territory

_____ 6. Agreement between the United States and the revolutionary government of Panama granting America the right to build a canal

_____ 7. Questionable extension of a traditional American policy; declared an American right to intervene in Latin American nations under certain circumstances

_____ 8. War concluded by Roosevelt-mediated treaty that earned TR the Nobel Peace Prize but caused much ill will toward America from the two signatories

_____ 9. Diplomatic understanding of 1907–1908 that ended a Japanese-American crisis over treatment of Japanese immigrants to the U.S.

_____ 10. Large U.S. naval force sent on a peaceful but highly visible voyage to Japan and elsewhere in 1907

D. Matching People, Places, and Events

Match the person, place, or event in the left column with the proper description in the right column by inserting the correct letter on the blank line.

___ 1. Emilio Aguinaldo
___ 2. John Hay
___ 3. William Jennings Bryan
___ 4. Theodore Roosevelt
___ 5. Philippe Bunau-Varilla
___ 6. Thomas Platt
___ 7. George Washington Goethals
___ 8. Portsmouth, New Hampshire
___ 9. San Francisco, California
___ 10. Algeciras, Spain

A. American engineer who organized the building of the Panama Canal
B. Site of a Roosevelt-mediated international conference on Morocco
C. Place where a local school board's attempt to segregate Japanese children created an international incident
D. American secretary of state who attempted to preserve Chinese independence and protect American interests in China
E. Site of Roosevelt-sponsored negotiations that ended the Russo-Japanese War
F. Scheming French engineer who helped stage a revolution in Panama and then became the new country's "instant" foreign minister
G. Filipino leader of a guerilla war against American rule from 1899 to 1901
H. Diplomat, moralizer, wielder of the big stick, "a combination of St. Paul and St. Vitus"
I. Politician who successfully schemed to get TR out of New York and off to Washington
J. Candidate who waged an unsuccessful presidential campaign on the issue of American imperialism in the Philippines

E. **Putting Things in Order**

Put the following events in correct order by numbering them from 1 to 5.

___ TR mediates a peace treaty between two combatants in the Far East.

___ A Chinese uprising against foreigners brings American troops to Beijing (Peking).

___ "That damn cowboy" becomes president of the United States after an assassination.

___ A school-spawned crisis provokes the end of Japanese immigration to America and a flurry of diplomacy to smooth relations between U.S. and Japan.

___ Questionable Roosevelt actions in Central America help create a new republic and pave the way for a U.S.-built canal.

F. **Matching Cause and Effect**

Match the historical cause in the left column with the proper effect in the right column by writing the correct letter on the blank line.

Cause

___ 1. The Filipino rebellion against the United States

___ 2. The threat of European partition of China

___ 3. The Boxer Rebellion

___ 4. Boss Platt's desire to get Roosevelt out of New York

___ 5. The Colombian Senate's refusal to ratify a canal treaty

___ 6. The "Roosevelt corollary" to the Monroe Doctrine and U.S. intervention in Cuba and the Dominican Republic

___ 7. The Russo-Japanese War

___ 8. West Coast fear of the "yellow peril" of Japanese immigration

___ 9. Roosevelt's intervention in the San Francisco School Board crisis

___ 10. The Great White Fleet's visit to Japan

Effect

A. Led to John Hay's energetic and clever Open Door diplomacy

B. Paved the way for the Root-Takahira agreement between the United States and Japan

C. Sent TR to the vice presidency and from there to the White House

D. Convinced the San Francisco School Board to allow Japanese children into the city's schools

E. Led to a costly, dirty war that shocked and dismayed Americans

F. Resulted in a pro-American and procanal revolution that declared an independent Panama

G. Sent waves of new Japanese immigrants into California

H. Brought a foreign expedition into China and forced China to pay an indemnity to the United States

I. Created strong anti-American feeling in Latin America

J. Prompted the San Francisco school segregation crisis of 1906

Name_____ Section_____ Date_____

G. Developing Historical Skills

Main Ideas and Supporting Evidence

Historical writing, like many other kinds of writing, develops a main idea with supporting detailed evidence. Each of the five statements below is the main idea of one section of Chapter 28. For each main idea in these headed subsections, list three factual details from the text that support it.

1. *"Little Brown Brothers" in the Philippines* (pp.646–648)

    Assuming control of the Philippines caused terrible military and political conflict between the American government and the Filipinos.

2. *TR: Brandisher of the Big Stick* (pp. 653–655)

    Theodore Roosevelt was a very energetic and able politician who overcame all kinds of obstacles.

3. *Uncle Sam Creates Puppet Panama* (pp. 655–656)

    Frustrated by Colombian opposition, Theodore Roosevelt encouraged a group of Panamanians to stage a revolution and pave the way for an American canal.

4. *TR's Perversion of the Monroe Doctrine* (pp. 657–658)

    Roosevelt's "corollary" to the Monroe Doctrine distorted traditional American policy, aroused Latin American resentment, and led to frequent American interventions in the region.

5. *Roosevelt on the World Stage* (pp. 658–659)

    Roosevelt successfully resolved the Russo-Japanese War, but at some cost to American relations with the two countries.

PART III: Applying What You Have Learned

1. What were the effects of America's new East Asian involvement in both the Philippines and China in 1899–1901?
2. What were the essential principles of Theodore Roosevelt's foreign policy, and how did he apply them to specific situations?
3. How did Roosevelt's policies in Latin America demonstrate American power in the region, and why did they arouse opposition from Latin Americans?
4. What were the central issues in America's relations with China and Japan? How did Roosevelt handle tense relations with Japan?
5. What were the strengths and weaknesses of Theodore Roosevelt's aggressive foreign policy? What were the benefits of TR's activism and what were its drawbacks?
6. The text states that the Roosevelt corollary to the Monroe Doctrine distorted the original policy statement of 1823. How did it do so? (See Chapter 10.) Compare the circumstances and purposes of the two policies.

Name_____ Section_____ Date_____

29

Progressivism and the Republican Roosevelt, 1901–1912

PART I: Reviewing the Chapter

A. Checklist of Learning Objectives

After mastering this chapter, you should be able to

1. discuss the origins and nature of the progressive movement.
2. describe how the early progressive movement developed its roots at the city and state level.
3. identify the critical role that women played in progressive social reform.
4. tell how President Roosevelt began applying progressive principles to the national economy.
5. explain why Taft's policies offended progressives, including Roosevelt.
6. describe how Roosevelt led a progressive revolt against Taft that openly divided the Republican party.

B. Glossary

To build your social science vocabulary, familiarize yourself with the following terms.

1. **progressive** In politics, one who believes in continuing social advancement, improvement, or reform. "The new crusaders, who called themselves 'progressives,' waged war on many evils. . . ." (p. 664)
2. **conspicuous consumption** The theory, developed by economist Thorstein Veblen, that much spending by the affluent occurs primarily to display wealth and status to others rather than from enjoyment of the goods or services. " . . . a savage attack on 'predatory wealth' and 'conspicuous consumption.'" (p. 665)
3. **direct primary** In politics, the nomination of a party's candidates for office through a special election of that party's voters. "These ardent reformers pushed for direct primary elections. . . ." (p. 667)
4. **initiative** In politics, the procedure whereby voters can, through petition, present proposed legislation directly to the electorate. "They favored the 'initiative' so that voters could directly propose legislation. . . ." (p. 667)
5. **referendum** The submission of a law, proposed or already in effect, to a direct vote of the electorate. "Progressives also agitated for the 'referendum.'" (p. 667)
6. **recall** In politics, a procedure for removing an official from office through popular election or other means. "The 'recall' would enable the voters to remove faithless elected officials. . . ." (p. 667)
7. **city manager** An administrator appointed by the city council or other elected body to manage affairs, supposedly in a nonpartisan or professional way. "Other communities adopted the city-manager system. . . ." (p. 669)

8. **red-light district** A section of a city where prostitution is officially or unofficially tolerated. "... wide-open prostitution (vice-at-a-price) ... flourished in red-light districts...." (p. 669)
9. **franchise** In government, a special privilege or license granted to a company or group to perform a specific function. "Public-spirited city-dwellers also moved to halt the corrupt sale of franchises for streetcars...." (p. 669)
10. **bureaucracy (bureaucrat)** The management of government or business through departments and subdivisions manned by a system of officials (bureaucrats) following defined rules and processes. (The term is often though not necessarily disparaging.) "These wedges into the federal bureaucracy, however small, gave female reformers a national stage...." (p. 670)
11. **workers' (workmen's) compensation** Insurance, provided either by government or employers or both, providing benefits to employees suffering work-related injury or disability. "... by 1917 thirty states had put workers' compensation laws on the books...." (p. 672)
12. **reclamation** The process of bringing or restoring wasteland to productive use. "Settlers repaid the cost of reclamation...." (p. 676)
13. **collectivism** A political or social system in which individuals are subordinated to mass organization and direction. "He strenuously sought the middle road between unbridled individualism and paternalistic collectivism." (p. 683)
14. **insubordination** Deliberate disobedience to proper authority. "... Taft dismissed Pinchot on the narrow grounds of insubordination...." (p. 685)

PART II: Checking Your Progress

A. True-False

Where the statement is true, mark **T**. Where it is false, mark **F**, and correct it in the space immediately below.

____ 1. The progressive movement believed that social and economic problems should be solved at the community level without involvement by the federal government.

____ 2. Muckraking journalists, social-gospel ministers, and women reformers all aroused Americans' concern about economic and social problems.

____ 3. The leading progressive reformers were primarily immigrants and urban industrial workers.

____ 4. Many female progressives saw the task of improving life in factories and slums as an extension of their traditional roles as wives and mothers.

____ 5. President Theodore Roosevelt ended the anthracite coal strike by threatening to use federal troops to break the miners' union.

____ 6. Roosevelt promoted stronger federal legislation to regulate the railroads and other major industries.

____ 7. Roosevelt believed that all the monopolistic corporate trusts should be broken up and competition restored among smaller businesses.

____ 8. Upton Sinclair's novel *The Jungle* was intended to arouse consumers' concern about unsanitary practices in the meat industry.

____ 9. Conservation policies like land reclamation and forest preservation were probably Theodore Roosevelt's most popular and enduring presidential achievement.

Name_____ Section_____ Date_____

_____ 10. Defenders of nature became divided between fervent "preservationists" who wanted to stop all human intrusions and more moderate "conservationists."

_____ 11. Roosevelt effectively used the power of the presidency and the federal government to tame unrestricted capitalism while preserving the basic foundations of American business.

_____ 12. Taft's "dollar diplomacy" was a successful attempt to mobilize American business to support U.S. foreign policy in East Asia and Latin America.

_____ 13. Progressive Republicans became angry with President Taft because he began to form alliances with Democrats and Socialists.

_____ 14. The Ballinger-Pinchot conservation controversy pushed Taft into alliance with the Republican "Old Guard" against the pro-Roosevelt progressives.

_____ 15. President Taft used his control of the Republican party machinery to deny Roosevelt the nomination in 1912.

B. Multiple Choice

Select the best answer and write the proper letter in the space provided.

_____ 1. The primary emphasis of the progressive movement was on
   a. freeing individuals and business from federal control.
   b. protecting farmers and small business from corporate power.
   c. strengthening government as an instrument of social betterment.
   d. organizing workers into a unified and class-conscious political party.

_____ 2. Prominent among those who aroused the progressive movement by stirring the public's sense of concern were
   a. socialists, social gospelers, women, and muckraking journalists.
   b. union leaders, machine politicians, immigrant spokespeople, and engineers.
   c. bankers, advertising people, congressmen, and scientists.
   d. athletes, entertainers, filmmakers, and musicians.

_____ 3. Which of the following was *not* among the targets of muckraking journalistic exposés?
   a. urban politics and government
   b. the oil, insurance, and railroad industries
   c. the U.S. Army and Navy
   d. child labor and the "white slave" traffic in women

_____ 4. Most progressives were
   a. poor farmers.
   b. urban workers.
   c. urban middle-class people.
   d. wealthy people.

5. Among the political reforms sought by the progressives were
   a. an end to political parties, political conventions, and the Supreme Court's right to judicial review of legislation.
   b. an Equal Rights Amendment, federal financing of elections, and restrictions on negative campaigning.
   c. civil-service reform, racial integration, and free silver.
   d. initiative and referendum, direct election of senators, and women's suffrage.

6. The states where progressivism first gained great influence were
   a. Massachusetts, Maine, and New Hampshire.
   b. Wisconsin, Oregon, and California.
   c. Michigan, Kansas, and Nevada.
   d. New York, Florida, and Texas.

7. The Supreme Court case of *Muller v. Oregon* was seen as a victory for both progressivism and women's rights because
   a. it upheld the constitutionality of laws granting special protection to women in the workplace.
   b. it held that women should receive "equal pay for equal work."
   c. it upheld workplace safety regulations to prevent disasters like the Triangle Shirtwaist fire.
   d. it opened almost all categories of the new industrial employment to women.

8. Roosevelt ended the Pennsylvania coal strike by
   a. urging labor and management to negotiate a settlement.
   b. passing federal legislation legalizing unions.
   c. forcing mediation by threatening to seize the coal mines and operate them with federal troops.
   d. declaring a national state of emergency and ordering the miners back to work.

9. The Roosevelt-backed Elkins Act and Hepburn Act were aimed at
   a. better protection for industrial workers.
   b. more effective regulation of the railroad industry.
   c. protection for consumers of beef and produce.
   d. breaking up the Standard Oil monopoly.

10. The controversy over the Hetch Hetchy Valley in Yosemite National Park revealed
    a. a philosophical disagreement between wilderness "preservationists" and more moderate "conservationists."
    b. President Roosevelt's hostility toward creating any more national parks.
    c. a political conflict between the lumber industry and conservationists.
    d. a split between urban California's need for water and environmentalists' concerns to preserve free-flowing streams..

11. Two areas where Roosevelt's progressivism made its substantial headway were
    a. agricultural and mining legislation.
    b. stock-market and securities legislation.
    c. immigration and racial legislation.
    d. consumer and conservation legislation.

___ 12. Roosevelt was blamed for the "Panic of 1907" because
   a. his "boat-rocking tactics" had allegedly unsettled industry.
   b. his policies of regulating and protecting industrial workers had caused a depression.
   c. his inability to establish a stable monetary policy led to a wall street crash.
   d. the public wanted him to run again for president in 1908.

___ 13. As a result of his successful campaign in 1908, William Howard Taft was expected to
   a. continue and extend Roosevelt's progressive policies.
   b. forge a coalition with William Jennings Bryan and the Democrats.
   c. emphasize foreign policy instead of Roosevelt's domestic reforms.
   d. turn away from Roosevelt and toward the conservative wing of the Republican party.

___ 14. Progressive Republicans grew disillusioned with Taft primarily over the issues of
   a. dollar diplomacy and military intervention in the Caribbean and Central America.
   b. labor union rights and women's concerns.
   c. trust-busting, tariffs, and conservation.
   d. regulation of the banking and railroad industries.

___ 15. Roosevelt finally decided to break with the Republicans and form a third party because
   a. he had always regarded the Republican party as too conservative.
   b. he could no longer stand to be in the same party with Taft.
   c. Taft used his control of the Republican convention to deny Roosevelt the nomination.
   d. Roosevelt believed that he would have a better chance of winning the presidency as a third-party candidate.

C. Identification

Supply the correct identification for each numbered description.

_____ 1. A largely middle-class movement that aimed to use the power of government to correct the economic and social problems of industrialism

_____ 2. Popular journalists who used publicity to expose corruption and attack abuses of power in business and government

_____ 3. Progressive proposal to allow voters to bypass state legislatures and propose legislation themselves

_____ 4. Progressive device that would enable voters to remove corrupt or ineffective officials from office

_____ 5. Roosevelt's policy of having the federal government promote the public interest by dealing evenhandedly with both labor and business

_____ 6. Effective railroad-regulation law of 1906 that greatly strengthened the Interstate Commerce Commission

_____ 7. Disastrous industrial fire of 1911 that spurred workmen's compensation laws and some state regulation of wages and hours in New York

_____ 8. Upton Sinclair's novel that inspired proconsumer federal laws regulating meat, food, and drugs

_____ 9. Powerful women's reform organization led by Frances Willard

_____ 10. Brief but sharp economic downturn of 1907, blamed by conservatives on the supposedly dangerous president

_____ 11. Generally unsuccessful Taft foreign policy in which government attempted to encourage overseas business ventures

_____ 12. Powerful corporation broken up by a Taft-initiated antitrust suit in 1911

D. Matching People, Places, and Events

Match the person, place, or event in the left column with the proper description in the right column by inserting the correct letter on the blank line.

___ 1. Jacob Riis
___ 2. Lincoln Steffens
___ 3. Ida Tarbell
___ 4. Seventeenth Amendment
___ 5. Robert La Follette
___ 6. Triangle Shirtwaist Company fire
___ 7. Anthracite coal strike
___ 8. Meat Inspection Act of 1906
___ 9. *Muller* v. *Oregon*
___ 10. William Howard Taft
___ 11. *Lochner* v. *New York*
___ 12. Gifford Pinchot

A. Politically inept inheritor of the Roosevelt legacy who ended up allied to the reactionary Republican "Old Guard"

B. Case that upheld protective legislation on the grounds of women's supposed physical weakness

C. New York City disaster that underscored urban workers' need for government protection

D. The most influential of the state-level progressive governors and a presidential aspirant in 1912

E. Author of *How the Other Half Lives*, a shocking description of the New York slums

F. Leading muckraking journalist whose articles documented the Standard Oil Company's abuse of power

G. Proconservation federal official whose dismissal by Taft angered Roosevelt progressives

H. Dangerous labor conflict resolved by Rooseveltian negotiation and threats against business people

I. Early muckraker who exposed the political corruption in many American cities

J. Progressive law aimed at curbing practices like those exposed in Upton Sinclair's *The Jungle*

K. Progressive measure that required U.S. senators to be elected directly by the people rather than by state legislatures

L. Supreme court ruling that overturned a progressive law mandating a ten-hour workday

E. Putting Things in Order

Put the following events in correct order by numbering them from 1 to 5.

___ A former president opposes his handpicked successor for the Republican presidential nomination.

___ Sensational journalistic accounts of corruption and abuse of power in politics and business spur the progressive movement.

___ A progressive forestry official feuds with Taft's secretary of the interior, deepening the division within the Republican party.

___ A novelistic account of Chicago's meat-packing industry sparks new federal laws to protect consumers.

___ A brief but sharp financial crisis leads to conservative criticism of Roosevelt's progressive policies.

F. Matching Cause and Effect

Match the historical cause in the left column with the proper effect in the right column by writing the correct letter on the blank line.

Cause

___ 1. Old-time Populists, muckraking journalists, social-gospel ministers, and European socialist immigrants

___ 2. Progressive concern about political corruption

___ 3. Governors like Robert La Follette

___ 4. Roosevelt's threat to seize the anthracite coal mines

___ 5. Settlement Houses and women's clubs

___ 6. Upton Sinclair's *The Jungle*

___ 7. Roosevelt's personal interest in conservation

___ 8. Taft's political mishandling of tariff and conservation policies

___ 9. Russia's and Japan's hostility to an American role in China

___ 10. Roosevelt's feeling that he was cheated out of the Republican nomination by the Taft machine

Effect

A. Ended the era of uncontrolled exploitation of nature and involved the federal government in preserving natural resources

B. Led to reforms like the initiative, referendum, and direct election of senators

C. Forced a compromise settlement of a strike that threatened the national well-being

D. Outraged consumers and led to the Meat Inspection Act and the Pure Food and Drug Act

E. Laid the basis for a third-party crusade in the election of 1912

F. Incensed pro-Roosevelt progressives and increased their attacks on the Republican "Old Guard"

G. Led the way in using universities and regulatory agencies to pursue progressive goals

H. Made Taft's dollar-diplomacy policy a failure

I. Provided the pioneering forces who laid the foundations for the Progressive movement.

J. Served as the launching pads for widespread female involvement in progressive reforms

G. Developing Historical Skills

Classifying Historical Information

Often a broad historical movement, such as progressivism, can best be understood by breaking it down into various component parts. Among the varieties of progressive reform discussed in this chapter are (A) political progressivism, (B) economic or industrial progressivism, (C) consumer progressivism, and (D) environmental progressivism.

Put each of the following progressive acts, policies, or court cases into one of those categories by writing in the correct letter.

___ 1. The Newlands Act of 1902

___ 2. The ten-hour law for bakers

___ 3. The movement for women's suffrage

___ 4. The anthracite coal strike of 1902

___ 5. Direct election of senators

___ 6. The Meat Inspection Act of 1906

___ 7. The Pure Food and Drug Act

___ 8. Initiative, referendum, and recall

___ 9. *Muller* v. *Oregon*

___ 10. The Hepburn Act of 1906

___ 11. Yosemite and Grand Canyon National Parks

___ 12. Workmen's compensation laws

Name_____ Section_____ Date_____

PART III: Applying What You Have Learned

1. What caused the progressive movement, and how did it get under way?
2. What did the progressive movement accomplish at the local, state, and national levels?
3. What made women such central forces in the progressive crusade? What specific backgrounds and ideologies did they bring to the public arena? What were the strengths and limitations of the progressive emphasis on providing special protection to children and women?
4. Discuss Roosevelt's support for conservation and consumer protection. Why were these among the most successful progressive achievements?
5. What caused the Taft-Roosevelt split, and how did it reflect the growing division between "Old Guard" and "progressive" Republicans?
6. How was progressivism a response to the development of the new urban and industrial order in American? (See Chapters 24 and 25.)

30

Wilsonian Progressivism at Home and Abroad, 1912–1916

PART I: Reviewing the Chapter

A. Checklist of Learning Objectives

After mastering this chapter, you should be able to

1. discuss the key issues of the pivotal 1912 election and the basic principles of Wilsonian progressivism.
2. describe how Wilson successfully reformed the "triple wall of privilege."
3. state the basic features of Wilson's foreign policy and explain how they drew him into intervention in Latin America.
4. describe America's response to World War I and explain the increasingly sharp conflict over America's policies toward Germany.
5. explain how domestic and foreign controversies played into Wilson's narrow victory over Hughes in 1916.

B. Glossary

To build your social science vocabulary, familiarize yourself with the following terms.

1. **entrepreneurship** The process whereby an individual initiates a business at some risk in order to expand it and thereby earn a profit. "Wilson's New Freedom, by contrast, favored small enterprise, entrepreneurship, and the free functioning of . . . markets." (p. 688)
2. **self-determination** In politics, the right of a people to shape its own national identity and form of government, without outside coercion or influence. ". . . [the Confederacy] . . . partly inspired his ideal of self-determination for people of other countries." (p. 690)
3. **piety** Devotion to religious duty and practices. ". . . Wilson was reared in an atmosphere of fervent piety." (p. 690)
4. **graduated income tax** A tax on income in which the taxation rates grow progressively higher for those with higher income. "Congress enacted a graduated income tax. . . ." (p. 691)
5. **levy** A forcible tax or other imposition. ". . . [the] income tax [began] with a modest levy on income over $3,000. . . ." (p. 691)
6. **inelasticity** The inability to expand or contract rapidly. "[The] most serious shortcoming [of the country's financial structure] was the inelasticity of the currency." (p. 691)
7. **commercial paper** Any business document having monetary or exchangeable value. "The . . . paper money [was] backed by commercial paper. . . ." (p. 692)
8. **promissory note** A written pledge to pay a certain person a specified sum of money at a certain time. "The . . . paper money [was] backed by commercial paper, such as promissory notes of business people." (p. 692)

9. **Magna Carta** The "Great Charter" of England, which feudal nobles of England forced King John I to sign in 1215. As the first written guarantee of certain traditional rights, such as trial by a jury of peers, against arbitrary royal power, it served as a model for later assertions of Anglo-Saxon liberties. "Union leader Samuel Gompers hailed the [Clayton] act as the Magna Carta of labor...." (p. 692)

10. **agricultural extension** The system of providing services and advice to farmers through dispersed local agents. "Other laws benefited rural American by providing for . . . the establishment of agricultural extension work in the state colleges." (p. 693)

11. **enclave** A small territory surrounded by foreign or hostile territory. "Though often segregated in Spanish-speaking enclaves, they helped to create a unique borderland culture...." (p. 695)

12. **gringo** Contemptuous Latin American term for North Americans. "Challenging Carranza's authority while also punishing the gringos...." (p. 696)

13. **censor** An official who examines publications, mail, literature, and so forth in order to remove or prohibit the distribution of material deemed dangerous or offensive. "Their censors sheared away war stories harmful to the Allies . . . ." (p. 697)

14. **torpedo** To launch from a submarine or airplane a self-propelled underwater explosive designed to detonate on impact. ". . . the British passenger liner *Lusitania* was torpedoed and sank. . . ." (p. 699)

15. **draft** In politics, to choose an individual to run for office without that person's prior solicitation of the nomination. (A *military* draft, or conscription, legally compels individuals into the armed services.) "Instead, they drafted Supreme Court Justice Charles Evans Hughes, a cold intellectual who had achieved a solid record as governor of New York." (p. 701)

PART II: Checking Your Progress

A. True-False

Where the statement is true, mark **T**. Where it is false, mark **F**, and correct it in the space immediately below.

1. Wilson won the election of 1912 largely because the Republican party split in two.

2. In the 1912 campaign, Wilson's "New Freedom" favored a socially activist government and preserving large regulated trusts, while Roosevelt's "New Nationalist" favored small enterprise and breaking up a big business by antitrust action.

3. Wilson believed that the president should provide national leadership by appealing directly to the people.

4. Wilson successfully used his popular appeal to push through progressive reforms of the tariff, monetary systems, and trusts.

5. Wilson's progressive outlook showed itself clearly in his attempt to improve the conditions and treatment of blacks.

6. Wilson attempted to reverse the big-stick and dollar-diplomacy foreign policies of Roosevelt and Taft, especially in Latin America.

7. Wilson consistently refused to send American troops to intervene in the Caribbean.

8. In his policy toward the revolutionary Mexican government of Huerta, Wilson attempted to walk a middle line between recognition and intervention.

Name_____ Section_____ Date_____

_____ 9. The mediation of three Latin American nations saved Wilson from a full-scale war with Mexico.

_____ 10. General Pershing's expedition into Mexico was an attempt to bring the pro-American faction of Mexican revolutionaries to power.

_____ 11. In the early days of World War I, more Americans sympathized with Germany than with Britain.

_____ 12. The American economy benefited greatly from supplying goods to the Allies.

_____ 13. After the *Lusitania*'s sinking, the Midwest and West favored war with Germany, while the East generally favored attempts at negotiation.

_____ 14. After the sinking of the *Sussex*, Wilson successfully pressured Germany into stopping submarine attacks against neutral shipping.

_____ 15. In the 1916 campaign, Wilson ran on the slogan "He Kept Us Out of War," while his opponent Hughes tried to straddle the issue of a possible war with Germany.

B. Multiple Choice

Select the best answer and write the proper letter in the space provided.

_____ 1. The basic contrast between the two progressive candidates, Roosevelt and Wilson, was that
   a. Roosevelt wanted genuine political and social reforms, while Wilson wanted only to end obvious corruption.
   b. Roosevelt wanted to promote free enterprise and competition, while Wilson wanted the federal government to regulate the economy and promote social welfare.
   c. Roosevelt wanted the federal government to regulate the economy and promote social welfare, while Wilson wanted to restore economic competition and social equality.
   d. Roosevelt wanted to focus on issues of jobs and economic growth, while Wilson wanted social legislation to protect women, children, and city-dwellers.

_____ 2. Wilson won the election of 1912 primarily because
   a. his policies were more popular with the public.
   b. Taft and Roosevelt split the former Republican vote.
   c. the Socialists took nearly a million votes from Roosevelt.
   d. he was able to win over many of the Roosevelt supporters to his cause.

_____ 3. Wilson's primary weakness as a politician was
   a. his lack of skill in public speaking.
   b. his inability to grasp the complexity of governmental issues.
   c. his tendency to be inflexible and refuse to compromise.
   d. his lack of overarching political ideals.

____ 4. The "triple wall of privilege" that Wilson set out to reform consisted of
   a. farmers, shippers, and the military.
   b. the tariffs, the banks, and the trusts.
   c. the universities, private dining clubs, and political bosses.
   d. congressional leaders, lobbyists, and lawyers.

____ 5. During the Wilson administration, Congress exercised the authority granted by the newly enacted Sixteenth Amendment to pass
   a. prohibition of liquor.
   b. women's suffrage.
   c. voting rights for blacks.
   d. a federal income tax.

____ 6. The new regulatory agency created by the Wilson administration in 1914 that attacked monopolies, false advertising, and consumer fraud was
   a. the Federal Trade Commission.
   b. the Interstate Commerce Commission.
   c. the Federal Reserve System.
   d. the Consumer Products Safety Commission.

____ 7. While it attacked business monopolies, the Clayton Anti-Trust Act exempted from anti-trust prosecution
   a. industries essential to national defense.
   b. agricultural and labor organizations.
   c. the oil and steel industries.
   d. professional organizations of doctors and lawyers.

____ 8. Wilson effectively reformed the banking and financial system by
   a. establishing a third Bank of the United States to issue and regulate the currency.
   b. taking the United States off the gold standard.
   c. establishing a publicly controlled Federal Reserve Board with regional banks under bankers' control.
   d. transferring authority to regulate banking and currency to the states and the private sector.

____ 9. Wilson's progressive measures substantially aided all of the following groups *except*
   a. workers.
   b. blacks.
   c. farmers.
   d. children.

____ 10. Wilson's initial attitude toward the Mexican revolutionary government was
   a. a refusal to recognize the legitimacy of General Huerta's regime.
   b. a willingness to intervene with troops on behalf of threatened American business interests.
   c. strong support and provision of economic assistance to the Huerta regime.
   d. an attempt to mobilize other Latin American governments to help oust Huerta.

Name_____ Section_____ Date_____

___ 11. The threatened war between the United States and Mexico in 1914 was avoided by the mediation of the ABC powers, which consisted of
   a. Australia, Britain, and Canada.
   b. Antigua, Brazil, and Cuba.
   c. Argentina, Brazil, and Chile.
   d. the Association of British Commonwealth nations.

___ 12. General Pershing's expedition into Mexico was sent in direct response to
   a. the refusal of Huerta to abandon power.
   b. the threat of German intervention in Mexico.
   c. the arrest of American sailors in the Mexican port of Tampico.
   d. the killing of American citizens in New Mexico by "Pancho" Villa.

___ 13. The sympathy of a majority of Americans for the Allies and against Germany was especially conditioned by
   a. British bribes and payoffs to American journalists.
   b. the Germans' involvement in overseas imperialism.
   c. the German invasion of neutral Belgium.
   d. the British refusal to use poison gas in warfare.

___ 14. After the *Lusitania, Arabic,* and *Sussex* sinkings, Wilson successfully pressured the German government to
   a. end the use of the submarine against British warships.
   b. end its attempt to blockade the British Isles.
   c. publish warnings to all Americans considering traveling on unarmed ships.
   d. cease from sinking neutral merchant and passenger ships without warning.

___ 15. Wilson's most effective slogan in the campaign of 1916 was
   a. "The full dinner pail."
   b. "Free and unlimited coinage of silver in the ratio of sixteen to one."
   c. "A war to make the world safe for democracy."
   d. "He kept us out of war."

C. Identification

Supply the correct identification for each numbered description.

_____ 1. Four-footed symbol of Roosevelt's Progressive third party in 1912

_____ 2. A fourth political party, led by a former labor union leader, that garnered nearly a million votes in 1912

_____ 3. Wilson's political philosophy of restoring democracy through trust-busting and economic competition

_____ 4. A twelve-member agency appointed by the president to oversee the banking system under a new federal law of 1913

_____ 5. New presidentially appointed regulatory commission designed to prevent monopoly and guard against unethical trade practices

_____ 6. Wilsonian law that tried to curb business monopoly while permitting labor and agricultural organizations

_____ 7. Wilsonian reform law that established an eight-hour day for railroad workers

_____ 8. Troubled Caribbean island nation where a president's murder led Wilson to send in the marines and assume American control of the police and finances

_____ 9. Term for the three Latin American nations whose mediation prevented war between the United States and Mexico in 1914

_____ 10. World War I alliance headed by Germany and Austria-Hungary

_____ 11. The coalition of powers—led by Britain, France, and Russia—that opposed Germany and its partners in World War I

_____ 12. New underwater weapon that threatened neutral shipping and seemed to violate all traditional norms of international law

_____ 13. Large British passenger liner whose sinking in 1915 prompted some Americans to call for war against Germany

_____ 14. Germany's carefully conditional agreement in 1916 not to sink passenger and merchant vessels without warning

_____ 15. Key electoral state where a tiny majority for Wilson tipped the balance against Hughes in 1916

D. Matching People, Places, and Events

Match the person, place, or event in the left column with the proper description in the right column by inserting the correct letter on the blank line.

___ 1. Thomas Woodrow Wilson
___ 2. Theodore Roosevelt
___ 3. Samuel Gompers
___ 4. Louis D. Brandeis
___ 5. Virgin Islands
___ 6. General Huerta
___ 7. Venustiano Carranza
___ 8. Tampico and Vera Cruz
___ 9. "Pancho" Villa
___ 10. John J. Pershing
___ 11. Belgium
___ 12. Serbia
___ 13. Kaiser Wilhelm II
___ 14. Haiti

A. Small European nation in which an Austro-Hungarian heir was killed, leading to the outbreak of World War I
B. Mexican revolutionary whose assaults on American citizens and territory provoked a U.S. expedition into Mexico
C. Ports where clashes between Mexicans and American military forces nearly led to war in 1914
D. Caribbean territory purchased by the United States from Denmark in 1917
E. Narrowly unsuccessful presidential candidate who tried to straddle both sides of the fence regarding American policy toward Germany
F. Small European nation whose neutrality was violated by Germany in the early days of World War I
G. Commander of the American military expedition into Mexico in 1916–1917
H. Southern-born intellectual who pursued strong moral goals in politics and the presidency
I. Leading progressive reformer and the first Jew named to the U.S. Supreme Court
J. Caribbean nation where Wilson sent American marines in 1915
K. Energetic progressive and vigorous nationalist who refused to wage another third-party campaign in 1916
L. Labor leader who hailed the Clayton Anti-Trust Act as the "Magna Carta of labor"
M. Second revolutionary Mexican president, who took aid from the United States but strongly resisted American military intervention in his country

Name_____ Section_____ Date_____

____ 15. Charles Evans Hughes

N. Autocratic ruler who symbolized ruthlessness and arrogance to many pro-Allied Americans

O. Mexican revolutionary whose bloody regime Wilson refused to recognize and nearly ended up fighting

E. Putting Things in Order

Put the following events in correct order by numbering them from 1 to 5.

____ Wilson extracts a dangerously conditional German agreement to halt submarine warfare.

____ Wilson's superb leadership pushes major reforms of the tariff and monetary system through Congress.

____ The bull moose and the elephant are both electorally defeated by a donkey bearing the banner of "New Freedom."

____ The heavy loss of American lives to German submarines nearly leads the United States into war with Germany.

____ Despite efforts to avoid involvement in the Mexican revolution, Wilson's occupation of a Mexican port raises the threat of war.

F. Matching Cause and Effect

Match the historical cause in the left column with the proper effect in the right column by writing the correct letter on the blank line.

____ 1. The split between Taft and Roosevelt

____ 2. Wilson's presidential appeals to the public over the heads of Congress

____ 3. The Federal Reserve Act

____ 4. Conservative justices of the Supreme Court

____ 5. Political turmoil in Haiti and Santo Domingo (Dominican Republic)

____ 6. The Mexican revolution

____ 7. "Pancho" Villa's raid on Columbus, New Mexico

____ 8. America's close cultural and economic ties with Britain

____ 9. Germany's sinking of the *Lusitania*, *Arabic*, and *Sussex*

____ 10. Wilson's apparent success in keeping America at peace through diplomacy

A. Caused most Americans to sympathize with the Allies rather than the Central Powers

B. Helped push through sweeping reforms of the tariff and the banking system in 1913

C. Enabled the Democrats to win a narrow presidential victory in the election of 1916

D. Allowed Wilson to win a minority victory in the election of 1912

E. Declared unconstitutional progressive Wilsonian measures dealing with labor unions and child labor

F. Caused President Wilson and other outraged Americans to demand an end to unrestricted submarine warfare

G. Created constant political instability south of the border and undermined Wilson's hopes for better U.S. relations with Latin America

H. Was the immediate provocation for General Pershing's punitive expedition into Mexico

I. Finally established an effective national banking system and a flexible money supply

J. Caused Wilson to send in U.S. marines to restore order and supervise finances

G. Developing Historical Skills

Understanding Documents in Context

Historical documents cannot usually be understood in isolation. Awareness of the circumstances and conditions under which they were written is essential to comprehending their importance. The text reproduces on p. 701 the advertisement with notice from the German government that appeared in the New York *Herald* on May 1, 1915, six days before the *Lusitania* was sunk. Read the ad carefully, and reread text pp. 698–703 to understand and evaluate the context in which the warning appeared. Then answer the following questions.

1. What was the *policy* of the German government regarding submarine use at the time the ad was taken out?

2. Why might the German government be particularly concerned about warning American passengers thinking of traveling on a British liner? How would the notice be useful even if some Americans did travel on the ship?

3. What fact about the *Lusitania*'s cargo did the German government know that it did not put into the warning?

4. Why were many Americans outraged about the *Lusitania* sinking despite the warning?

Name_____ Section_____ Date_____

PART III: Applying What You Have Learned

1. What were the essential qualities of Wilson's presidential leadership, and how did he display them in 1913–1914?
2. What were the results of Wilson's great reform assault on the "triple wall of privilege"—the tariff, the banks, and the trusts?
3. How was Wilson's foreign policy an attempt to expand idealistic progressive principles from the domestic to the international arena? Why did Wilson's progressive democratic idealism lead to the kind of U.S. interventions he professed to dislike?
4. What were the causes and consequences of U.S. entanglement with Mexico in the wake of the Mexican Revolution? Could the U.S. have avoided involvement in Mexican affairs?
5. Why was it so difficult for Wilson to maintain America's neutrality from 1914–1916?
6. How did Wilson's foreign policy differ from that of the other great progressive president, Theodore Roosevelt? (See Chapter 29.) Which president was more effective in foreign policy and why?

31

The War to End War, 1917–1918

PART I: Reviewing the Chapter

A. Checklist of Learning Objectives

After mastering this chapter, you should be able to

1. explain what caused America to enter World War I.
2. describe how Wilsonian idealism turned the war into an ideological crusade that inspired fervor and overwhelmed dissent.
3. discuss the mobilization of America for war.
4. explain the consequences of World War I for labor, women, and African-Americans.
5. describe America's economic and military role in the war.
6. analyze Wilson's attempt to forge a peace based on his Fourteen Points and explain why developments at home and abroad forced him to compromise.
7. discuss the opposition of Lodge and others to Wilson's League and show how Wilson's refusal to compromise doomed the Treaty of Versailles.

B. Glossary

To build your social science vocabulary, familiarize yourself with the following terms.

1. **isolationism** In American diplomacy, the traditional belief that the United States should refrain from involvement in overseas politics, alliances, or wars, and confine its national security interest to its own borders (sometimes along with the Caribbean and Central America). **Internationalism** or **Wilsonianism** is the contrasting belief that America's national security requires involvement and sometimes diplomatic or military alliances overseas. "But their obstruction was a powerful reminder of the continuing strength of American isolationism." (p. 706)
2. **collective security** In international affairs, reliance on a group of nations or an international organization as protection against aggressors, rather than on national self-defense alone. " . . . an international organization that Wilson dreamed would provide a system of collective security." (p. 707)
3. **mobilization** The organization of a nation and its armed forces for war. "Creel typified American war mobilization. . . ." (p. 708)
4. **pardon** The official release of a person from punishment for a crime. ". . . presidential pardons were rather freely granted. . . ." (p. 709)
5. **ration** A fixed allowance of food or other scarce commodity. "He deliberately rejected issuing ration cards. . . ." (p. 713)
6. **conscientious objector** A person who refuses to participate in war on grounds of conscience or belief. ". . . about 4,000 conscientious objectors were excused." (p. 715)
7. **Bolshevik** The radical majority faction of the Russian Socialist party that seized power in the October 1917 revolution; they later took the name *Communist*. (Bolshevik is the Russian word

for "majority;" their rivals for power were **Mensheviks**, or minority.) "The Bolsheviks long resented these 'capitalistic' interventions...." (p. 716)

8. **salient** A portion of a battle line that extends forward into enemy territory. "... nine American divisions ... joined four French divisions to push the Germans from the St. Mihiel salient...." (p. 717)

9. **parliamentary** Concerning political systems in which the government is constituted from the controlling party's members in the legislative assembly. "Unlike all the parliamentary statesmen at the table, [Wilson] did not command a legislative majority at home." (p. 719)

10. **protectorate** In international affairs, a weaker or smaller country held to be under the guidance or protection of a major power; the arrangement is a weaker form of imperialism or colonialism. (A **colony** is a territory owned outright by a more powerful nation.) "... preventing any vengeful parceling out of the former colonies and protectorates of the vanquished powers." (p. 720)

11. **trustee** A nation that holds the territory of a former colony as the conditional agent of an international body under defined terms. "The victors would ... receive the conquered territory ... only as trustees of the League of Nations." (p. 720)

12. **mandate** Under the League of Nations (1919–1939), a specific commission that authorized a trustee to administer a former colonial territory. "Japan was conceded the strategic Pacific islands under a League of Nations mandate...." (p. 720)

13. **self-determination** The Wilsonian doctrine that each people should have the right to freely choose its own political affiliation and national future, e.g., independence or incorporation into another nation. "Faced with fierce Wilsonian opposition to this violation of self-determination...." (p. 721)

14. **reservation** A portion of a deed, contract, or treaty that places conditions or restrictions on the general obligations. "... he finally came up with fourteen formal reservations...." (p. 723)

15. **demagogue** A politician who arouses fervor by appealing to the lowest emotions of a mass audience, such as fear, hatred, and greed. " ... a debacle that played into the hands of the German demagogue Adolf Hitler." (p. 725)

PART II: Checking Your Progress

A. True-False

Where the statement is true, mark **T**. Where it is false, mark **F**, and correct it in the space immediately below.

_____ 1. Germany responded to Wilson's call for "peace without victory" by proposing a temporary armistice.

_____ 2. Wilson's proclamation of the war as a crusade to end all war and spread democracy around the world inspired intense ideological enthusiasm among Americans.

_____ 3. Among Wilson's Fourteen Points were freedom of the seas, national self-determination for minorities, and an international organization to secure peace.

_____ 4. The Committee on Public Information used an aroused American patriotism more than formal laws and censorship to promote the war cause.

_____ 5. The primary targets of prosecution under the Espionage and Sedition Acts were German and Austrian agents in the United States.

_____ 6. Even during the war mobilization, Americans were extremely reluctant to grant the federal government extensive powers over the economy.

___ 7. Despite bitter and sometimes violent strikes, American labor made economic and organizational gains as a result of World War I.

___ 8. War-inspired black migration into northern cities led to major racial riots in 1917–1919.

___ 9. The passage of the Nineteenth Amendment granting women's suffrage guaranteed the permanence of women's wartime economic gains.

___ 10. American troops actually played only a small role in the Allies' final victory.

___ 11. Before he would negotiate an armistice, President Wilson insisted that the Germans overthrow Kaiser Wilhelm II.

___ 12. Wilson's skillful handling of Republican political opposition strengthened his hand at the Paris Peace Conference.

___ 13. Other Allied leaders forced Wilson to make serious compromises in his Fourteen Points in order to keep the League of Nations in the Treaty of Versailles.

___ 14. Wilson's unwillingness to compromise and accept Republican reservations to the Treaty of Versailles sent the whole treaty down to defeat.

___ 15. In the election of 1920, Republican Harding supported the League of Nations while Democrat Cox tried to evade the issue.

B. Multiple Choice

Select the best answer and write the proper letter in the space provided.

___ 1. The immediate cause of American entry into World War I was
   a. German support for a possible Mexican invasion of the southwestern United States.
   b. Germany's resumption of unrestricted submarine warfare.
   c. the German defeat of France.
   d. desire of American munitions makers for large profits.

___ 2. Wilson aroused the somewhat divided American people to fervent support of the war by
   a. seizing control of the means of communication and demanding national unity.
   b. declaring the German people to be immoral Huns and barbarians.
   c. proclaiming an ideological war to end war and make the world safe for democracy.
   d. proclaiming the war a religious crusade.

___ 3. The capstone "Fourteenth Point" of Wilson's declaration of war aims called for
   a. the establishment of parliamentary democracies throughout Europe.
   b. guarantees of basic human rights for all people in the world.
   c. an international organization to guarantee collective security.
   d. freedom of travel without restrictions.

4. The purpose of George Creel's Committee on Public Information was
   a. to develop information on American wartime industrial production.
   b. to whip up public support for the war and promote anti-German propaganda.
   c. to develop counterintelligence information on German spies and saboteurs in the United States.
   d. to recruit volunteers for the armed forces.

5. The two key laws aimed at enforcing loyalty and suppressing antiwar dissent were
   a. the War Mobilization Act and the National Defense Act.
   b. the Selective Service Act and the Public Information Act.
   c. the Eighteenth Amendment and the Anti-German Language Act.
   d. the Espionage Act and the Sedition Act.

6. Among the primary victims of the prowar propaganda campaign to enforce loyalty were
   a. German-Americans and socialists.
   b. Russian-Americans and communists.
   c. Mexican-Americans and immigrants.
   d. African-Americans and feminists.

7. Among the political changes the war helped bring about was
   a. a constitutional amendment granting women the right to vote.
   b. a law granting labor unions the right to strike.
   c. a constitutional amendment guaranteeing African-Americans the right to travel freely.
   d. a constitutional amendment prohibiting child labor.

8. Particularly violent strikes erupted during and after World War I in the
   a. shipping and railroad industries.
   b. mining and steel industries.
   c. textile and clothing manufacturing industries.
   d. factories employing women war workers.

9. During World War I, African-American military men served primarily in
   a. segregated, non-combat support units.
   b. the navy and the coast guard.
   c. the most dangerous trenches in northern France.
   d. in northern cities where their presence did not threaten the system of segregation.

10. A major difference between the World War I Selective Service Act and the Civil War draft was that
    a. in World War I women as well as men were drafted.
    b. in World War I it was not possible to purchase an exemption or to hire a substitute.
    c. in World War I draftees were sent immediately into front line combat.
    d. in World War I draftees received the same training as professional soldiers.

11. American soldiers were especially needed in France in the spring of 1918 because
    a. the Allied invasion of Germany was faltering short of its goal.
    b. Britain had moved many of its soldiers from the western front to Russia.
    c. a renewed German offensive was threatening to break through to Paris.
    d. the Russians were threatening to enter the war on the Germans' side.

12. Most of the military supplies for General Pershing's expeditionary force came from
    a. America's European allies.
    b. factories in the United States.
    c. captured German matériel.
    d. Britain's colonies in Africa.

13. Wilson blundered when choosing the American peace delegation by failing to
    a. have a set of clear diplomatic goals.
    b. include any Republicans in the delegation.
    c. consult with his key Allies, Britain and France.
    d. include experts who would understand the intricate politics of Europe.

14. The European powers and Japan weakened Wilson at the peace conference by
    a. refusing to support his proposed League of Nations.
    b. supporting the Republicans who were criticizing Wilson at home.
    c. demanding continuing American aid and involvement in European affairs.
    d. forcing him to compromise his ideals on matters of self-determination and punishment of Germany.

15. Wilson bore considerable responsibility for the failure of the United States to join the League of Nations because
    a. he linked the League too closely to European politics.
    b. he ordered Democratic senators to defeat the pro-League treaty with the Lodge reservations.
    c. he failed to take the case for the League to the American public.
    d. he had agreed that America would pay most of the cost of the League.

C. Identification

Supply the correct identification for each numbered description.

1. Wilson's appeal to all the belligerents in January 1917, just before the Germans resumed submarine warfare

2. Message that contained a German proposal to Mexico for an anti-American alliance

3. Wilson's idealistic statement of American war aims in January 1918 that inspired the Allies and demoralized their enemies

4. American government propaganda agency that aroused zeal for Wilson's ideals and whipped up hatred for the kaiser

5. Radical antiwar labor union whose members were prosecuted under the Espionage and Sedition Act

6. Weak federal agency designed to organize and coordinate U.S. industrial production for the war effort

7. Constitutional provision endorsed by Wilson as a war measure whose ratification achieved a long-sought goal for American women

8. Treasury Department bond-selling drives that raised about $21 billion to finance the American war effort

_____ 9. The nations that dominated the Paris Peace Conference—namely, Britain, France, Italy, and the United States

_____ 10. Wilson's proposed international body that constituted the key provision of the Versailles treaty

_____ 11. Controversial peace agreement that compromised many of Wilson's Fourteen Points but retained his League

_____ 12. Senatorial committee whose chairman used delaying tactics and hostile testimony to develop opposition to Wilson's treaty and League of Nations

_____ 13. A hard core of isolationist senators who bitterly opposed any sort of league; also called the "Battalion of Death"

_____ 14. Amendments to the proposed Treaty of Versailles, sponsored by Wilson's hated senatorial opponent, that attempted to guarantee America's sovereign rights in relation to the League of Nations

_____ 15. Wilson's belief that the presidential election of 1920 should constitute a direct popular vote on the League of Nations

D. Matching People, Places, and Events

Match the person, place, or event in the left column with the proper description in the right column by inserting the correct letter on the blank line.

___ 1. George Creel
___ 2. Eugene V. Debs
___ 3. Bernard Baruch
___ 4. Herbert Hoover
___ 5. John J. Pershing
___ 6. Alice Paul
___ 7. Meuse-Argonne
___ 8. Kaiser Wilhelm II
___ 9. Woodrow Wilson
___ 10. Henry Cabot Lodge
___ 11. Georges Clemenceau
___ 12. William Borah
___ 13. Ludlow, Colorado
___ 14. East St. Louis, Illinois
___ 15. Warren G. Harding

A. Inspirational leader of the Western world in wartime who later stumbled as a peacemaker
B. Senatorial leader of the isolationist "irreconcilables" who absolutely opposed all American involvement in Europe.
C. Climactic final battle of World War I
D. The "tiger" of France, whose drive for security forced Wilson to compromise at Versailles
E. Head of the American propaganda agency that mobilized public opinion for World War I
F. Folksy Ohio senator whose 1920 presidential victory ended the last hopes for U.S. participation in the League of Nations
G. Hated leader of America's enemy in World War I
H. Head of the Food Administration who pioneered successful voluntary mobilization methods
I. Leader of the pacifist National Women's Party who opposed U.S. involvement in World War I
J. Site where state police killed 39 striking miners and their families in 1917
K. Commander of the overseas American Expeditionary Force in World War I
L. Site of one of the largest World War I-era race riots.
M. Wilson's great senatorial antagonist who fought to keep America out of the League of Nations
N. Head of the War Industries Board, which attempted to impose some order on U.S. war production
O. Socialist leader who won nearly a million votes as a presidential candidate while in federal prison for antiwar activities

Name_____ Section_____ Date_____

E. **Putting Things in Order**

Put the following events in correct order by numbering them from 1 to 5.

___ Germany's resumption of submarine warfare forces the United States onto a declaration of war.

___ The Senate's final defeat of the Versailles treaty and a Republican election victory end Wilson's last hopes for American entry into the League of Nations.

___ The United States takes the first hesitant steps toward preparedness in the event of war.

___ The effectiveness of American combat troops in crucial battles helps bring about an Allied victory in World War I.

___ Wilson struggles with other Allied leaders in Paris to hammer out a peace treaty and organize the postwar world.

F. **Matching Cause and Effect**

Match the historical cause in the left column with the proper effect in the right column by writing the correct letter on the blank line.

Cause

___ 1. Germany's resumption of unrestricted submarine warfare

___ 2. Wilson's Fourteen Points

___ 3. The wartime atmosphere of emotional patriotism and fear

___ 4. Women's labor in wartime factories

___ 5. The migration of African-Americans to northern cities

___ 6. American troops' entry into combat in the spring and summer of 1918

___ 7. Wilson's political blunders in the fall of 1918

___ 8. The strong diplomatic demands of France, Italy, and Japan

___ 9. Senator Lodge's tactics of delaying and proposing reservations in the Versailles treaty

___ 10. Wilson's refusal to accept any reservations supported by Lodge

Effect

A. Led to major racial violence in Chicago and East St. Louis, Illinois

B. Forced Democrats to vote against a modified treaty and killed American participation in the League of Nations

C. Stopped the final German offensive and turned the tide toward Allied victory

D. Allowed domestic disillusionment and opposition to the treaty and League to build strength

E. Finally pushed the United States into World War I

F. Weakened the president's position during the peacemaking process

G. Caused harsh attacks on German-Americans and other Americans who opposed the war

H. Lifted Allied and American spirits and demoralized Germany and its allies

I. Forced Wilson to compromise his Fourteen Points in order to keep the League as part of the peace treaty

J. Helped pass the Nineteenth Amendment but did not really change society's emphasis on the maternal role

G. Developing Historical Skills

Analyzing Visual Propaganda

This exercise involves analyzing visual propaganda designed to make emotional appeals on behalf of a cause. In this case, the propaganda was designed to enlist the American public's support for the war effort against Germany. The kinds of propaganda used on behalf of a cause can tell the historian a great deal about what issues were perceived to be at stake and what public values were being appealed to.

Answer the following questions about the cartoons and drawings in this chapter.

1. *Anti-German Propaganda* (p. 708): How do the words and image of this poster work together to persuade an American audience to buy liberty loans? Besides the specific message, what general portrait of Germany, the war, and America's reasons for fighting are conveyed?

2. *A Universal Draft, 1917*: How do the visual and verbal symbols in this cartoon convey the combination of invitation and threat implied in the War Department's 1918 wartime manpower rules? How would you characterize the depiction of "Uncle Sam's" mood here?

3. *Food for Thought* (p. 713): How does this poster visually make the connection between the patriotic war effort and gardens"? What specific words or phrases create the link between women's food-growing effort and military service on fields of combat? What specific appeal is this image making to women?

PART III: Applying What You Have Learned

1. What caused American entry into World War I, and how did Wilson turn the war into an ideological crusade?
2. Did World War I substantially alter American society and culture (e.g., ethnic, class, gender, and race relations), or were its effects primarily an "affair of the mind," i.e., altering American ideas and world views?
3. What was America's military and ideological contribution to the Allied victory?
4. How were the goals of the war presented to the American public? What does the text mean when it says that the war and Wilson's ideals may have been "oversold?" (p. 708)
5. How was Wilson forced to compromise during the peace negotiations, and why did America in the end refuse to ratify the treaty and join the League of Nations?
6. Apart from such immediate factors as the Lodge-Wilson antagonism, what general features of earlier American history worked against American involvement in European affairs and participation in the League of Nations?

32

American Life in the "Roaring Twenties," 1919–1929

PART I: Reviewing the Chapter

A. Checklist of Learning Objectives

After mastering this chapter, you should be able to

1. analyze the movement toward social conservatism following World War I.
2. describe the cultural conflicts over such issues as prohibition and evolution.
3. discuss the rise of the mass-consumption economy, led by the automobile industry.
4. describe the cultural revolution brought about by radio, films, and changing sexual standards.
5. explain how new ideas and values were reflected and promoted in the American literary renaissance of the 1920s.
6. explain how the era's cultural changes affected women and African-Americans.

B. Glossary

To build your social science vocabulary, familiarize yourself with the following terms.

1. **syndicalism** A theory or movement that advocates bringing all economic and political power into the hands of labor unions by means of strikes. ". . . a number of legislatures . . . passed criminal syndicalism laws." (p. 729)
2. **Bible Belt** The region of the American South, extending roughly from North Carolina west to Oklahoma and Texas, where Protestant Fundamentalism and belief in literal interpretation of the Bible have traditionally been strongest. ". . . the Klan spread with astonishing rapidity, especially in the Midwest and the 'Bible Belt' South." (p. 730)
3. **provincial** Narrow and limited; isolated from cosmopolitan influences. "Isolationist America of the 1920s, ingrown and provincial, had little use for the immigrants. . . ." (p. 730)
4. **racketeer** A person who obtains money illegally by fraud, bootlegging, gambling, or threats of violence. "Racketeers even invaded the ranks of local labor unions. . . ." (pp. 736–737)
5. **underworld** Those who live outside society's laws, by vice or crime. ". . . the annual 'take' of the underworld was estimated to be from $12 billion to $18 billion. . . ." (p. 737)
6. **credit** In business, the arrangement of purchasing goods or services immediately but making the payment at a later date. "Buying on credit was another innovative feature of the postwar economy." (p. 739)
7. **installment plan** A credit system by which goods already acquired are paid for in a series of payments at specified intervals. ". . . encouraged by tempting installment-plan buying, countless Americans with shallow purses acquired the habit of riding as they paid." (p. 741)
8. **magnate** An influential person in a large-scale enterprise. ". . . an outraged public forced the screen magnates to set up their own rigorous code of censorship." (pp. 744–745)

9. **repression** In psychology, the forcing of instincts or ideas painful to the conscious mind into the unconscious, where they continue to exercise influence. "The Viennese physician appeared to argue that sexual repression was responsible for a variety of nervous and emotional ills." (p. 746)
10. **charismatic** Concerning the personal magnetism or appeal of a leader for his or her followers; literally, "gift of grace." "Harlem in the 1920s also spawned a charismatic political leader, Marcus Garvey." (p. 748)
11. **functionalism** The theory that a plan or design should be derived from practical purpose. "Architecture also married itself to the new materialism and functionalism." (p. 750)
12. **surtax** A special tax, usually involving a raised rate on an already existing tax. ". . . Congress . . . abolish[ed] the surtax, the income tax, and estate taxes." (p. 752)

PART II: Checking Your Progress

A. True-False

Where the statement is true, mark **T**. Where it is false, mark **F**, and correct it in the space immediately below.

___ 1. The "red scare" of 1919–1920 led the U.S. government to threaten military assault on the Communist government of Russia.

___ 2. The Sacco-Vanzetti case aroused liberal and radical protest because of alleged prejudice by the judge and jury against the atheistic immigrant defendants.

___ 3. The Ku Klux Klan of the 1920s was strongest in the East and the West.

___ 4. The Immigration Act of 1924 reflected nativist prejudice against the new immigrants from southern and eastern Europe.

___ 5. The Eighteenth Amendment and the Volstead Act were frequently violated, especially by big-city dwellers and immigrants.

___ 6. The Scopes trial verdict acquitted biology teacher Scopes and overturned the Tennessee law prohibiting the teaching of evolution in the schools.

___ 7. The 1920s saw a shift from heavy industrial production toward a mass-consumption economy.

___ 8. Henry Ford's great economic achievement was the production of a cheap, reliable, mass-produced automobile.

___ 9. The automobile's large social and cultural effects in such areas as family life and gender relations were comparable to its economic importance.

___ 10. The radio and film industries initially emphasized non-commercial and public service uses of the mass media.

___ 11. The 1920s saw attempts to restore stricter standards of sexual behavior, especially for women.

_____ 12. Jazz was initially pioneered by blacks but was eventually taken up and promoted by whites.

_____ 13. The center of black literacy and cultural achievement in the 1920s was Atlanta, Georgia.

_____ 14. The most prominent writers of the 1920s upheld the moral virtues of small-town American life against the critical attitudes and moral questioning of the big cities.

_____ 15. The real estate and stock market booms of the 1920s included large elements of speculation and excessive credit risk.

B. Multiple Choice

Select the best answer and write the proper letter in the space provided.

_____ 1. The "red scare" of the early 1920s was initially set off by
   a. the Sacco-Vanzetti case.
   b. the rise of the radical Industrial Workers of the World.
   c. the Bolshevik revolution in Russia.
   d. an influx of radical immigrants.

_____ 2. Besides attacking minorities like Catholics, blacks, and Jews, the Ku Klux Klan of the 1920s opposed contemporary cultural and social changes such as
   a. evolution and birth control.
   b. prohibition and higher education.
   c. automobiles and airplanes.
   d. patriotism and immigration restriction.

_____ 3. The quota system established for immigration in the 1920s was based partly on the idea that
   a. America could accept the refugees created by war and revolution in Europe.
   b. immigrants from northern and western Europe were superior to those from southern and eastern Europe.
   c. immigration from Europe would be largely replaced by immigration from Asia.
   d. priority in immigration would be based on family relations, profession, and education.

_____ 4. The concentration of many American ethnic groups in separate neighborhoods with their own distinct institutions, cultures, and values meant that
   a. English was no longer the dominant language in the United States.
   b. the United States was intolerant of ethnic differences.
   c. Catholics and Jews had a political base from which to gain the presidency.
   d. it was almost impossible to organize the American working class across ethnic and religious lines.

_____ 5. One clear result of prohibition was
   a. a rise in criminal organizations that supplied illegal liquor.
   b. an improvement in family relations and the general moral tone of society.
   c. a turn from alcohol to other forms of substance abuse.
   d. the rise of voluntary self-help organizations like Alcoholics Anonymous.

6. The American city where gangsterism flourished most blatantly in the 1920s was
   a. New York City.
   b. Harlem.
   c. Chicago.
   d. New Orleans.

7. The essential issue in the Scopes trial was whether
   a. scientists ought to be allowed to investigate the biological origins of humanity.
   b. the teachings of Darwin could be reconciled with those of religion.
   c. Darwinian evolutionary science could be taught in the public schools.
   d. Fundamentalist Protestantism could be taught in the public schools.

8. The most highly acclaimed industrial innovator of the new mass-production economy was
   a. Babe Ruth.
   b. Bruce Barton.
   c. Ransom E. Olds.
   d. Henry Ford.

9. Two major American industries that benefited economically from the widespread use of the automobile were
   a. plastics and synthetic fibers.
   b. rubber and petroleum.
   c. textiles and leather.
   d. electronics and aluminum.

10. One of the primary *social* effects of the new automobile age was
    a. a weakening of traditional family ties between parents and youth.
    b. a strengthening of intergenerational ties among parents, children, and grandchildren.
    c. a tightening of restrictions on women.
    d. a closing of the gap between the working class and the wealthy.

11. Radio and the movies both had the cultural effect of
    a. increasing Americans' interest in history and literature.
    b. increasing mass standardization and weakening traditional forms of culture.
    c. undermining the tendency of industry toward big business and mass production.
    d. encouraging creativity and cultural independence among the people.

12. In the 1920s, the major changes pursued by American women were
    a. voting rights and political equality.
    b. economic equality and equal pay for equal work.
    c. social reform and family welfare.
    d. cultural freedom and expanded sexual experience.

13. The primary achievement of Marcus Garvey's Universal Negro Improvement Association was
    a. its promotion of black jazz and blues.
    b. its positive impact on black racial pride.
    c. its economic development program in Harlem.
    d. its transportation of numerous blacks to Liberia.

___ 14. The literary figure who promoted many new writers of the 1920s in his magazine, *The American Mercury*, was
   a. H. L. Mencken.
   b. W. C. Handy.
   c. F. Scott Fitzgerald.
   d. Henry Adams.

___ 15. Many of the prominent new writers of the 1920s were
   a. fascinated by their historical roots in old New England.
   b. disgusted with European domination of American culture.
   c. interested especially in nature and social reform.
   d. highly critical of traditional American "Puritanism" and small-town life.

C. Identification

Supply the correct identification for each numbered description.

_____ 1. The movement of 1919–1920, spawned by fear of Bolshevik revolution, that resulted in the arrest and deportation of many political radicals

_____ 2. Hooded defenders of Anglo-Saxon and "Protestant" values against immigrants, Catholics, and Jews

_____ 3. Restrictive legislation of 1924 that reduced the number of newcomers to the United States and discriminated against immigrants from southern and eastern Europe

_____ 4. New constitutional provision, popular in the Midwest and South, that encouraged lawbreaking and gangsterism in big cities

_____ 5. Term for area of the South where traditional evangelical and Fundamentalist religion remained strong

_____ 6. Legal battle over teaching evolution that pitted modern science against Fundamentalist religion

_____ 7. New industry spawned by the mass-consumption economy that encouraged still more consumption

_____ 8. Henry Ford's cheap, mass-produced automobile

_____ 9. Invented in 1903 and first used primarily for stunts and mail carrying

_____ 10. One of the few new consumer products of the 1920s that encouraged people to stay at home rather than pulling them away from home and family

_____ 11. Feminist Margaret Sanger's cause that contributed to changing sexual behaviors, especially for women

_____ 12. Syncopated style of music created by blacks that attained national popularity in the 1920s

_____ 13. Marcus Garvey's self-help organization that proposed leading blacks to Africa.

_____ 14. H. L. Mencken's monthly magazine that led the literary attack on traditional moral values, the middle class, and "Puritanism"

_____ 15. The New York institution in which continuously rising prices and profits were fueled by speculation in the 1920s

D. Matching People, Places, and Events

Match the person, place, or event in the left column with the proper description in the right column by inserting the correct letter on the blank line.

___ 1. A. Mitchell Palmer
___ 2. Nicola Sacco and Bartolomeo Vanzetti
___ 3. Al Capone
___ 4. John Dewey
___ 5. William Jennings Bryan
___ 6. Henry Ford
___ 7. Bruce Barton
___ 8. Langston Hughes
___ 9. Charles A. Lindbergh
___ 10. Marcus Garvey
___ 11. Sigmund Freud
___ 12. H. L. Mencken
___ 13. F. Scott Fitzgerald
___ 14. Ernest Hemingway
___ 15. Andrew Mellon

A. The "Poet Laureate" of Harlem and author of *The Weary Blues*
B. Innovative writer whose novels reflected the disillusionment of many Americans with propaganda and patriotic idealism
C. Italian-American anarchists whose trial and execution aroused widespread protest
D. Mechanical genius and organizer of the mass-produced automobile industry
E. U.S. attorney general who rounded up thousands of alleged Bolsheviks in the red scare of 1919–1920
F. Baltimore writer who criticized the supposedly narrow and hypocritical values of American society
G. Top gangster of the 1920s, eventually convicted of income-tax evasion
H. Former presidential candidate who led the fight against evolution at the 1925 Scopes trial
I. U. S. treasury secretary who attempted to promote business investment by reducing taxes on the rich
J. A leader of the advertising industry and author of a new interpretation on Christ in *The Man Nobody Knows*
K. Viennese psychologist whose writings were interpreted by Americans as a call for sexual liberation and gratification
L. Leading American philosopher and proponent of "progressive education"
M. Humble aviation pioneer who became a cultural hero of the 1920s
N. Minnesota-born writer whose novels were especially popular with young people in the 1920s
O. Jamaican-born leader who enhanced African-American pride despite his failed migration plans

E. Putting Things in Order

Put the following events in correct order by numbering them from 1 to 5.

___ The trial of a Tennessee high-school biology teacher symbolizes a national conflict over values of religion and science.

___ Fear of the Bolshevik revolution sparks a crusade against radicals and Communists in America.

___ A modest young man becomes a national hero by accomplishing a bold feat of aviation.

___ Two Italian immigrants are convicted of murder and robbery, provoking charges of prejudice against the judge and jury.

___ A new immigration law tightens up earlier emergency restrictions and imposes discriminatory quotas against the "New Immigrants."

Name_____ Section_____ Date_____

F. Matching Cause and Effect

Match the historical cause in the left column with the proper effect in the right column by writing the correct letter on the blank line.

Cause

___ 1. American fear of Bolshevism

___ 2. Nativist American fear of immigrants and Catholics

___ 3. Prohibition

___ 4. The automobile industry

___ 5. The radio

___ 6. Rising prosperity, new technologies, and the ideas of Sigmund Freud

___ 7. Resentment against conventional small-town morality

___ 8. The economic boom of the 1920s

___ 9. The ability to buy stocks with only a small down payment

___ 10. Andrew Mellon's tax policies

Effect

A. Caused the rise of the Ku Klux Klan and the imposition of immigration restrictions

B. Caused many influential writers of the 1920s to criticize traditional values and search for new moral standards

C. Caused the red scare and the deportation of foreign radicals

D. Enabled many ordinary citizens to join in a speculative Wall Street boom

E. Stimulated highway construction, petroleum production, and other related industries

F. Helped stimulate mass attention to sports and entertainment while spreading the reach of advertising

G. Reduced the tax burden on the wealthy and contributed to the stock-market boom

H. Greatly raised the incomes and living standards of many Americans

I. Created a new atmosphere of sexual frankness and liberation, especially among the young

J. Helped spawn "bootlegging" and large-scale organized crime

G. Developing Historical Skills

Understanding Cultural Developments in Historical Context

The first part of this chapter describes the major social and economic changes of the 1920s. The second part describes the cultural developments that also occurred in the 1920s. Since the artists, writers, and others who produced the culture and ideas of the period were living amidst these very same social changes, your knowledge of the historical context can help you understand why they created the kind of works they did.

Answer the following questions.

1. In what ways were the "movies," for all their glamour, similar to the automobile industry as developed by Henry Ford?

2. How did new technological and economic innovations like the automobile (pp. 739–742) and social changes like urbanization help bring about the cultural liberation of women?

3. In what ways did the novels of F. Scott Fitzgerald (pp. 749–750)) or musical developments like jazz (p. 746–747) especially appeal to people living amid the social and economic changes of the 1920s? Did these cultural developments simply mirror existing politics and society, or were they in some ways a challenge to them?

4. Why were writers like H. L. Mencken, Sinclair Lewis, and Sherwood Anderson so harshly critical of American rural and small-town life in their work? Why would writers with such attitudes have been unlikely to succeed in any period before the 1920s?

PART III: Applying What You Have Learned

1. How and why did America turn toward domestic isolation and social conservatism in the 1920s?
2. How was the diverse American "melting pot" affected by the political and cultural changes of the 1920s? (Include both white ethnic groups and blacks in your discussion.)
3. How did some of the events of the 1920s reflect national conflicts over social, cultural, and religious values?
4. How did the automobile and other new products create a mass-consumption economy in the 1920s?
5. How did the new films, literature, and music of the 1920s affect Americans' values in areas of religion, sexuality, and family life? Were African-American cultural developments fundamentally different, or were they part of the *same* cultural movement?
6. In what ways were the twenties a social and cultural reaction against the progressive idealism that held sway before and during World War I? (See Chapters 29, 30, and 31.)

33

The Politics of Boom and Bust, 1920–1932

PART I: Reviewing the Chapter

A. Checklist of Learning Objectives

After mastering this chapter, you should be able to

1. analyze the domestic political conservatism and economic prosperity of the 1920s.
2. explain the Republican administrations' policies of isolationism, disarmament, and high-tariff protectionism.
3. compare the easygoing corruption of the Harding administration with the straight-laced uprightness of his successor Coolidge.
4. describe the international economic tangle of loans, war debts, and reparations, and indicate how the United States dealt with it.
5. discuss how Hoover went from being a symbol of twenties business success to a symbol of depression failure.
6. explain how the stock-market crash set off the deep and prolonged Great Depression.
7. indicate how Hoover's response to the depression was a combination of old-time individualism and the new view of federal responsibility for the economy.

B. Glossary

To build your social science vocabulary, familiarize yourself with the following terms.

1. **nationalization** Ownership of the major means of production by the national or federal government. "... wartime government operation of the lines might lead to nationalization." (p. 755)
2. **dreadnought** A heavily armored battleship with large batteries of twelve-inch guns. "... Secretary Hughes startled the delegates ... with a comprehensive, concrete plan for ... scrapping some of the huge dreadnoughts. ..." (p. 757)
3. **accomplice** An associate or partner of a criminal who shares some degree of guilt. "... he and his accomplices looted the government to the tune of about $200 million. ..." (p. 759)
4. **reparations** Compensation by a defeated nation for damage done to civilians and their property during a war. "Overshadowing all other foreign-policy problems ... was ... a complicated tangle of private loans, Allied war debt, and German reparations payments." (p. 763)
5. **pump-priming** In economics, the spending or lending of a small amount of funds in order to stimulate a larger flow of economic activity. " 'Pump-priming' loans by the RFC were no doubt of widespread benefit. ..." (p. 772)

PART II: Checking Your Progress

A. True-False

Where the statement is true, mark **T**. Where it is false, mark **F**, and correct it in the space immediately below.

_____ 1. The most corrupt members of Harding's cabinet were the secretaries of state and the treasury.

_____ 2. The Republican administrations of the 1920s believed in strict enforcement of antitrust laws to maintain strong business competition.

_____ 3. The Republican administrations of the 1920s pursued their isolationist approach to national security by engaging in a large military buildup.

_____ 4. The high tariff policies of the 1920s enhanced American prosperity but hindered Europe's economic recovery from World War I.

_____ 5. Calvin Coolidge's image of honesty and thrift helped restore public confidence in the government after the Harding administration scandals.

_____ 6. Farmers looked unsuccessfully to the federal government to help relieve their severe economic troubles in the 1920s.

_____ 7. The main sources of support for liberal third-party presidential candidate Robert La Follette in 1924 were urban workers and social reformers.

_____ 8. The main exception to America's isolationist foreign policy in the 1920s was continuing U.S. armed intervention in the Caribbean and Central America.

_____ 9. Britain and France did not begin to repay their war debts to the United States until the Dawes plan provided American loans to Germany.

_____ 10. In the election of 1928, Democratic nominee Al Smith's urban, Catholic, and "wet" background cost him support from traditionally Democratic southern voters.

_____ 11. The Hawley-Smoot Tariff strengthened the trend toward expanded international trade and economic cooperation.

_____ 12. The American economic collapse of the Great Depression was the most severe suffered by any major industrial nation in the 1930s.

_____ 13. The depression was caused partly by over-expansion of credit and excessive consumer debt.

_____ 14. Throughout his term, Hoover consistently followed his belief that the federal government should play no role in providing economic relief and assisting the recovery from the depression.

_____ 15. The Reconstruction Finance Corporation provided federal loans to business and governmental institutions but no aid to individuals.

B. Multiple Choice

Select the best answer and write the proper letter in the space provided.

1. As president, Warren G. Harding proved to be
   a. thoughtful and ambitious but rather impractical.
   b. an able administrator and diplomat but a poor politician.
   c. politically competent and concerned for the welfare of ordinary people.
   d. weak-willed and tolerant of corruption among his friends.

2. The general policy of the federal government toward industry in the early 1920s was
   a. a weakening of federal regulation and encouragement of trade associations.
   b. an emphasis on federal regulation rather than state and local controls.
   c. an emphasis on vigorous antitrust enforcement rather than on regulation.
   d. a turn toward direct federal control of key industries like the railroads.

3. Two groups who suffered severe political setbacks in the immediate post–World War I environment were
   a. Protestants and Jews.
   b. organized labor and blacks.
   c. small businesses and farmers.
   d. women and city dwellers.

4. Two terms that describe the Harding and Coolidge administrations' approach to foreign policy are
   a. internationalism and moralism.
   b. interventionism and militarism.
   c. isolationism and disarmament.
   d. balance of power and alliance-seeking.

5. The proposed ratio of "5-5-3" in the Washington Disarmament Conference of 1921–1922 referred to
   a. the allowable ratio of American, British, and Japanese troops in China.
   b. the respective number of votes Britain, France, and the United States would have in the League of Nations.
   c. the allowable ratio of battleships and carriers among the United States, Britain, and Japan.
   d. the number of nations from Europe, the Americas, and Asia, respectively, that would have to ratify the treaties before they went into effect..

6. The very high tariff rates of the 1920s had the economic effect of
   a. stimulating the formation of common markets among the major industrial nations.
   b. causing severe deflation in the United States and Europe.
   c. turning American trade away from Europe and toward Asia.
   d. causing the Europeans to erect their own tariff barriers and thus severely reduce international trade.

7. The central scandal of Teapot Dome involved members of Harding's cabinet who
   a. sold spoiled foodstuffs to the army and navy.
   b. took bribes for leasing federal oil lands.
   c. violated prohibition by tolerating gangster liquor deals.
   d. stuffed ballot boxes and played dirty tricks on campaign opponents.

8. The one major group that experienced hard economic times amidst the general prosperity of the 1920s was

   a. small business.
   b. farmers.
   c. bankers and stock brokers.
   d. the middle class.

9. Besides deep divisions within the Democratic party, the elections of 1924 revealed

   a. Coolidge's inability to attain Harding's level of popularity.
   b. the weakness of profarmer and prolabor Progressive reform..
   c. the turn of the solid South from the Democrats to the Republicans.
   d. The rise of liberalism within the Democratic party.

10. The international economic crisis caused by unpaid war reparations and loans was partially resolved by

    a. private American bank loans to Germany.
    b. forgiving the loans and reparations.
    c. the creation of a new international economic system by the League of Nations.
    d. the rise of Mussolini and Hitler.

11. Al Smith's Roman Catholicism and opposition to prohibition hurt him especially

    a. in the South.
    b. among ethnic voters.
    c. among African-Americans.
    d. among women voters.

12. The election of Hoover over Smith in 1928 seemed to represent a victory of

    a. northern industrial values over southern agrarianism.
    b. small business over the ideas of big government and big business.
    c. ethnic and cultural diversity over traditional Anglo-Saxon values.
    d. big business and efficiency over urban and Catholic values.

13. One important cause of the great stock market crash of 1929 was

    a. overexpansion of production and credit beyond the ability to pay for them.
    b. a "tight" money policy that made it difficult to obtain loans.
    c. the lack of tariff protection for American markets from foreign competitors.
    d. excessive government regulation of business.

14. The sky-high Hawley-Smoot Tariff of 1930 had the economic effect of

    a. providing valuable protection for hard-pressed American manufacturers.
    b. lowering the value of American currency in international money markets.
    c. crippling international trade and deepening the depression.
    d. forcing foreign governments to negotiate fairer trade agreements.

15. The federal agency that Hoover established to provide "pump-priming" loans to business was the

    a. Tennessee Valley Authority.
    b. Bonus Expeditionary Force.
    c. Reconstruction Finance Corporation.
    d. American Legion.

Name_____ Section_____ Date_____

C. **Identification**

Supply the correct identification for each numbered description.

_____ 1. Poker-playing cronies from Harding's native state who contributed to the morally loose atmosphere in his administration

_____ 2. Supreme Court ruling that removed workplace protection and invalidated a minimum wage for women

_____ 3. World War I veterans' group that promoted patriotism and economic benefits for former servicemen

_____ 4. Agreement emerging from the Washington Disarmament Conference that reduced naval strength and established a ratio of warships among the major shipbuilding powers

_____ 5. Toothless international agreement of 1928 that pledged nations to outlaw war

_____ 6. Naval oil reserve in Wyoming that gave its name to one of the major Harding administration scandals

_____ 7. Farm proposal of the 1920s, passed by Congress but vetoed by the president, that provided for the federal government to buy farm surpluses and sell them abroad

_____ 8. American-sponsored arrangement for rescheduling German reparations payments that only temporarily eased the international debt tangle of the 1920s

_____ 9. Southern Democrats who turned against their party's "wet," Catholic nominee and voted for the Republican in 1938

_____ 10. Sky-high tariff bill of 1930 that deepened the depression and caused international financial chaos

_____ 11. The climactic day of the October 1929 Wall Street stock-market crash

_____ 12. Depression shantytowns, named after the president whom many blamed for their financial distress

_____ 13. Hoover-sponsored federal agency that provided loans to hard-pressed banks and businesses after 1932

_____ 14. Encampment of unemployed veterans who were driven out of Washington by General Douglas MacArthur's forces in 1932

_____ 15. The Chinese province invaded and overrun by the Japanese army in 1932

D. **Matching People, Places, and Events**

Match the person, place, or event in the left column with the proper description in the right column by inserting the correct letter on the blank line.

___ 1. Warren G. Harding
___ 2. Charles Evans Hughes
___ 3. Andrew Mellon
___ 4. Henry Sinclair
___ 5. John Davis

A. The worst single event of the great stock market crash of 1929
B. Extremely high tariff act that killed international trade and deepened the Great Depression
C. The "Happy Warrior" who attracted votes in the cities but lost them in the South
D. Harding's interior secretary, convicted of taking bribes for leases on federal oil reserves

Chapter 33 *The Politics of Boom and Bust, 1920–1932* 329

___ 6. Albert B. Fall
___ 7. Harry Daugherty
___ 8. Calvin Coolidge
___ 9. Robert La Follette
___ 10. Herbert Hoover
___ 11. Al Smith
___ 12. Black Tuesday
___ 13. Hawley-Smoot Bill
___ 14. Douglas MacArthur
___ 15. Henry Stimson

E. Weak, compromise Democratic candidate in 1924
F. U.S. attorney general and a member of Harding's corrupt "Ohio Gang" who was forced to resign in administration scandals
G. Strong-minded leader of Harding's cabinet and initiator of major naval agreements
H. Wealthy industrialist and conservative secretary of the treasury in the 1920s
I. Weak-willed president whose easygoing ways opened the door to widespread corruption in his administration
J. Hoover's secretary of state, who sought sanctions against Japan for its aggression in Manchuria
K. Secretary of commerce through much of the 1920s whose reputation for economic genius became a casualty of the Great Depression
L. Leader of a liberal third-party insurgency who attracted little support outside the farm belt
M. Wealthy oilman who bribed cabinet officials in the Teapot Dome scandal
N. Commander of the troops who forcefully ousted the "army" of unemployed veterans from Washington in 1932
O. Tight-lipped Vermonter who promoted frugality and pro-business policies during his presidency

E. Putting Things in Order

Put the following events in correct order by numbering them from 1 to 5.

___ Amid economic collapse, Congress raises tariff barriers to new heights and thereby deepens the depression.

___ An American-sponsored plan to ease German reparations payments provides a temporarily successful approach to the international war-debt tangle.

___ An American-sponsored international conference surprisingly reduces naval armaments and stabilizes Far Eastern power relations.

___ The prosperous economic bubble of the 1920s suddenly bursts, setting off a sustained period of hardship.

___ A large number of corrupt dealings and scandals become public knowledge just as the president who presided over them is replaced by his impeccably honest successor.

F. Matching Cause and Effect

Match the historical cause in the left column with the proper effect in the right column by writing the correct letter on the blank line.

Cause

___ 1. Republican probusiness policies

___ 2. American concern about the arms race and the danger of war

Effect

A. Led to a Republican landslide in the election of 1928
B. Weakened labor unions and prevented the enforcement of progressive antitrust legislation

___ 3. The high-tariff Fordney-McCumber Law of 1922

___ 4. The loose moral atmosphere of Harding's Washington

___ 5. The improved farm efficiency and production of the 1920s

___ 6. America's demand for complete repayment of the Allies' war debt

___ 7. Hoover's media campaign and Smith's political liabilities

___ 8. The stock-market crash

___ 9. Domestic overexpansion of production and dried-up international trade

___ 10. Hoover's limited efforts at federally sponsored relief and recovery

C. Plunged the United States into the worst economic depression in its history

D. Drove crop prices down and created a rural economic depression

E. Led to the successful Washington Disarmament Conference and the Five Power Naval Agreement of 1922

F. Encouraged numerous federal officials to engage in corrupt dealings

G. Helped cause the stock-market crash and deepen the Great Depression

H. Failed to end the depression but did prevent more serious economic suffering

I. Sustained American prosperity but pushed Europe into economic protectionism and turmoil

J. Aroused British and French anger and toughened their demands for German war reparations

G. Developing Historical Skills

Reading Diagrams

Sometimes a schematic drawing or diagram can help explain a complicated historical process in a simpler way than words. The international financial tangle of the 1920s is an exceptionally complicated affair, but examining the diagram on p. 764 makes it much easier to understand.

Answer the following questions.

1. What two roles did Americans play in the process?

2. What economic relationship did Great Britain and France have with Germany?

3. To whom did Britain owe war debts? To whom did France owe war debts?

4. Why was credit from American bankers so essential to all the European powers? Can you explain what happened when that credit was suddenly cut off after the stock-market crash of 1929?

PART III: Applying What You Have Learned

1. What basic economic and political policies were pursued by the conservative Republican administrations of the 1920s?
2. What were the effects of America's international economic and political isolationism in the 1920s?
3. What weakness existed beneath the surface of the general 1920s prosperity, and how did these weaknesses help cause the Great Depression?
4. Why were liberal or "progressive" politics so weak in the 1920s? Discuss the strengths and weaknesses of La Follette and Smith as challengers to the Republicans in 1924 and 1928.
5. The three Republican presidents of the 1920s are usually lumped together as essentially identical in outlook. Is it right to see them that way, or were the personal or political differences between them at all significant?
6. What were the effects of the Great Depression on the American people, and how did President Hoover attempt to balance his belief in "rugged individualism" with the economic necessities of the time? Why do historians today tend to see Hoover as a more tragic figure than people of the time, who bitterly denounced him?
7. How did some of the economic policies of the 1920s and 1930s help cause and deepen the depression?

34

The Great Depression and the New Deal, 1933–1938

PART I: Reviewing the Chapter

A. Checklist of Learning Objectives

After mastering this chapter, you should be able to

1. describe the rise of Franklin Roosevelt to the presidency in 1932.
2. explain how the early New Deal pursued the "three Rs" of relief, recovery, and reform.
3. describe the New Deal's effect on labor and labor organizations.
4. discuss the early New Deal's efforts to organize business and agriculture in the NRA and the AAA and indicate what replaced those programs after they were declared unconstitutional.
5. describe the Supreme Court's hostility to many New Deal programs and explain why FDR's "Court-packing" plan failed.
6. explain the political coalition that Roosevelt mobilized on behalf of the New Deal and the Democratic Party.
7. discuss the changes the New Deal underwent in the late thirties and explain the growing opposition to it.
8. analyze the arguments presented by both critics and defenders of the New Deal.

B. Glossary

To build your social science vocabulary, familiarize yourself with the following terms.

1. **dispossessed** The economically deprived. ". . . she . . . emerged as a champion of the dispossessed. . . ." (p. 778)
2. **rubber-stamp** To approve a plan or law quickly or routinely, without examination. ". . . it was ready to rubber-stamp bills drafted by White House advisors. . . ." (p. 781)
3. **blank-check** Referring to permission to use an unlimited amount of money or authority. ". . . Congress gave the president extraordinary blank-check powers. . . ." (p. 781)
4. **foreign exchange** The transfer of credits or accounts between the citizens or financial institutions of different nations. "The new law clothed the president with power to regulate banking transactions and foreign exchange. . . ." (p. 782)
5. **hoarding** Secretly storing up quantities of goods or money. "Roosevelt moved swiftly . . . to protect the melting gold reserve and to prevent panicky hoarding." (p. 783)
6. **boondoggling** Engaging in trivial or useless work; any enterprise characterized by such work. "Tens of thousands of jobless were employed at . . . make-work tasks, which were dubbed 'boondoggling.' " (p. 785)
7. **Fascist (Fascism)** A political system or philosophy that advocates a mass-based party dictatorship, extreme nationalism, racism, and the glorification of war. "Fear of Long's becoming a fascist dictator ended. . . ." (p. 786)

8. **parity** Equivalence in monetary value under different conditions; specifically, in the United States, the price for farm products that would give them the same purchasing power as in the period 1909–1914. "... this agency was to establish 'parity prices' for basic commodities." (p. 788)
9. **holding company** A company that owns, and usually controls, the stocks and securities of another company. "New Dealers ... directed their fire at public utility holding companies...." (p. 791)
10. **collective bargaining** Bargaining between an employer and his or her organized work force over hours, wages, and other conditions of employment. "The NRA blue eagles, with their call for collective bargaining, had been a godsend...." (p. 795)
11. **jurisdictional** Concerning the proper sphere in which authority may be exercised. "... bitter and annoying jurisdictional feuding involving strikes continued...." (p. 797)
12. **checks and balances** In American politics, the interlocking system of divided and counterweighted authority among the executive, legislative, and judicial branches of government. "... Roosevelt was savagely condemned for attempting to break down the delicate checks and balances...." (p. 799)
13. **pinko** Disparaging term for someone who is not a "red," or Communist, but is presumed to be sympathetic to communism. "Critics deplored the employment of 'crackpot' college professors, leftist 'pinkos.'..." (p. 802)
14. **deficit spending** The spending of public funds beyond the amount of income. "Despite some $20 billion poured out in six years of deficit spending...." (p. 803)
15. **left** (or **left-wing**) In politics, groups or parties that traditionally advocate progress, social change, greater economic and social equality, and the welfare of the common worker. (The **right** or **right-wing** is traditionally groups or parties that advocate adherence to tradition, established authorities, and an acceptance of some degree of economic and social hierarchy.) "He may even have headed off a more radical swing to the left...." (p. 804)

PART II: Checking Your Progress

A. True-False

Where the statement is true, mark **T**. Where it is false, mark **F**, and correct it in the space immediately below.

_____ 1. Roosevelt's call for a "New Deal" in the 1932 campaign included attacks on the Hoover deficits and a promise to balance the federal budget.

_____ 2. The economy was beginning a turn upward in the months immediately before Roosevelt's inauguration.

_____ 3. Congress rushed to pass many of the early New Deal programs that granted large emergency powers to the president.

_____ 4. Roosevelt's monetary reforms were designed to maintain the gold standard and protect the value of the dollar.

_____ 5. The Civilian Conservation Corps (CCC) and the Public Works Administration (PWA) were designed to reform American business practices.

_____ 6. Two early New Deal programs, the National Recovery Administration (NRA) and the Agricultural Adjustment Administration (AAA), were both declared unconstitutional by the Supreme Court.

____ 7. The primary agricultural problem of the Great Depression was declining farm production caused by the natural disasters of the period.

____ 8. The Securities and Exchange Commission and the Public Utilities Holding Company Act both imposed new federal regulations to reform corrupt or self-serving business practices that injured the public.

____ 9. The Tennessee Valley Authority (TVA) was designed primarily to aid in conserving water and soil resources in eroded hill areas.

____ 10. The Committee for Industrial Organization (CIO) used sympathetic New Deal laws to unionize many unskilled workers previously ignored by the American Federation of Labor (AF of L).

____ 11. Roosevelt's political coalition rested heavily on lower-income groups, including African-Americans, Jews, Catholics, and southerners.

____ 12. After Roosevelt's Court-packing plan failed, the conservative Supreme Court continued to strike down New Deal legislation just as it had before.

____ 13. After 1938 the New Deal lost momentum and ran into increasing opposition from an enlarged Republican bloc in Congress.

____ 14. The New Deal more than doubled the U.S. national debt through "deficit spending."

____ 15. By 1939 the New Deal had largely solved the major depression problem of unemployment.

B. Multiple Choice

Select the best answer and write the proper letter in the space provided.

____ 1. Franklin Roosevelt's presidential campaign in 1932
   a. called for large-scale federal spending to reduce unemployment and restore prosperity.
   b. focused primarily on issues of international trade.
   c. promised to aid the ordinary person by balancing the federal budget and ending deficits.
   d. emphasized that there was no way out of the depression in the near future.

____ 2. Eleanor Roosevelt became and influential figure in the 1930s especially by advocating the cause of
   a. the impoverished and dispossessed.
   b. feminists and proponents of sexual liberation.
   c. farmers and ranchers.
   d. immigrant ethnic groups and Roman Catholics.

____ 3. The Roosevelt landslide of 1932 included the shift into the Democratic camp of traditionally Republican
   a. New Englanders.
   b. African-Americans.
   c. labor unions.
   d. southerners.

4. Roosevelt's first bold action during the Hundred Days was
   a. taking the nation off the gold standard.
   b. declaring a national bank holiday.
   c. legalizing labor strikes and job actions.
   d. doubling relief for the unemployed.

5. The *primary* purpose of the Civilian Conservation Corps (CCC) was
   a. to restore unproductive farmland to productive use.
   b. to protect wildlife and the environment.
   c. to provide better-trained workers for industry.
   d. to provide jobs and experience for unemployed young people.

6. Strong political challenges to Roosevelt came from extremist critics like
   a. Father Coughlin and Huey Long.
   b. Frances Perkins and Harry Hopkins.
   c. Henry Ford and Mary McLeod Bethune.
   d. John Steinbeck and John L. Lewis.

7. Roosevelt's National Recovery Administration (NRA) ended when
   a. Dr. Francis Townsend attacked it as unfair to the elderly.
   b. Congress refused to provide further funding for it.
   c. it came to be considered too expensive for the results achieved.
   d. the Supreme Court declared it unconstitutional.

8. Roosevelt's Agricultural Adjustment Administration met sharp criticism because
   a. it failed to raise farm prices.
   b. it actually contributed to soil erosion on the Great Plains.
   c. it raised prices by paying farmers to slaughter animals and not grow crops.
   d. it relied too much on private bank loans to aid farmers.

9. In addition to the natural forces of drought and wind, the Dust Bowl of the 1930s was also caused by
   a. Roosevelt's AAA farm policies.
   b. excessive use of dry farming and mechanization techniques on marginal land.
   c. the attempted shift from wheat and cotton growing to fruit and vegetable farming.
   d. the drying up of underground aquifers used to irrigate the Great Plains.

10. The so-called "Indian New Deal" included an emphasis on
    a. local tribal self-government and recovery of Indian identity and culture.
    b. the distribution of tribal lands to individual Indian landowners.
    c. the migration of Indians from rural reservations to the cities.
    d. programs to encourage businesses like gambling casinos to locate on Indian lands.

11. The major New Deal program that attempted to provide flood control, electric power, and economic development occurred in the valley of the
    a. Columbia River.
    b. Colorado River.
    c. Hudson River.
    d. Tennessee River.

_____ 12. The Social Security Act of 1935 provided for
   a. electricity and conservation for rural areas.
   b. pensions for older people, the blind, and other categories of citizens.
   c. assistance for low-income public housing and social services.
   d. unemployment and disability insurance for workers.

_____ 13. The new labor organization that flourished under depression conditions and New Deal sponsorship was
   a. the Knights of Labor.
   b. the American Federation of Labor.
   c. the National Labor Relations Board.
   d. the Committee for Industrial Organization.

_____ 14. Among the groups that formed part of the powerful "Roosevelt coalition" in the election of 1936 were
   a. African-Americans, southerners, and Catholics.
   b. Republicans, New Englanders, and "Old Immigrants."
   c. midwesterners, small-town residents, and Presbyterians.
   d. businessmen, prohibitionists, and Coughlinites.

_____ 15. Roosevelt's attempt to "pack" the Supreme Court proved extremely costly because
   a. the Court members he appointed still failed to support the New Deal.
   b. Congress began proceedings to impeach him.
   c. its failure ended much of the political momentum of the New Deal.
   d. many of his New Deal supporters turned to back Huey Long.

C. Identification

Supply the correct identification for each numbered description.

_____ 1. Term used by FDR in 1932 acceptance speech that came to describe his whole reform program

_____ 2. FDR's reform-minded intellectual advisers, who conceived much of the New Deal legislation

_____ 3. Popular term for the special session of Congress in early 1933 that passed vast quantities of Roosevelt-initiated legislation

_____ 4. The early New Deal agency that worked to solve the problems of unemployment and conservation by employing youth in reforestation and other socially beneficial tasks

_____ 5. Large federal employment program, established in 1935 under Harry Hopkins, that provided jobs in areas from road building to art

_____ 6. Widely displayed symbol of the National Recovery Administration (NRA), which attempted to reorganize and reform U.S. industry

_____ 7. New Deal farm agency that attempted to raise prices by paying farmers to reduce their production of crops and animals

_____ 8. The drought-stricken plains areas from which hundreds of thousands of "Okies" were driven during the Great Depression

_____ 9. New Deal agency that aroused strong conservative criticism by producing low-cost electrical power in competition with private utilities

_____ 10. New Deal program that financed old-age pensions, unemployment insurance, and other forms of income assistance

_____ 11. The new union group that organized large numbers of unskilled workers with the help of the Wagner Act and the National Labor Relations Board

_____ 12. New Deal agency established to provide a public watchdog against deception and fraud in stock trading

_____ 13. Organization of wealthy Republicans and conservative Democrats whose attacks on the New Deal caused Roosevelt to denounce them as "economic royalists" in the campaign of 1936

_____ 14. Roosevelt's scheme for gaining Supreme Court approval of New Deal legislation

_____ 15. Law of 1939 that prevented federal officials from engaging in campaign activities or using federal relief funds for political purposes

D. Matching People, Places, and Events

Match the person, place, or event in the left column with the proper description in the right column by inserting the correct letter on the blank line.

___ 1. Franklin D. Roosevelt
___ 2. Eleanor Roosevelt
___ 3. Banking holiday
___ 4. Harry Hopkins
___ 5. Father Coughlin
___ 6. Huey ("Kingfish") Long
___ 7. *Schechter* case
___ 8. Harold Ickes
___ 9. John Steinbeck
___ 10. John L. Lewis
___ 11. General Motors sit-down strike
___ 12. Alfred M. Landon
___ 13. Election of 1936
___ 14. John Maynard Keynes
___ 15. Justice Roberts

A. Republican who carried only two states in a futile campaign against "The Champ" in 1936

B. The "microphone messiah" of Michigan whose mass radio appeals turned anti–New Deal and anti-Semitic

C. Writer whose best-selling novel portrayed the suffering of dust bowl "Okies" in the Thirties

D. Supreme Court justice whose "switch in time" to support New Deal legislation helped undercut FDR's Court-packing scheme

E. Presidential wife who became an effective lobbyist for the poor during the New Deal

F. Louisiana senator and popular mass agitator who promised to make "every man a king" at the expense of the wealthy

G. Former New York governor who roused the nation to action against the depression with his appeal to the "forgotten man"

H. Dramatic CIO labor action in 1936 that forced the auto industry to recognize unions

I. Lopsided but bitter campaign that saw disadvantaged economic groups lined up in a kind of "class warfare" against those better off

J. Former New York social worker who became an influential FDR adviser and head of several New Deal agencies

K. Former bull moose progressive who spent billions of dollars on public building projects while carefully guarding against waste

L. Roosevelt-declared closing of all U.S. financial institutions on March 6–10, 1933, in order to stop panic and prepare reforms

Name_____ Section_____ Date_____

M. British economist whose theories helped justify New Deal deficit spending
N. Supreme Court ruling of 1935 that struck down a major New Deal industry-and-labor agency
O. Domineering boss of the mine workers' union who launched the CIO

E. Putting Things in Order

Put the following events in correct order by numbering them from 1 to 5.

____ FDR devalues the dollar to about sixty cents in gold in an attempt to raise domestic prices.

____ Congress passes numerous far-reaching laws under the pressure of a national crisis and strong presidential leadership.

____ Republican attempts to attack the New Deal fall flat, and FDR wins reelection in a landslide.

____ FDR's frustration at the conservative Supreme Court's overturning of New Deal legislation leads him to make a drastic proposal.

____ Passage of new federal prolabor legislation opens the way for a new union group and successful mass labor organizing.

F. Matching Cause and Effect

Match the historical cause in the left column with the proper effect in the right column by writing the correct letter on the blank line.

Cause

____ 1. The "lame-duck" period from November 1932 to March 1933

____ 2. Roosevelt's leadership during the Hundred Days

____ 3. The Civilian Conservation Corps, the Works Progress Administration, and the Civil Works Administration

____ 4. New Deal farm programs like the AAA

____ 5. The Tennessee Valley Authority

____ 6. The Wagner (National Labor Relations) Act

____ 7. FDR's political appeals to workers, African-Americans, southerners, and "New Immigrants"

Effect

A. Succeeded in raising farm prices but met strong opposition from many conservatives
B. Encouraged the CIO to organize large numbers of unskilled workers
C. May have pushed the Court toward more liberal rulings but badly hurt FDR politically
D. Caused a sharp "Roosevelt Depression" that brought unemployment back up to catastrophic levels
E. Caused a political paralysis that nearly halted the U.S. economy
F. Provided federal economic planning, conservation, cheap electricity, and jobs to a poverty-stricken region
G. Provided federal jobs for unemployed workers in conservation, construction, the arts, and other areas
H. Caused Roosevelt to propose a plan to "pack" the Supreme Court
I. Pushed a remarkable number of laws through Congress and restored the nation's confidence
J. Forged a powerful political coalition that made the Democrats the majority party

_____ 8. The Supreme Court's conservative rulings against New Deal legislation

_____ 9. Roosevelt's attempt to "pack" the Supreme Court

_____ 10. The rapid cutback in federal "pump-priming" spending in 1937

G. Developing Historical Skills

Reading Charts

Charts can classify complex information for ready reference. In this chapter they are an effective way to present the many New Deal laws, agencies, and programs. The chart dealing with the Hundred Days is on p. 781, and that dealing with the later New Deal on p. 784.

Answer the following questions.

1. Which Hundred Days agency whose primary purpose was recovery also contributed to relief and reform?

2. List three Hundred Days actions that were aimed *primarily* at recovery.

3. List three later New Deal measures aimed *primarily* at reform.

4. Which later New Deal law aimed primarily at relief also contributed to recovery and reform?

5. Which was the *last* of the later New Deal laws aimed primarily at providing relief?

6. Compare the two charts. What can you conclude about the Hundred Days compared to the later New Deal in relation to their relative emphasis on the three goals of relief, recovery, and reform? In which of the areas do you see the most continuity of purpose?

H. Map Mastery

Map Discrimination

Using the maps and charts in Chapter 34, answer the following questions.

1. *TVA Area*: In which four states was most of the Tennessee Valley Authority located?

2. *TVA Area*: How many major TVA dams were located in (a) Tennessee and (b) Alabama?

3. *The Rise and Decline of Organized Labor*: Before the organizing drives of the 1930s, which year saw the highest membership for organized labor?

4. *The Rise and Decline of Organized Labor*: About how many million members did the CIO *gain* between 1935 and 1945: 2 million, 4 million, 6 million, or 8 million?

Map Challenge

Using the graph of *The Rise and Decline of Organized Labor* on p. 797, write a brief essay explaining the changing fortunes of (a) organized labor in general and (b) the different types of unions—craft, industrial, and independent—from 1900 to 1998.

PART III: Applying What You Have Learned

1. What qualities did FDR bring to the presidency, and how did he display them during the New Deal years? What particular role did Eleanor Roosevelt play in FDR's political success?
2. How did the early New Deal legislation attempt to achieve the three goals of relief, recovery, and reform?
3. How did Roosevelt's programs develop such a strong appeal for the "forgotten man," and why did the New Deal arouse such opposition from conservatives, including those on the Supreme Court?
4. Discuss the political components of the "Roosevelt coalition" formed in the 1930s. What did the New Deal offer to the diverse elements of this coalition?
5. Was the New Deal essentially a conservative attempt to save American capitalism from collapse, a radical change in traditional American anti-government beliefs, or a moderate liberal response to a unique crisis?
6. How was the New Deal a culmination of the era of progressive reform, and how did it differ from the pre–World War I progressive era? (See Chapters 29 and 30.)

35

Franklin D. Roosevelt and the Shadow of War, 1933–1941

PART I: Reviewing the Chapter

A. Checklist of Learning Objectives

After mastering this chapter, you should be able to

1. describe the isolationist motives and effects of FDR's early foreign policies.
2. explain how American isolationism dominated U.S. policy in the mid-1930s.
3. explain how America gradually began to respond to the threat from totalitarian aggression while still trying to stay neutral.
4. describe Roosevelt's increasingly bold moves toward aiding Britain in the fight against Hitler and the sharp disagreements these efforts caused at home.
5. discuss the events and diplomatic issues in the Japanese-American conflict that led up to Pearl Harbor.

B. Glossary

To build your social science vocabulary, familiarize yourself with the following terms.

1. **Exchange rate** The monetary ratio according to which one currency is convertible into another, e.g., American dollars vis-à-vis German deutschmarks, which determines their value relative to one another. "Exchange-rate stabilization was essential to revival of world trade . . ." (p. 806)
2. **militarist** Someone who glorifies military values or institutions and extends them into the political and social spheres. "Yet in Tokyo, Japanese militarists were calculating that they had little to fear. . . ." (p. 807)
3. **totalitarianism** A political system of absolute control, in which all social, moral, and religious values and institutions are put in direct service of the state. "Post-1918 chaos in Europe, followed by the Great Depression, fostered the ominous spread of totalitarianism." (p. 809)
4. **quarantine** In politics, isolating a nation by refusing to have economic or diplomatic dealings with it. ". . . they feared that a moral quarantine would lead to a shooting quarantine." (p. 812)
5. **division** The major unit of military organization, usually about 3,000 to 10,000 strong, into which most modern armies are organized. " . . . he sent his mechanized divisions crashing into Poland at dawn on September 1, 1939." (p. 813)
6. **unilateral** In politics, concerning a policy or action undertaken by only one nation. "This ancient dictum [was] hitherto unilateral. . . ." (p. 815)
7. **multilateral** In politics, referring to a policy or action undertaken by more than one nation. "Now multilateral, [the Monroe Doctrine bludgeon] was to be wielded by twenty-one pairs of American hands. . . ." (p. 815)
8. **steppes** The great plains of southeastern Europe and Asia. "The two fiends could now slit each other's throats on the icy steppes of Russia." (p 822)

9. **convoy** (v.) To escort militarily, for purposes of protection. (The escorting ships or troops is called a convoy.) "Roosevelt made the fateful decision to convoy in July 1941." (p. 823)
10. **warlord** A leader or ruler who maintains power by continually waging war, often against other similar rulers or local military leaders. ". . . Roosevelt had resolutely held off an embargo, lest he goad the Tokyo warlords. . . ." (p. 824)
11. **hara-kiri** Traditional Japanese ritual suicide. "Japan's *hara-kiri* gamble in Hawaii paid off only in the short run." (p. 825)

PART II: Checking Your Progress

A. True-False

Where the statement is true, mark **T**. Where it is false, mark **F**, and correct it in the space immediately below.

___ 1. Roosevelt's policy toward the 1933 London Economic Conference showed his concern for establishing a stable international economic order.

___ 2. Roosevelt adhered to his Good Neighbor principle of nonintervention in Latin America even when Mexico seized American oil companies in 1938.

___ 3. American isolationism was caused partly by deep disillusionment with U.S. participation in World War I.

___ 4. The Neutrality Acts of the mid-1930s prevented Americans from lending money or selling weapons to warring nations and from sailing on belligerent ships.

___ 5. Despite the neutrality laws, the United States provided some assistance to the Spanish Loyalist government in its Civil War with the Fascistic General Franco.

___ 6. The United States reacted strongly when Japan sank the American gunboat *Panay* in Chinese waters.

___ 7. The United States attempted to dissuade the Western democracies from pursuing their policy of appeasing Hitler's aggressive demands.

___ 8. The "cash-and-carry" Neutrality Act of 1939 allowed America to aid the Allies without making loans or transporting weapons on U.S. ships.

___ 9. The fall of France to Hitler in 1940 strengthened U.S. determination to stay neutral.

___ 10. Isolationists argued that economic and military aid to Britain would inevitably lead to U.S. involvement in the European war.

___ 11. Republican presidential nominee Willkie joined the isolationist attack on Roosevelt's pro-Britain policy in the 1940 campaign.

___ 12. The 1941 Lend-Lease Act marked the effective abandonment of U.S. neutrality and the beginning of naval clashes with Germany.

___ 13. The Atlantic Charter was an agreement on future war aims signed by Great Britain, the United States, and the Soviet Union.

Name_____ Section_____ Date_____

___ 14. U.S. warships were already being damaged and sunk in clashes with the German navy before Pearl Harbor.

___ 15. The focal point of conflict between the United States and Japan in the pre–Pearl Harbor negotiations was Japan's refusal to withdraw from the Dutch East Indies.

B. Multiple Choice

Select the best answer and write the proper letter in the space provided.

___ 1. Roosevelt torpedoed the London Economic Conference of 1933 because
   a. he wanted to concentrate primarily on the recovery of the American domestic economy.
   b. he saw the hand of Hitler and Mussolini behind the conference's proposals.
   c. he was firmly committed to the gold standard.
   d. he wanted economic cooperation only between the United States and Britain, not the rest of Europe.

___ 2. Seeking to withdraw from overseas commitments and colonial expense, the United States in 1934 promised future independence to
   a. Puerto Rico.
   b. the Virgin Islands.
   c. the Philippines.
   d. Cuba.

___ 3. Roosevelt's Good Neighbor policy toward Latin America included
   a. a substantial program of American economic aid for Latin American countries.
   b. a renunciation of American intervention in Mexico or elsewhere in the region.
   c. an American military presence to block German influence in Argentina and Brazil.
   d. an American pledge to transfer the Panama Canal to Panama by the year 2000.

___ 4. The immediate response of most Americans to the rise of the Fascist dictators Mussolini and Hitler was
   a. a call for a new military alliance to contain aggression.
   b. a focus on political cooperation with Britain and the Soviet Union.
   c. support for the Spanish government against Fascist rebels.
   d. a deeper commitment to remain isolated from European problems.

___ 5. The Neutrality Acts of 1935, 1936, and 1937 provided that
   a. the United States would remain neutral in any war between Britain and Germany.
   b. Americans could not sail on belligerent ships, sell munitions, or make loans to nations at war.
   c. no belligerent could conduct propaganda campaigns, sell goods, or make loans within the United States.
   d. the United States would take the lead in neutral efforts to end the wars in China and Ethiopia.

6. The effect of the strict American arms embargo during the civil war between the Loyalist Spanish government and Franco's Fascist rebels was
   a. to encourage a negotiated political settlement between the warring parties.
   b. to strengthen the Spanish government's ability to resist Franco.
   c. to push Britain and the Soviet Union to intervene in the Spanish Civil War.
   d. to cripple the Loyalist government while the Italians and Germans armed Franco.

7. The policy of appeasing the Fascist dictators reached its low point in 1938 when Britain and France sold out Czechoslovakia to Hitler in the conference at
   a. Geneva.
   b. Versailles.
   c. Munich.
   d. Prague.

8. The "cash-and-carry" Neutrality Act of 1939 was cleverly designed to
   a. guarantee that American policy would not benefit either side in World War II.
   b. enable American merchants to provide loans and ships to the Allies.
   c. prepare America for involvement in the war.
   d. help Britain and France by letting them buy supplies and munitions in the United States.

9. The "destroyers-for-bases" deal of 1940 provided that
   a. the United States would give Britain fifty American destroyers in exchange for eight British bases in North America.
   b. the United States would give Britain new bases in North America in exchange for fifty British destroyers.
   c. if America entered the war it would receive eight bases in Britain in exchange for American destroyers.
   d. the British would transfer captured French destroyers to the United States in exchange for the use of American bases in East Asia.

10. The twin events that precipitated the reversal of American policy from neutrality to active, though nonbelligerent, support of the Allied cause were
    a. the Munich Conference and the invasion of Poland.
    b. the fall of France and the Battle of Britain.
    c. the fall of Poland and the invasion of Norway.
    d. the invasion of the Soviet Union and the German submarine attacks on American shipping.

11. In the campaign of 1940, the Republican nominee Willkie essentially agreed with Roosevelt on the issue of
    a. the New Deal.
    b. the third term.
    c. Roosevelt's use of power in office.
    d. foreign policy.

___ 12. The Lend-Lease Act clearly marked
   a. the end of isolationist opposition to Roosevelt's foreign policy.
   b. an end to the pretense of American neutrality between Britain and Germany.
   c. a secret Roosevelt plan to involve the United States in war with Japan.
   d. the beginning of opposition in Congress to Roosevelt's foreign policy.

___ 13. The provisions of the Atlantic Charter signed by Roosevelt and Churchill in 1941 included
   a. self-determination for oppressed peoples and a new international peacekeeping organization.
   b. a permanent alliance between Britain, the United States, and the Soviet Union.
   c. a pledge to rid the world of dictators and to establish democratic governments in Germany and Italy.
   d. an agreement to oppose Soviet communism, but only after Hitler was defeated.

___ 14. By the fall of 1940, American warships were being attacked by German destroyers near the coast of
   a. Spain.
   b. Ireland.
   c. Iceland.
   d. Canada.

___ 15. The key issue in the failed negotiations with Japan just before Pearl Harbor was
   a. the refusal of the Japanese to withdraw their navy from Hawaiian waters.
   b. Americans' insistence on their right to expand naval power in Asia.
   c. the Japanese refusal to withdraw from China.
   d. the Japanese refusal to guarantee the security of the Philippines.

C. Identification

Supply the correct identification for each numbered description.

_____ 1. International economic conference on stabilizing currency that was sabotaged by FDR

_____ 2. Nation to which the U.S. promised independence in the Tydings-McDuffie Act of 1934

_____ 3. FDR's repudiation of Theodore Roosevelt's corollary to the Monroe Doctrine, stating his intention to work cooperatively with Latin American nations

_____ 4. A series of laws enacted by Congress in the mid-1930s that attempted to prevent any American involvement in future overseas wars

_____ 5. Conflict between the rebel Fascist forces of General Francisco Franco and the Loyalist government that severely tested U.S. neutrality legislation

_____ 6. Roosevelt's 1937 speech that proposed strong U.S. measures against overseas aggressors

_____ 7. European diplomatic conference in 1938 where Britain and France conceded to Hitler's demands for Czechoslovakia

_____ 8. Term for the British-French policy of attempting to prevent war by granting German demands

_____ 9. Leading U.S. group advocating American support for Britain in the fight against Hitler

_____ 10. Leading isolationist group advocating that America focus on continental defense and non-involvement with the European war

_____ 11. Controversial 1941 law that made America the "arsenal of democracy" by providing supposedly temporary military material assistance to Britain

_____ 12. Communist nation invaded by Hitler in June 1941 that was also aided by American lend-lease

_____ 13. U.S.–British agreement of August 1941 to promote democracy and establish a new international organization for peace

_____ 14. U.S. destroyer sunk by German submarines off the coast of Iceland in October 1941, with the loss of over a hundred men

_____ 15. Major American Pacific naval base devastated in a surprise attack in December 1941

D. Matching People, Places, and Events

Match the person, place, or event in the left column with the proper description in the right column by inserting the correct letter on the blank line.

____ 1. Cordell Hull
____ 2. Adolf Hitler
____ 3. Benito Mussolini
____ 4. Gerald Nye
____ 5. Francisco Franco
____ 6. Ethiopia
____ 7. Czechoslovakia
____ 8. Poland
____ 9. France
____ 10. Charles A. Lindbergh
____ 11. Wendell Willkie
____ 12. Winston Churchill
____ 13. Joseph Stalin
____ 14. Iceland
____ 15. Hawaii

A. Courageous prime minister who led Britain's lonely resistance to Hitler
B. Leader of the "America First" organization and chief spokesman for U.S. isolationism
C. African nation invaded by an Italian dictator in 1935
D. Dynamic dark horse Republican presidential nominee who attacked FDR only on domestic policy
E. Fanatical Fascist leader of Germany whose aggressions forced the United States to abandon its neutrality
F. Instigator of 1934 Senate hearings that castigated World War I munitions manufacturers as "merchants of death"
G. Nation whose sudden fall to Hitler in 1940 pushed the United States closer to direct aid to Britain
H. Site of a naval base where Japan launched a devastating surprise attack on the United States
I. North Atlantic nation near whose waters U.S. destroyers came under Nazi submarine attack
J. Small East European democracy betrayed into Hitler's hands at Munich
K. The lesser partner of the Rome-Berlin Axis who invaded Ethiopia and joined the war against France and Britain
L. FDR's secretary of state, who promoted reciprocal trade agreements, especially with Latin America
M. Russian dictator who first helped Hitler destroy Poland before becoming a victim of Nazi aggression in 1941
N. East European nation whose September 1939 invasion by Hitler set off World War II in Europe
O. Fascist rebel against the Spanish Loyalist government

Name_____ Section_____ Date_____

E. Putting Things in Order

Put the following events in correct order by numbering them from 1 to 5.

____ FDR puts domestic recovery ahead of international economics, torpedoing a major monetary conference.

____ Western democracies try to appease Hitler by sacrificing Czechoslovakia, but his appetite for conquest remains undiminished.

____ Already engaged against Hitler in the Atlantic, the United States is plunged into World War II by a surprise attack in the Pacific.

____ The fall of France pushes FDR into providing increasingly open aid to Britain.

____ Japan invades China and attacks an American vessel, but the United States sticks to its neutrality principles.

F. Matching Cause and Effect

Match the historical cause in the left column with the proper effect in the right column by writing the correct letter on the blank line.

Cause

____ 1. FDR's refusal to support international economic cooperation in the 1930s

____ 2. Roosevelt's Good Neighbor policy

____ 3. Bad memories of World War I and revelations about arms merchants

____ 4. The U.S. Neutrality Acts of the 1930s

____ 5. Japanese aggression against China in 1937

____ 6. Hitler's invasion of Poland

____ 7. The fall of France in 1940

____ 8. Willkie's support for FDR's pro-British foreign policy

____ 9. The U.S. embargo on oil and other supplies to Japan

____ 10. Roosevelt's decision to convoy lend-lease shipments

Effect

A. Thrust the United States into an undeclared naval war with Nazi German in the North Atlantic

B. Prompted FDR to make his "Quarantine Speech," proposing strong action against aggressors

C. Brought new respect for the United States and for democracy in Latin America

D. Shocked the United States into enacting conscription and making the "destroyers-for-bases" deal

E. Forced Japan to either accept U.S. demands regarding China or go to war

F. Caused the United States to institute a "cash-and-carry" policy for providing aid to Britain

G. Deepened the worldwide Depression and aided the rise of Fascist dictators

H. Actually aided Fascist dictators in carrying out their aggressions in Ethiopia, Spain, and China.

I. Promoted U.S. isolationism and the passage of several Neutrality Acts in the mid-1930s

J. Kept the 1940 presidential campaign from becoming a bitter national debate

G. Developing Historical Skills

Reading Text for Sequence and Context

In learning to read for and remember the historical sequence of events, it is often helpful to look for the context in which they occurred.

In the first list below are several major events discussed in the chapter. The second list contains the immediate contexts in which those events occurred. First, link the event to the appropriate context by putting a number from the bottom list to the right of the proper event. Then put the event-with-context in the proper sequence by writing numbers 1 to 7 in the spaces to the left.

Order	Event	Context
_____	Destroyer-for-bases deal	_____
_____	Atlantic Charter	_____
_____	Good Neighbor policy	_____
_____	U.S. Neutrality Acts of 1935–1936	_____
_____	Pearl Harbor	_____
_____	Lend-lease	_____
_____	Munich Conference	_____

Context

1. Failure of U.S.–Japanese negotiations
2. Decline of U.S. investment in Latin America
3. Nye Hearings and Italy's invasion of Ethiopia
4. Britain's near-defeat from German bombing
5. The fall of France
6. Hitler's threats to go to war
7. Hitler's invasion of Russia

H. Map Mastery

Map Discrimination

Using the maps and charts in Chapter 35, answer the following questions.

1. *Presidential Election of 1940*: In the 1940 election, how many electoral votes did Willkie win west of the Mississippi River?

2. *Presidential Election of 1940*: How many electoral votes did Willkie win east of the Mississippi?

Name_____ Section_____ Date_____

3. *Main Flow of Lend-Lease Aid*: Which *continent* received the most U.S. lend-lease aid?

4. *Main Flow of Lend-Lease Aid*: Which nation received lend-lease aid by way of both the Atlantic and Pacific oceans?

PART III: Applying What You Have Learned

1. How and why did the United States attempt to isolate itself from foreign troubles in the early and mid-1930s?
2. Discuss the effects of the U.S. neutrality laws of the 1930s on both American foreign policy and the international situation in Europe and East Asia.
3. How did the Fascist dictators' continually expanding aggression gradually erode the U.S. commitment to neutrality and isolationism?
4. How did Roosevelt manage to move the United States toward providing effective aid to Britain while slowly undercutting isolationist opposition?
5. Was American entry into World War II inevitable? Is it possible the U.S. might have been able to fight *either* Germany *or* Japan, while avoiding armed conflict with the other?
6. How did the process of American entry into World War II compare with the way the country got into World War I? (See Chapter 31.) How were the Neutrality Acts aimed at the conditions of 1914–1917, and why did they prove ineffective in the conditions of the 1930s?

Name_____ Section_____ Date_____

36

America in World War II, 1941–1945

PART I: Reviewing the Chapter

A. Checklist of Learning Objectives

After mastering this chapter, you should be able to

1. tell how America reacted to Pearl Harbor and prepared to wage war against both Germany and Japan.
2. describe the domestic mobilization for war.
3. describe the war's effects on American society, including regional migration, race relations, and women's roles.
4. explain the early Japanese successes in Asia and the Pacific and the American strategy for countering them.
5. describe the early Allied efforts against the Axis powers in North Africa and Italy.
6. discuss FDR's 1944 fourth-term election victory.
7. explain the final military efforts that brought Allied victory in Europe and Asia and the significance of the atomic bomb.

B. Glossary

To build your social science vocabulary, familiarize yourself with the following terms.

1. **concentration camp** A place of confinement for prisoners or others a government considers dangerous or undesirable. "The Washington top command . . . forcibly herded them together in concentration camps. . . ." (p. 829)
2. **bracero** A Mexican farm laborer temporarily brought into the United States. "The *bracero* program outlived the war by some twenty years. . . ." (p. 833)
3. **U-boat** A German submarine (from the German *Unterseeboot*). "Not until the spring of 1943 did the Allies . . . have the upper hand against the U-boat." (p. 841)
4. **depose(d); deposition** Forcibly remove from office or position. "Mussolini was deposed, and Italy surrendered unconditionally soon thereafter." (p. 843)
5. **beachhead** The first position on a beach secured by an invading force and used to land further troops and supplies. "The Allied beachhead, at first clung to with fingertips, was gradually enlarged, consolidated, and reinforced." (p. 846)
6. **underground** A secret or illegal movement organized in a country to resist or overthrow the government. "With the assistance of the French 'underground,' Paris was liberated. . . ." (p. 846)
7. **acclamation** A general and unanimous action of approval or nomination by a large public body, without a vote. "He was nominated at Chicago on the first ballot by acclamation." (p. 847)

8. **bastion** A fortified stronghold, often including earthworks or stoneworks, that guards against enemy attack. ". . . the 101st Airborne Division had stood firm at the vital bastion of Bastogne." (p. 848)
9. **genocide** The systematic extermination or killing of an entire people. "The Washington government had long been informed about Hitler's campaign of genocide against the Jews. . . ." (p. 849)
10. **bazooka** A metal-tubed weapon from which armor-piercing rockets are electronically fired. "The enemy was almost literally smothered by bayonets, bullets, bazookas, and bombs." (p. 854)

PART II: Checking Your Progress

A. True-False

Where the statement is true, mark **T**. Where it is false, mark **F**, and correct it in the space immediately below.

___ 1. America's major strategic decision in World War II was to fight Japan first and then attack Hitler's Germany.

___ 2. A substantial minority of Americans, particularly those of Germans and Italian descent, questioned the wisdom of fighting World War II.

___ 3. Government-run rationing and wage-price controls enabled the United States to meet the economic challenges of the war.

___ 4. New sources of labor such as women and Mexican *braceros* helped overcome the human-resources shortage during World War II.

___ 5. World War II stimulated massive black migration to the North and West and encouraged black demands for greater equality.

___ 6. A majority of women who worked in wartime factories stayed in the labor force after the war ended.

___ 7. American citizens at home had to endure serious economic deprivations during World War II.

___ 8. The Japanese navy established its domination of the Pacific sea-lanes in the 1942 battles of Coral Sea and Midway.

___ 9. The American strategy in the Pacific was to encircle Japan by flank movements from Burma and Alaska.

___ 10. In the first years of the war in Europe, Britain and the United States bore the heaviest burden of Allied ground fighting against Hitler.

___ 11. Britain was reluctant to attack Germany directly across the English Channel because of its memory of World War I's heavy losses.

___ 12. At the Teheran Conference in 1943, Stalin, Churchill, and Roosevelt planned the D-Day invasion and the final strategy for winning the war.

___ 13. Liberal Democrats rallied to dump Vice President Henry Wallace from FDR's ticket in 1944 and replace him with Senator Harry S Truman.

___ 14. Roosevelt died just a few weeks before the dropping of the atomic bomb and the surrender of Japan.

___ 15. The United States modified its demand for "unconditional surrender" by allowing Japan to keep its emperor, Hirohito.

B. Multiple Choice

Select the best answer and write the proper letter in the space provided.

___ 1. The fundamental American strategic decision of World War II was
   a. to attack Germany and Japan simultaneously with equal force.
   b. to concentrate naval forces in the Pacific and ground forces in Europe.
   c. to attack Germany first while using just enough strength to hold off Japan.
   d. to attack Germany and Japan from the "back door" routes of North Africa and China.

___ 2. The major exception to the relatively good American civil liberties record during World War II was the treatment of
   a. American Fascist groups.
   b. Japanese-Americans.
   c. Mexican-Americans.
   d. German-Americans.

___ 3. Wartime inflation and food shortages were kept partly in check by
   a. price controls and rationing.
   b. government operation of factories and railroads.
   c. special bonuses to farmers and workers to increase production.
   d. importation of additional fuel and food from Latin America.

___ 4. The wartime shortage of labor was partly made up by bringing into the work force such groups as
   a. teenage and elderly laborers.
   b. Japanese and Chinese immigrants.
   c. Mexican *braceros* and women.
   d. sharecroppers and inner-city residents.

___ 5. Compared with British and Soviet women during World War II, more American women
   a. did not work for wages in the wartime economy.
   b. worked in heavy-industry war plants.
   c. served in the armed forces.
   d. worked in agriculture.

___ 6. The Fair Employment Practices Commission was designed to
   a. prevent discrimination against blacks in wartime industries.
   b. guarantee all regions of the country an opportunity to compete for defense contracts.
   c. prevent discrimination in employment against women.
   d. guarantee that those who had been unemployed longest would be the first hired.

7. The wartime migration of rural African-Americans to northern urban factories was further accelerated after the war by the invention of
   a. the cotton gin.
   b. the gasoline-powered mechanical combine.
   c. synthetic fibers such as nylon that largely replaced cotton cloth.
   d. the mechanical cotton picker.

8. Besides African-Americans, another traditionally rural group who used service in the armed forces as a springboard to postwar urban life were
   a. Scandinavian-Americans.
   b. New England farmers.
   c. Indians.
   d. Japanese-Americans.

9. The Japanese advance in the Pacific was finally halted at the battles of
   a. Guadalcanal and Tarawa.
   b. Bataan and Corregidor.
   c. Guam and Wake Island.
   d. Coral Sea and Midway.

10. The essential American strategy in the Pacific called for
    a. securing bases in China from which to bomb the Japanese home islands.
    b. carrying the war into Southeast Asia from Australia and New Guinea.
    c. advancing on as broad a front as possible all across the Pacific.
    d. "island hopping" by capturing only the most strategic Japanese bases and bypassing the rest.

11. The U.S.–British demand for "unconditional surrender" was
    a. a sign of the Western Allies' confidence in its ultimate victory.
    b. designed to weaken Japan's and Germany's will to resist.
    c. a weak verbal substitute for the promised "Second Front."
    d. developed in close cooperation with the Soviet Union.

12. The American conquest of Guam and other islands in the Marianas in 1944 was especially important because
    a. it halted the Japanese advance in the Pacific.
    b. it made possible round-the-clock bombing of Japan from land bases.
    c. it paved the way for the American reconquest of the Philippines.
    d. it indicated that the Japanese would surrender without an invasion of the home island.

13. The most difficult European fighting for American forces through most of 1943 occurred in
    a. France.
    b. Italy.
    c. North Africa.
    d. Belgium.

Name_____ Section_____ Date_____

___ 14. Hitler's last-ditch effort to stop the British and American advance in the west occurred at
   a. the Battle of Normandy.
   b. the Battle of Château-Thierry.
   c. the Battle of Rome.
   d. the Battle of the Bulge.

___ 15. The *second* American atomic bomb was dropped on the Japanese city of
   a. Nagasaki.
   b. Hiroshima.
   c. Kyoto.
   d. Okinawa.

C. Identification

Supply the correct identification for each numbered description.

_____ 1. A U.S. minority that was forced into concentration camps during World War II

_____ 2. A federal agency that coordinated U.S. industry and successfully mobilized the economy to produce vast quantities of military supplies

_____ 3. Women's units of the army and navy during World War II

_____ 4. Mexican-American workers brought into the United States to provide an agricultural labor supply

_____ 5. Symbolic personification of female laborers who took factory jobs in order to sustain U.S. production during World War II

_____ 6. The federal agency established to guarantee opportunities for African-American employment in World War II industries

_____ 7. U.S.–owned Pacific archipelago seized by Japan in the early months of World War II

_____ 8. Crucial naval battle of June 1942, in which U.S. Admiral Chester Nimitz blocked the Japanese attempt to conquer a strategic island near Hawaii

_____ 9. Controversial U.S.–British demand on Germany and Japan that substituted for a "second front"

_____ 10. Site of 1943 Roosevelt-Churchill conference in North Africa, at which the Big Two planned the invasion of Italy and further steps in the Pacific war

_____ 11. Iranian capital where Roosevelt, Churchill, and Stalin met to plan D-Day in coordination with Russian strategy against Hitler in the East

_____ 12. The beginning of the Allied invasion of France in June 1944

_____ 13. The December 1944 German offensive that marked Hitler's last chance to stop the Allied advance

_____ 14. The last two heavily defended Japanese islands conquered by the United States in 1945

_____

_____ 15. The devastating new weapon used by the United States against Japan in August 1945

D. Matching People, Places, and Events

Match the person, place, or event in the left column with the proper description in the right column by inserting the correct letter on the blank line.

_____ 1. Henry J. Kaiser
_____ 2. John L. Lewis
_____ 3. A. Philip Randolph
_____ 4. Detroit
_____ 5. Jiang Jieshi (Chiang Kai-shek)
_____ 6. Douglas MacArthur
_____ 7. Chester W. Nimitz
_____ 8. Dwight D. Eisenhower
_____ 9. Winston Churchill
_____ 10. Joseph Stalin
_____ 11. Thomas Dewey
_____ 12. Henry A. Wallace
_____ 13. Harry S Truman
_____ 14. Albert Einstein
_____ 15. Hirohito

A. Commander of the Allied military assault against Hitler in North Africa and France
B. Japanese emperor who was allowed to stay on his throne, despite unconditional surrender policy
C. FDR's liberal vice president during most of World War II, dumped from the ticket in 1944
D. The Allied leader who constantly pressured the United States and Britain to open a "second front" against Hitler
E. Site of a serious racial disturbance during World War II
F. Leading American industrialist and shipbuilder during World War II
G. Commander of the U.S. Army in the Pacific during World War II, who fulfilled his promise to return to the Philippines
H. Inconspicuous former senator from Missouri who was suddenly catapulted to national and world leadership on April 12, 1945
I. Tough head of the United Mine Workers, whose work stoppages precipitated antistrike laws
J. Commander of the U.S. naval forces in the Pacific and brilliant strategist of the "island-hopping" campaign
K. Allied leader who met with FDR to plan strategy at Casablanca and Teheran
L. German-born physicist who helped persuade Roosevelt to develop the atomic bomb
M. Republican presidential nominee in 1944 who failed in his effort to deny FDR a fourth term
N. Head of the Brotherhood of Sleeping Car Porters whose threatened march on Washington opened job opportunities for blacks during World War II
O. U.S. ally who resisted Japanese advances in China during World War II

E. Putting Things in Order

Put the following events in correct order by numbering them from 1 to 4.

_____ The United States and Britain invade Italy and topple Mussolini from power.

_____ Japan surrenders after two atomic bombs are dropped.

_____ The United States enters World War II and begins to "fight Hitler first."

_____ The United States stops the Japanese advance in the Pacific and attacks Germany in North Africa.

Name_____ Section_____ Date_____

F. Matching Cause and Effect

Match the historical cause in the left column with the proper effect in the right column by writing the correct letter on the blank line.

Cause

___ 1. The surprise Japanese attack at Pearl Harbor

___ 2. Fear that Japanese-Americans would aid Japan in invading the United States

___ 3. Efficient organization by the War Production Board

___ 4. The mechanical cotton picker and wartime labor demand

___ 5. Women's role in wartime production

___ 6. American resistance in the Philippines and the Battle of the Coral Sea

___ 7. The American strategy of "leapfrogging" toward Japan

___ 8. The British fear of sustaining heavy casualties in ground fighting

___ 9. Conservative Democrats' hostility to liberal Vice President Henry Wallace

___ 10. Japan's refusal to surrender after the Potsdam Conference in July 1945

Effect

A. Kept the Western Allies from establishing a "second front" in France until June 1944

B. Slowed the powerful Japanese advance in the Pacific in 1942

C. Enabled the United States to furnish itself and its allies with abundant military supplies

D. Enabled the United States to set up key bomber bases while bypassing heavily fortified Japanese-held islands

E. Drew millions of African-Americans from the rural South to the urban North

F. Resulted in Senator Harry S Truman's becoming FDR's fourth-term running mate in 1944

G. Created a temporary but not a permanent transformation in gender roles for most women

H. Caused innocent American citizens to be rounded up and put in concentration camps

I. Created a strong sense of American national unity during World War II

J. Led the United States to drop the atomic bomb on Hiroshima in August 1945

G. Developing Historical Skills

Reading Maps for Routes and Strategy

In order to understand the events and strategies of war, careful reading of military maps is essential. Attention to the routes and dates of the Allied armies, presented in the map of *World War II in Europe and North Africa, 1939–1945* on p. 844, will help you grasp the essentials of Allied strategy and the importance of the postponement of the "second front" in the west, as described in the text. Answer the following questions.

1. Where were (a) the Russians and (b) the Western Allies Britain and America each fighting in January and February of 1943?

2. Approximately where were the central Russian armies when the British and Americans invaded Sicily?

3. Approximately where were the central Russian armies when the British and Americans invaded Normandy in June 1944?

4. It took approximately ten months for the British and Americans to get from the Normandy beaches to the Elbe River in central Germany. How long did it take the Russians to get from Warsaw to Berlin?

5. Besides north-central Germany, where else did the British, American, and Russian invasion routes converge? From what two countries were the British and Americans coming? From what country was the southern Russian army coming?

H. Map Mastery

Map Discrimination

Using the maps and charts in Chapter 36, answer the following questions.

1. *Internal Migration in the United States During World War II*: During World War II, what was the approximate *net* migration of civilian population from the East to the West? (Net migration is the number of westward migrants minus the number of those who moved east.)

2. *Internal Migration in the United States During World War II*: Of the nine fastest-growing cities during the 1940s, how many were located in the West and South? (Consider Washington, D.C., as a southern city.)

3. *Internal Migration in the United States During World War II*: Which were the two fastest-growing cities in the North?

4. *United States Thrusts in the Pacific, 1942–1945*: Which *two* of the following territories were not wholly or partially controlled by Japan at the height of Japanese conquest: India, Philippines, Australia, Netherlands Indies, Thailand, and New Guinea?

5. *World War II in Europe and North Africa, 1939–1945*: From which North African territory did the Allies launch their invasion of Italy?

6. *World War II in Europe and North Africa, 1939–1945*: As the Russian armies crossed into Germany from the east, which three Axis-occupied East European countries did they move through?

7. *World War II in Europe and North Africa, 1939–1945*: As the Western Allied armies crossed into Germany from the west, which three Axis-occupied West European countries did they liberate and move through? (Do not count Luxembourg.)

8. *World War II in Europe and North Africa, 1939–1945*: Along which river in Germany did the Western Allied armies meet the Russians?

Map Challenge

Using the maps of both the Pacific (p. 840) and European (p. 844) theaters in World War II, write an essay explaining the principal movements of Allied armies and navies in relation to the principal Allied strategies of the war determined in the ABC–1 agreement and the various wartime exchanges and meetings among American, British, and Soviet leaders.

PART III: Applying What You Have Learned

1. What effects did World War II have on the American economy? What role did American industry and agriculture play in the war?
2. Discuss the effects of World War II on women and on racial and ethnic minorities. Is it accurate to see the war as a key turning point in the movement toward equality for some or all of these groups?
3. Ever since World War II, historians and other scholars have commonly spoken of "postwar American society." How was American society different after the war than before? Were these changes all direct or indirect results of the war, or would many have occurred without it?
4. How did the United States and its allies develop and carry out their strategy for defeating Italy, Germany, and Japan?
5. What were the costs of World War II, and what were its effects on America's role in the world?
6. Compare America's role in World War I—domestically, militarily, and diplomatically—with its role in World War II. (See Chapter 31.) What accounts for the differences in America's participation in the two wars?

Name_____ Section_____ Date_____

37

The Cold War Begins, 1945–1952

PART I: Reviewing the Chapter

A. Checklist of Learning Objectives

After mastering this chapter, you should be able to

1. describe the economic transformation of the immediate post–World War II era.
2. describe the postwar migrations to the "Sunbelt" and the suburbs.
3. explain changes in the American population structure brought about by the "baby boom."
4. explain the growth of tensions between the United States and the Soviet Union after Roosevelt's death and Germany's defeat.
5. describe the early Cold War conflicts over Germany and Eastern Europe.
6. discuss American efforts to "contain" the Soviets through the Truman Doctrine, the Marshall Plan, and NATO.
7. describe the expansion of the Cold War to Asia and the Korean War.
8. analyze the postwar domestic climate in America and explain the growing fear of internal communist subversion.

B. Glossary

To build your social science vocabulary, familiarize yourself with the following terms.

1. **gross national product** The total value of a nation's annual output of goods and services. "Real gross national product (GNP) slumped sickeningly in 1946 and 1947. . . ." (p. 858)
2. **agribusiness** Farming and related activities considered as commercial enterprises, especially large corporate agricultural ventures. ". . . consolidation produced giant agribusinesses able to employ costly machinery." (p. 862)
3. **population curve** The varying size and age structure of a given nation or other group, measured over time. "This boom-or-bust cycle of births begot a bulging wave along the American population curve." (p. 866)
4. **precinct** The smallest subdivision of a city, as it is organized for purposes of police administration, politics, voting, and so on. "He then tried his hand at precinct-level Missouri politics. . . ." (p. 866)
5. **protégé** Someone under the patronage, protection, or tutelage of another person or group. "Though a protégé of a notorious political machine in Kansas City, he had managed to keep his own hands clean." (p. 866)
6. **superpower** One of the two overwhelmingly dominant international powers after World War II—the United States and the Soviet Union. "More specific understandings among the wartime allies—especially the two emerging superpowers—awaited the arrival of peace." (p. 870)
7. **exchange rates** The ratios at which the currencies of two or more countries are traded, which express their values relative to one another. ". . . the International Monetary Fund (IMF) [was established] to encourage world trade by regulating currency exchange rates." (p. 871)

8. **underdeveloped** Economically and industrially deficient. "They also founded the International Bank for Reconstruction and Development . . . to promote economic growth in war-ravaged and underdeveloped areas." (p. 871)
9. **military occupation** The holding and control of a territory and its citizenry by the conquering forces of another nation. ". . . Germany had been divided at war's end into four military occupation zones. . . ." (p. 873)
10. **containment** In international affairs, the blocking of another nation's expansion through the application of military and political pressure short of war. "Truman's piecemeal responses . . . took on intellectual coherence in 1947, with the formulation of the 'containment doctrine.' " (p. 874)
11. **communist-fronter** One who belongs to an ostensibly independent political, economic, or social organization that is secretly controlled by the Communist party. ". . . he was nominated . . . by . . . a bizarre collection of disgruntled former New Dealers . . . and communist-fronters." (p. 881)
12. **Politburo** The small ruling executive body that controlled the Central Committee of the Soviet Communist party, and hence dictated the political policies of the Soviet, Chinese, and other Communist parties (from "Political Bureau"). "This so-called Pied Piper of the Politburo took an apparently pro-Soviet line. . . ." (p. 881)
13. **perimeter** The outer boundary of a defined territory. ". . . Korea was outside the essential United States defense perimeter in the Pacific." (p. 883)

PART II: Checking Your Progress

A. True-False

Where the statement is true, mark **T**. Where it is false, mark **F**, and correct it in the space immediately below.

_____ 1. The American consumer economy began to grow dramatically as soon as the war ended, during the years 1945 to 1950.

_____ 2. The postwar economic boom was fueled by military spending and cheap energy.

_____ 3. Labor unions continued to grow rapidly in the industrial factories throughout the 1940s and 1950s.

_____ 4. The economic and population growth of the Sunbelt occurred because the South relied less than the North did on federal government spending for its economic well-being.

_____ 5. After World War II, American big cities became heavily populated with minorities, while most whites lived in the suburbs.

_____ 6. Government policies sometimes encouraged residential segregation in the cities and new suburbs.

_____ 7. Harry S Truman brought extensive experience and confidence to the presidency he assumed in April 1945.

_____ 8. The growing Cold War broke down the strong bonds of trust and common ideals that America and Russia had shared as World War II allies.

____ 9. The Western Allies pushed to establish a separate nation of West Germany, while the Russians wanted to restore a unified German state.

____ 10. The Truman Doctrine was initiated in response to threatened Soviet gains in Iran and Afghanistan.

____ 11. The Marshall Plan was developed primarily as a response to the possible Soviet military invasion of Western Europe.

____ 12. The fundamental purpose of NATO was to end the historical feuds among the European nations of Britain, France, Italy, and Germany.

____ 13. The postwar hunt for communist subversion was supposedly aimed at rooting out American communists from positions in government and teaching.

____ 14. Truman defeated Dewey in 1948 partly because of the deep splits within the Republican party that year.

____ 15. Truman fired General MacArthur because MacArthur wanted to expand the Korean War into China.

B. Multiple Choice

Select the best answer and write the proper letter in the space provided.

____ 1. Besides giving educational benefits to returning veterans, the Servicemen's Readjustment Act of 1944 (the GI Bill of Rights) was partly intended to
   a. prevent returning soldiers from flooding the job market.
   b. provide the colleges with a new source of income.
   c. keep the GIs' military skills in high readiness for the Cold War.
   d. help to slow down the inflationary economy that developed at the end of World War II.

____ 2. Among the greatest beneficiaries of the post–World War II economic "boom" were
   a. the industrial inner cities.
   b. farm laborers.
   c. labor unions.
   d. women.

____ 3. Among the causes of the long postwar economic expansion were
   a. foreign investment and international trade.
   b. military spending and cheap energy.
   c. labor's wage restraint and the growing number of small businesses.
   d. government economic planning and investment.

4. The two regions that gained most in population and new industry in the postwar economic expansion were
   a. the Northwest and New England.
   b. the Northeast and South.
   c. the Midwest and West.
   d. the South and West.

5. The federal government played a large role in the growth of the Sunbelt through
   a. federal subsidies to southern and western agriculture.
   b. its policies supporting civil rights and equal opportunity for minorities.
   c. housing loans to veterans.
   d. its financial support of the aerospace and defense industries.

6. Among the federal policies that contributed to the postwar migration from the cities to the suburbs were
   a. housing-mortgage tax deductions and federally built highways.
   b. public housing and Social Security.
   c. military and public-works spending.
   d. direct subsidies to suburban homebuilders.

7. The postwar "baby-boom" population expansion contributed to
   a. the sharp rise in elementary school enrollments in the 1970s.
   b. the strains on the Social Security system in the 1950s.
   c. the popular "youth culture" of the 1960s.
   d. the expanding job opportunities of the 1980s.

8. Among President Harry Truman's most valuable qualities as a leader were
   a. his considerable experience in international affairs.
   b. his personal courage, authenticity, and sense of responsibility for big decisions.
   c. his intolerance of pettiness or corruption among his subordinates.
   d. his patience and willingness to compromise with honest critics.

9. The primary reason that Franklin Roosevelt made concessions to Stalin at the Yalta Conference was that
   a. he sympathized with the Soviet need to dominate Eastern Europe.
   b. he wanted the Soviet Union to enter the war against Japan.
   c. he wanted the Soviets to agree to American domination of Central America and the Caribbean.
   d. he was afraid of a postwar confrontation with the Soviet Union over China.

10. Before World War II, both the United States and the Soviet Union
    a. had competed with Germany for the role of leading power in Europe.
    b. had concentrated on practical achievements rather than ideological issues.
    c. had attempted to build powerful armies and navies in order to gain global power.
    d. had been largely inward-looking and isolated from international affairs.

11. A crucial early development of the Cold War occurred when
    a. Germany was divided into an East Germany under Soviet control and a pro-American West Germany.
    b. American and Soviet forces engaged in armed clashes in Austria.
    c. the Soviets crushed anticommunist rebellions in Poland and Hungary.
    d. the French and Italian Communist parties attempted revolutions against their governments.

12. The NATO alliance represented an historic transformation in American foreign policy because
    a. it departed from the principles of the Monroe Doctrine.
    b. it put the United States into the position of guaranteeing the permanent subordination of Germany.
    c. it committed the United States to a permanent peacetime alliance with other nations.
    d. it meant establishing military bases outside the territory of the continental United States.

13. The Truman Doctrine originally developed because of the communist threat to
    a. Turkey and Greece.
    b. France and West Germany.
    c. Iran and Afghanistan.
    d. Poland and Hungary.

14. The crusade of Senator Joseph McCarthy was first directed especially at
    a. the Soviet Union
    b. potential communist takeovers of Western Europe.
    c. Republicans who refused to support Dwight Eisenhower.
    d. alleged communists inside the United States government.

15. The Korean War broke out in 1950 when
    a. Chinese communists invaded South Korea.
    b. the Soviet Union threatened to blockade Japan and South Korea.
    c. South Korea invaded North Korea.
    d. North Korea invaded South Korea.

C. Identification

Supply the correct identification for each numbered description.

_____ 1. Popular name for the Servicemen's Readjustment Act, which provided assistance to former soldiers

_____ 2. Shorthand name for the southern and western regions of the U.S. that experienced the highest rates of growth after World War II

_____ 3. New York suburb where postwar builders pioneered the techniques of mass home construction

_____ 4. Term for the dramatic rise in U.S. births that began immediately after World War II

_____ 5. Big Three wartime conference that later became the focus of charges that Roosevelt had "sold out" Eastern Europe to the Soviet communists

_____ 6. The extended post–World War II confrontation between the United States and the Soviet Union that stopped just short of a shooting war

_____ 7. Meeting of Western Allies during World War II that established the economic structures to promote recovery and enhance FDR's vision of an "open world"

_____ 8. New international organization that experienced some early successes in diplomatic and cultural areas but failed in areas like atomic arms control

_____ 9. Term for the barrier that Stalin erected to block off Soviet-dominated nations of Eastern Europe from the West

_____ 10. American-sponsored effort that provided funds for the economic relief and recovery of Western Europe

_____ 11. The new anti-Soviet organization of Western nations that ended the long-time American tradition of not joining permanent military alliances

_____ 12. Jiang Jieshi's (Chiang Kai-shek's) pro-American forces, which lost the Chinese civil war to Mao Zedong's (Mao Tse-tung's) communists in 1949

_____ 13. Key U.S. government memorandum that militarized American foreign policy and indicated national faith in the economy's capacity to sustain large military expenditures

_____ 14. U.S. House of Representatives committee that took the lead in investigating alleged procommunist agents such as Alger Hiss

_____ 15. The dividing line between North and South Korea, across which the fighting between communists and United Nations forces ebbed and flowed during the Korean War

D. Matching People, Places, and Events

Match the person, place, or event in the left column with the proper description in the right column by inserting the correct letter on the blank line.

___ 1. Benjamin Spock
___ 2. Hermann Goering
___ 3. Joseph Stalin
___ 4. Berlin
___ 5. Iran
___ 6. George F. Kennan
___ 7. Greece
___ 8. George C. Marshall
___ 9. Japan
___ 10. Nuremberg

A. Top Nazi official who committed suicide after being convicted in war-crimes trials
B. Physician who provided advice on child rearing to baby-boomers' parents after World War II.
C. Young California congressman whose investigation of Alger Hiss spurred fears of communist influence in America
D. Oil-rich Middle Eastern nation that became an early focal point of Soviet-American conflict
E. Originator of a massive program for the economic relief and recovery of devastated Europe
F. American military commander in Korea fired by President Harry Truman
G. Former vice president of the United States whose 1948 campaign as a pro-Soviet liberal split the Democratic party
H. Site of a series of controversial war-crimes trials that led to the execution of twelve Nazi leaders
I. Wisconsin senator whose charges of communist infiltration of the U.S. government deepened the anti-red atmosphere of the early 1950s

___ 11. Richard Nixon

___ 12. Joseph McCarthy

___ 13. Henry A. Wallace

___ 14. Strom Thurmond

___ 15. Douglas MacArthur

J. Nation that was effectively converted from dictatorship to democracy by the strong leadership of General Douglas MacArthur

K. The tough leader whose violation of agreements in Eastern Europe and Germany helped launch the Cold War

L. Southern European nation whose threatened fall to communism in 1947 precipitated the Truman Doctrine

M. Territory deep inside the Soviet zone of Germany that was itself divided into four zones of occupation

N. Southern segregationist who led "Dixiecrat" presidential campaign against Truman in 1948

O. Brilliant U.S. specialist on the Soviet Union and originator of the theory that U.S. policy should be to "contain" the Soviet Union

E. Putting Things in Order

Put the following events in correct order by numbering them from 1 to 5.

___ The threatened communist takeover of Greece prompts a presidential request for aid and a worldwide effort to stop communism.

___ The collapse of Jiang Jieshi's (Chiang Kai-shek's) corrupt government means victory for Mao Zedong's (Mao Tse-tung's) communists and a setback for U.S. policy in Asia.

___ A new president takes charge of American foreign policy amid growing tension between America and its ally the Soviet Union.

___ A "give-'em-hell" campaign by an underdog candidate overcomes a three-way split in his own party and defeats his overconfident opponent.

___ Communists go on the offensive in a divided Asian nation, drawing the United States into a brutal and indecisive war.

F. Matching Cause and Effect

Match the historical cause in the left column with the proper effect in the right column by writing the correct letter on the blank line.

Cause

___ 1. Cheap energy, military spending, and rising productivity

___ 2. The mechanization and consolidation of agriculture

___ 3. Job opportunities, warm climates, and improved race relations

___ 4. "White flight" to the suburbs

___ 5. The post–World War II "baby boom"

___ 6. The American airlift to West Berlin

Effect

A. Caused an era of unprecedented growth in American prosperity from 1950 to 1970

B. Drew millions of white and black Americans to the Sunbelt after World War II

C. Led to the proclamation of the Truman Doctrine and hundreds of millions of dollars in aid for anticommunist governments

D. Led to organization of the permanent NATO alliance

E. Caused the rise of big commercial agribusiness and spelled the near-disappearance of the traditional family farm

F. Aroused Republican charges that Democrats Truman and Acheson had "lost China"

_____ 7. The British withdrawal from communist-threatened Greece

_____ 8. The threat of Soviet invasion or U.S. isolationist withdrawal from Europe

_____ 9. General MacArthur's reform-oriented rule of occupied Japan

_____ 10. Mao Zedong's (Mao Tse-tung's) defeat of Jiang Jieshi (Chiang Kai-shek)

G. Broke a Soviet ground blockade and established American determination to resist further Soviet advance

H. Left America's cities heavily populated by racial minorities

I. Led to the firm establishment of Japanese democracy and the beginnings of a great Japanese economic advance

J. Caused much school-building in the 1950s, a "youth culture" in the 1960s, and a growing concern about "aging" in the 1980s

G. Developing Historical Skills

Reading a Bar Graph

Read the bar graph of *National Defense Budget* on p. 861 and answer the following questions.

1. In what census year after World War II did the defense budget first decline as a percentage of the federal budget and a percentage of GNP?

2. In what census year after 1960 was the defense budget the same fraction of GNP as it was in 1950?

3. Which decade after World War II saw the largest increase in actual dollar outlays for defense?

4. By approximately what percentage of the federal budget did the defense budget increase from 1950 to 1960? By roughly what percentage did it decrease from 1970 to 1980? By what percentage did it increase from 1980 to 1990? By about what percentage did it decrease from 1990 to 1999?

Name_____ Section_____ Date_____

H. **Map Mastery**

Map Discrimination

Using the maps and charts in Chapter 37, answer the following questions.

1. *Postwar Partition of Germany*: Which of the Big Four had the smallest occupation zone in postwar Germany?

2. *Postwar Partition of Germany*: Which of the three *Western* occupation zones was closest to Berlin?

3. *Postwar Partition of Germany*: Which two other nations did the American occupation zone border on?

4. *The Shifting Front in Korea*: When General MacArthur attacked at Inchon, did he land above or below the thirty-eighth parallel?

5. *The Shifting Front in Korea*: Besides China, what other nation bordering North Korea presented a potential threat to American forces?

6. *The Shifting Front in Korea*: After the armistice—signed on July 27, 1953—which of the two Koreas had made very slight territorial gains in the Korean War?

Map Challenge

Using the map of *Population Increase, 1950–2000* on p. 863, write an essay explaining the differences in the regional impact of post–World War II migration and population growth from 1950 to 1998. What states and regions exhibited exceptions to the general patterns of growth?

Chapter 37 *The Cold War Begins, 1945–1952* 371

PART III: Applying What You Have Learned

1. How and why did the American economy soar from 1950 to 1970?
2. How have economic and population changes shaped American society since World War II?
3. What were the immediate conflicts and deeper causes that led the United States and the Soviet Union to go from being allies to bitter Cold War rivals?
4. Explain the steps that led to the long-term involvement of the United States in major overseas military commitments, including NATO and the Korean War. How did expanding military power and the Cold War affect American society and ideas?
5. Discuss President Harry Truman's role as a leader in both international and domestic affairs from 1945–1952. Does Truman deserve to be considered a "great" president? Why or why not?
6. Why did World War II—unlike World War I—lead to a permanent end to American isolationism? (See Chapter 31.) How did the long American tradition of isolation from permanent foreign entanglements create tensions in U.S. policy during the early Cold War?

38

The Eisenhower Era, 1952–1960

PART I: Reviewing the Chapter

A. Checklist of Learning Objectives

After mastering this chapter, you should be able to

1. explain how Eisenhower's leadership coincided with the American mood of the 1950s.
2. describe Ike's initially hesitant reactions to McCarthyism and the early civil rights movement.
3. describe the approach that Eisenhower and Dulles took to the Cold War and nuclear policy.
4. list the basic elements of Eisenhower's foreign policy in Vietnam, Europe, and the Middle East.
5. describe the vigorous challenges Eisenhower faced from the Soviet Union and indicate how he responded to them.
6. describe the new American economy of the 1950s.
7. explain the changes in American "mass culture" in the 1950s, including the rise of television and the computer.

B. Glossary

To build your social science vocabulary, familiarize yourself with the following terms.

1. **plebiscite** In politics, a single-question universal election or referendum, in which a ruler or government seeks approval of a policy or a mandate to continue in office. "In future years, television made possible a kind of 'plebiscitarian' politics. . . ." (p. 888)
2. **McCarthyism** The practice of making sweeping, unfounded charges against innocent people with consequent loss of reputation, job, and so on. "But 'McCarthyism' has passed into the English language as a label for the dangerous forces of unfairness. . . ." (p. 891)
3. **brass** High-ranking military officers. "The military brass at first protested. . . ." (p. 894)
4. **taboo** A social prohibition or rule that results from strict tradition or convention. ". . . Warren shocked the president and other traditionalists with his active judicial intervention in previously taboo social issues." (p. 895)
5. **self-incrimination** Sworn testimony in a trial or other legal proceeding that forces a person to admit to criminally indictable acts; the Fifth Amendment to the U.S. Constitution forbids compelling such testimony. "The millionaire Teamster chief . . . invoked the Fifth Amendment against self-incrimination 209 times. . . ." (p. 902)
6. **embezzlement** The fraudulent appropriation or theft of funds entrusted to one's care. "He was later sentenced to prison for embezzlement." (p. 903)
7. **secondary boycott** A boycott of goods, aimed not at the employer or company directly involved in a dispute but at those who do business with that company. ". . . antilaborites also forced into the bill prohibitions against 'secondary boycotts'. . . ." (p. 903)
8. **thermonuclear** Concerning the heat released in nuclear fission; specifically, the use of that heat in hydrogen bombs. "Thermonuclear suicide seemed nearer in July 1958. . . ." (p. 904)
9. **confiscation** The seizure of property by a public authority, often as a penalty. "Castro retaliated with further wholesale confiscations of Yankee property. . . ." (p. 905)

10. **Pentecostal** A family of Protestant Christian churches that emphasize a "second baptism" of the holy spirit, speaking in tongues, faith healing, and intense emotionalism in worship. "'Televangelists' like the Baptist Billy Graham, the Pentecostal Holiness preacher Oral Roberts. . . ." (p. 911)

PART II: Checking Your Progress

A. True-False

Where the statement is true, mark **T**. Where it is false, mark **F**, and correct it in the space immediately below.

____ 1. Eisenhower presented himself to the country as a strongly partisan Republican president.

____ 2. Eisenhower initially hesitated to oppose Senator Joseph McCarthy because of McCarthy's political popularity and power.

____ 3. McCarthy lost his power when he attacked alleged communist influence in the U.S. Army.

____ 4. The Supreme Court ruled in *Brown* v. *Board of Education* that blacks should be provided additional educational benefits in order to equalize public education.

____ 5. Eisenhower used his influence as president to support blacks' push for civil rights in the schools and elsewhere.

____ 6. Eisenhower endorsed a major growth of military spending on conventional and nuclear forces to counteract the Soviet Union in the Cold War.

____ 7. Eisenhower tried but failed to repeal most of the New Deal economic and social legislation.

____ 8. In the Hungarian crisis, the United States retreated from Secretary of State Dulles's talk of "rolling back" communism and liberating the "captive peoples" of Eastern Europe.

____ 9. Eisenhower sent the first contingent of American troops to Vietnam in 1954 in order to prevent the communist Vietnamese from defeating the French.

____ 10. The Suez crisis was caused by Egyptian President Nasser's nationalization of the Suez Canal.

____ 11. The Soviet *Sputnik* satellite raised American fears that the Soviet Union had forged ahead of the United States in rocketry, science, and education.

____ 12. In the 1950s Latin Americans sometimes demonstrated hostility toward the United States for supporting anticommunist dictators and ignoring Latin American interests.

____ 13. Senator Kennedy was able to successfully neutralize the issue of his Roman Catholicism during the 1960 campaign.

____ 14. Feminist Betty Friedan's manifesto *The Feminine Mystique* was aimed primarily at reviving labor militancy among working-class women in factories and shops.

_____ 15. Social critics like David Riesman and Daniel Bell attacked the conformity and consumerism that they believed was undermining the older American character and work ethic.

B. Multiple Choice

Select the best answer and write the proper letter in the space provided.

_____ 1. In the 1952 campaign, the Eisenhower-Nixon ticket made the first really effective use of
   a. the Cold War as a campaign issue.
   b. television.
   c. political advertising.
   d. political appeals targeted at special-interest groups.

_____ 2. As president, Eisenhower enjoyed great popularity by presenting a leadership style of
   a. reassurance, sincerity, and optimism.
   b. aggressiveness, boldness, and energy.
   c. political shrewdness, economic knowledge, and hands-on management.
   d. vision, imagination, and moral leadership.

_____ 3. The Korean War ended with
   a. an agreement to unify and neutralize Korea.
   b. a peace treaty that provided for withdrawal of American and Chinese forces from Korea.
   c. an American and South Korean military victory.
   d. a stalemated armistice and continued division of North and South Korea.

_____ 4. Senator Joseph McCarthy's anticommunist crusade finally collapsed when
   a. the Cold War wound down.
   b. Eisenhower publicly attacked him as a threat to the Republican party.
   c. McCarthy failed to force the alleged communists out of the federal government.
   d. McCarthy attacked the U.S. Army for alleged communist influence.

_____ 5. The precipitating event that made Dr. Martin Luther King, Jr. the most prominent civil rights leader was
   a. the lynching of Emmett Till.
   b. the Little Rock school crisis.
   c. the Montgomery bus boycott.
   d. the passage of the 1957 Civil Rights Act.

_____ 6. The primary impetus for civil rights within the federal government came from
   a. the Supreme Court.
   b. Congress.
   c. President Eisenhower.
   d. the armed forces.

___ 7. Martin Luther King, Jr.'s civil rights organization, the SCLC, rested on the institutional foundation of
   a. black business.
   b. the black churches.
   c. black colleges.
   d. northern philanthropic foundations.

___ 8. Eisenhower's basic approach to domestic economic policy was
   a. to seek to overturn the Democratic New Deal.
   b. to propose major new federal social programs.
   c. to turn most New Deal programs over to the states.
   d. to trim back some New Deal programs but keep most in place.

___ 9. Despite his fiscal conservatism, Eisenhower actually outdid the New Deal with his massive federal spending on
   a. a continental interstate highway system.
   b. a system of medical care for the elderly.
   c. intercontinental military bombers and civilian aircraft.
   d. agricultural subsidies for American farmers.

___ 10. The United States first became involved in Vietnam by
   a. providing economic aid to the democratic Vietnamese government of Ngo Dinh Diem.
   b. providing economic aid to the French colonialists fighting Ho Chi Minh.
   c. providing aid to Ho Chi Minh in his fight against the French colonialists.
   d. sending American bombers to defend the French at Dien Bien Phu.

___ 11. Senator John F. Kennedy's main issue in the campaign of 1960 was that
   a. as a Catholic he would better be able to deal with Catholic Latin America.
   b. the United States should seek nuclear disarmament agreement with the Soviets.
   c. the United States had fallen behind the Soviet Union in prestige and power.
   d. the Eisenhower administration had failed to work hard enough for desegregation.

___ 12. When the 1950s began, a majority of American women were
   a. working in blue-collar factory or service jobs.
   b. raising children and not employed outside the home.
   c. pursuing training and education to prepare them for the new positions in service and high technology.
   d. agitating for federal child care and other assistance to enable them to assume a larger place in the work force.

___ 13. The primary force shaping the new consumerism and popular culture of the 1950s was
   a. the computer.
   b. magazines like *Playboy*.
   c. television.
   d. evangelical Protestantism.

Name_____ Section_____ Date_____

___ 14. One major breakthrough in American literature in the early post–World War II years was
   a. the realistic depiction of war and industrial poverty.
   b. angry social criticism of the "American dream."
   c. satirical and comic novels by Jewish writers.
   d. an optimistic vision of nature and love in the work of American poets and playwrights.

___ 15. A key economic transformation of the 1950s was
   a. the displacement of large corporations by smaller entrepeneurial businesses.
   b. the growth of "white collar" jobs into a majority that increasingly replaced "blue collar" factory labor.
   c. the turn from World War II military and defense industries to civilian production.
   d. the replacement of "mass consumer production" by "target marketing" aimed at particular segments of the population.

C. Identification

Supply the correct identification for each numbered description.

_____ 1. Term for making ruthless and unfair charges against opponents, such as those leveled by a red-hunting Wisconsin senator in the 1950s

_____ 2. Supreme Court ruling that overturned the old *Plessy* v. *Ferguson* principle that black public facilities could be "separate but equal"

_____ 3. The doctrine upon which Eisenhower and Dulles based American nuclear policy in the 1950s

_____ 4. An Asian alliance, set up by Secretary Dulles on the model of NATO, to help support the anticommunist regime in South Vietnam

_____ 5. The British-and-French-owned waterway whose nationalization by Egyptian President Nasser triggered a major Middle East crisis

_____ 6. A soviet scientific achievement that set off a wave of American concern about Soviet superiority in science and education

_____ 7. Major international corporation that symbolized the early computer and "information age"

_____ 8. High-flying American spy plane, whose downing in 1960 destroyed a summit and heightened Cold War tensions

_____ 9. Latin American nation where a 1959 communist revolution ousted a U.S.-backed dictator

_____ 10. Betty Friedan's 1963 book that launched a revolution against the suburban "cult of domesticity" that reigned in the 1950s

D. Matching People, Places, and Events

Match the person, place, or event in the left column with the proper description in the right column by inserting the correct letter on the blank line.

___ 1. Dwight D. Eisenhower
___ 2. Joseph R. McCarthy
___ 3. Earl Warren
___ 4. Martin Luther King, Jr.
___ 5. Ho Chi Minh
___ 6. Ngo Dinh Diem
___ 7. Betty Friedan
___ 8. Adlai E. Stevenson
___ 9. Billy Graham
___ 10. James R. Hoffa
___ 11. John Foster Dulles
___ 12. Nikita Khrushchev
___ 13. Fidel Castro
___ 14. Richard Nixon
___ 15. John F. Kennedy

A. Eloquent Democratic presidential candidate who was twice swamped by a popular Republican war hero
B. Anticommunist leader who set up a pro-American government to block Ho Chi Minh's expected takeover of all Vietnam
C. Latin American revolutionary who became economically and militarily dependent on the Soviet Union
D. Eisenhower's tough-talking secretary of state who wanted to "roll back" communism
E. Red-hunter turned world-traveling diplomat who narrowly missed becoming president in 1960
F. Black minister whose 1955 Montgomery bus boycott made him the leader of the civil rights movement
G. The soldier who kept the nation at peace for most of his two terms and ended up warning America about the "military-industrial complex"
H. Popular religious evangelical who effectively used the new medium of television
I. Youthful politician who combined television appeal with traditional big-city Democratic politics to squeak out a victory in 1960
J. Blustery Soviet leader who frequently challenged Eisenhower with both threats and diplomacy
K. Reckless and power-hungry demagogue who intimidated even President Eisenhower before his bubble burst
L. A Vietnamese nationalist and communist whose defeat of the French led to calls for American military intervention in Vietnam
M. Writer whose 1963 book signaled the beginnings of more extensive feminist protest
N. Tough Teamster-union boss whose corrupt actions helped lead to passage of the Landrum-Griffin Act
O. Controversial jurist who led the Supreme Court into previously off-limits social and racial issues

E. Putting Things in Order

Put the following events in correct order by numbering them from 1 to 5.

___ Major crises in Eastern Europe and the Middle East create severe challenges for Eisenhower's foreign policy.

___ An American plane is downed over the Soviet Union, disrupting a summit and rechilling the Cold War.

___ Eisenhower refuses to use American troops to prevent a communist victory over a colonial power in Asia.

___ Eisenhower orders federal troops to enforce a Supreme Court ruling over strong resistance from state officials.

___ Eisenhower's meeting with Soviet leader Khrushchev marks the first real sign of a thaw in the Cold War.

F. Matching Cause and Effect

Match the historical cause in the left column with the proper effect in the right column by writing the correct letter on the blank line.

Cause

___ 1. Joseph McCarthy's attacks on the U.S. Army

___ 2. *Brown* v. *Board of Education*

___ 3. Governor Orval Faubus's use of the National Guard to prevent integration

___ 4. The 1956 Hungarian revolt

___ 5. The Communist Vietnamese victory over the French in 1954

___ 6. Nasser's nationalization of the Suez Canal

___ 7. The fears of both the United States and the Soviet Union that the other nation was gaining a lead in rocketry and weapons

___ 8. The downing of the U-2 spy plane

___ 9. American intervention in Latin America and support for anti-communist dictators in that region

___ 10. Kennedy's television glamour and traditional political skills

Effect

A. Set off "massive resistance" to integration in most parts of the Deep South

B. Led to continuing nuclear tests and the extension of the arms race

C. Caused the United States to begin backing an anticommunist regime in South Vietnam

D. Created widespread resentment of the United States in parts of the Western Hemisphere

E. Forced Secretary of State Dulles to abandon his plans to "roll back" communism

F. Exposed the senator's irresponsibility and brought about his downfall

G. Forced President Eisenhower to send federal troops to Little Rock

H. Undermined the Paris summit and weakened Eisenhower's goodwill diplomacy

I. Enabled the Democrats to win a narrow electoral victory in 1960

J. Led to the 1956 British-French-Israeli invasion of Egypt

G. Developing Historical Skills

Comparing and Interpreting Election Maps

Read carefully the maps for the elections of 1956 (p. 902) and 1960 (p. 907). Answer the following questions.

1. Which was the only nonsouthern state to vote for Democrats Stevenson in 1956 and Kennedy in 1960?

2. Which three southern states (states of the old Confederacy) voted for Republicans Eisenhower in 1956 and Nixon in 1960?

3. Which two southern states switched from Republican in 1956 to Democratic in 1960?

4. How many more electoral votes did Kennedy get in the West (not counting Texas) in 1960 than Stevenson got in the same region in 1956?

5. How many electoral votes did Kennedy win from states that Stevenson also carried in 1956? (Note the divided electoral vote in one state.)

PART III: Applying What You Have Learned

1. In what ways was the Eisenhower era a time of caution and conservatism, and in what ways was it a time of dynamic economic, social, and cultural change?
2. How did Eisenhower balance assertiveness and restraint in his foreign policies in Vietnam, Europe, and the Middle East?
3. What were the dynamics of the Cold War with the Soviet Union in the 1950s, and how did Eisenhower and Khrushchev combine confrontation and conversation in their relationship?
4. How did America's far-flung international responsibilities shape the U.S. economy and society in the Eisenhower era? Was the American way of life fundamentally altered by the nation's new superpower status, or did it remain largely sheltered from world affairs?
5. How did television and other innovations of the "consumer age" affect American politics, society, and culture in the 1950s?
6. Despite widespread power and affluence, the 1950s were often described as an "age of anxiety." What were the major sources of anxiety and conflict that stirred beneath the surface of the time? Could they have been addressed more effectively by Eisenhower and other national leaders? Why or why not?

Name_____ Section_____ Date_____

39

The Stormy Sixties, 1960–1968

PART I: Reviewing the Chapter

A. Checklist of Learning Objectives

After mastering this chapter, you should be able to

1. describe the high expectations Kennedy's New Frontier aroused and the political obstacles it encountered.
2. analyze the theory and practice of Kennedy's doctrine of "flexible response" in Asia and Latin America.
3. describe Johnson's succession to the presidency in 1963, his electoral landslide over Goldwater in 1964, and his Great Society successes of 1965.
4. discuss the course of the black movement of the 1960s, from civil rights to Black Power.
5. indicate how Johnson led the United States deeper into the Vietnam quagmire.
6. explain how the Vietnam war brought turmoil to American society and eventually drove Johnson and the divided Democrats from power in 1968.
7. describe the cultural rebellions of the 1960s, and indicate their short-term and long-term consequences.

B. Glossary

To build your social science vocabulary, familiarize yourself with the following terms.

1. **free world** The noncommunist democracies of the Western world, as opposed to the communist states. "But to the free world the 'Wall of Shame' looked like a gigantic enclosure around a concentration camp." (p. 919)
2. **nuclear proliferation** The spreading of nuclear weapons to nations that have not previously had them. "Despite the perils of nuclear proliferation or Soviet domination, de Gaulle demanded an independent Europe. . . ." (p. 919)
3. **exile** A person who has been banished or driven from her or his country by the authorities. "He had inherited . . . a CIA-backed scheme to topple Fidel Castro from power by invading Cuba with anticommunist exiles." (p. 921)
4. **peaceful coexistence** The principle or policy that communists and noncommunists—specifically, the United States and the Soviet Union—ought to live together without trying to dominate or destroy each other. "Kennedy thus tried to lay the foundations for a realistic policy of peaceful coexistence with the Soviet Union." (p. 923)
5. **détente** In international affairs, a period of relaxed agreement in areas of mutual interest. "Here were the modest origins of the policy that later came to be known as 'détente.'" (p. 923)
6. **sit-in** A demonstration in which people occupy a facility for a sustained period to achieve political or economic goals. "Following the wave of sit-ins that surged across the South. . . ." (p. 923)

7. **establishment** The ruling inner circle of a nation and its principal institutions. "Goldwater's forces had . . . rid[den] roughshod over the moderate Republican 'eastern establishment.'" (p. 929)
8. **literacy test** A literacy examination that a person must pass before being allowed to vote. "Ballot-denying devices like the poll tax, literacy tests, and barefaced discrimination still barred black people from the political process." (p. 931)
9. **ghetto** The district of a city where members of a religious or racial minority are forced to live, either by legal restriction or by informal social pressure. (Originally, ghettoes were enclosed Jewish districts in Europe.) ". . . a bloody riot exploded in Watts, a black ghetto in Los Angeles." (p. 932)
10. **black separatism** The doctrine that blacks in the United States ought to separate themselves from whites, either in separate institutions or in a separate political territory. ". . . Malcolm X trumpeted black separatism. . . ." (p. 932)
11. **hawk** During the Vietnam War, someone who favored vigorous prosecution or escalation of the conflict. "If the United States were to cut and run from Vietnam, claimed prowar 'hawks,' other nations would doubt America's word. . . ." (p. 935)
12. **dove** During the Vietnam War, someone who opposed the war and favored de-escalation or withdrawal by the United States. "New flocks of antiwar 'doves' were hatching daily." (p. 935)
13. **militant** In politics, someone who pursues political goals in a belligerent way, often using paramilitary means. "Other militants . . . shouted obscenities. . . ." (p. 938)
14. **dissident** Someone who dissents, especially from an established or normative institution or position. ". . . Spiro T. Agnew [was] noted for his tough stands against dissidents and black militants." (p. 939)
15. **coattails** In politics, the ability of a popular candidate at the top of a ticket to transfer some of his or her support to lesser candidates on the same ticket. "Nixon was . . . the first president-elect since 1848 not to bring in on his coattails at least one house of Congress. . . ." (pp. 939–940)

PART II: Checking Your Progress

A. True-False

Where the statement is true, mark **T**. Where it is false, mark **F**, and correct it in the space immediately below.

_____ 1. Kennedy's attempt to control rising steel prices met strong opposition from big business.

_____ 2. The Kennedy doctrine of "flexible response" was applied primarily to conflicts with Soviet communism in Europe.

_____ 3. The U.S.-supported coup against the corrupt Diem regime brought South Vietnam greater democracy and political stability.

_____ 4. Kennedy financed and trained the Cuban rebels involved in the Bay of Pigs invasion but refused to intervene directly with American troops or planes.

_____ 5. The Cuban missile crisis ended in a humiliating defeat for Khrushchev and the Soviet Union.

_____ 6. Kennedy encouraged the civil rights movement to become more outspoken in its opposition to segregation and discrimination.

_____ 7. Johnson's landslide victory came in every part of the country except the traditionally Republican Midwest.

_____ 8. The Gulf of Tonkin Resolution authorized the president to respond to naval attacks but kept the power to make war in Vietnam firmly in the hands of Congress.

_____ 9. Johnson's Great Society programs attempted to balance the federal budget and return power to the states.

_____ 10. The nonviolent civil rights movement, led by Martin Luther King, Jr., achieved great victories in integration and voting rights for blacks in 1964 and 1965.

_____ 11. The urban riots of the late 1960s demonstrated that the South had not been improved by the civil rights movement.

_____ 12. The campaigns of Senators McCarthy and Kennedy forced Johnson to withdraw as a presidential candidate and promoted de-escalation of the Vietnam War.

_____ 13. The deep Democratic divisions over Vietnam helped elect Nixon as president in 1968.

_____ 14. One major American institution largely unaffected by the cultural upheaval of the 1960s was the Roman Catholic Church.

_____ 15. The "sexual revolution" of the 1960s included the introduction of the birth control pill and the increasing visibility of gays and lesbians.

B. Multiple Choice

Select the best answer and write the proper letter in the space provided.

_____ 1. President Kennedy's proposals for increased educational aid and medical assistance
   a. succeeded because of his skill in legislative bargaining.
   b. were traded away in exchange for passage of the bill establishing the Peace Corps.
   c. were stalled by strong opposition in Congress.
   d. were strongly opposed by business interests.

_____ 2. The industry that engaged in a bitter conflict with President Kennedy over price increases was
   a. the aircraft industry.
   b. the meat industry.
   c. the steel industry.
   d. the oil industry.

_____ 3. The fundamental military doctrine of the Kennedy administration involved
   a. "flexible response" to "brushfire wars" in the Third World.
   b. a massive nuclear retaliation against communist advances.
   c. a heavy buildup of conventional armed forces in Western Europe.
   d. reliance on rapid-response jet and helicopter air power.

___ 4. The first major foreign-policy disaster of the Kennedy administration came when

   a. Middle East governments sharply raised the price of imported oil.
   b. American-backed Cuban rebels were defeated at the Bay of Pigs.
   c. Khrushchev threatened American interests in the Cuban missile crisis.
   d. American forces suffered severe battlefield losses in Vietnam.

___ 5. The Cuban missile crisis ended when

   a. the American-backed Cuban invaders were defeated at the Bay of Pigs.
   b. the United States agreed to allow Soviet missiles in Cuba as long as they were not armed with nuclear weapons.
   c. the Soviets agreed to pull all missiles out of Cuba and the United States agreed not to invade Cuba.
   d. The United States and the Soviet Union agreed that Cuba should become neutral in the Cold War.

___ 6. The Kennedy administration was pushed into a stronger stand on civil rights by

   a. the civil rights movement led by the Freedom Riders and Martin Luther King, Jr.
   b. the political advantages of backing civil rights.
   c. the pressure from foreign governments and the United Nations.
   d. the threat of violence in northern cities.

___ 7. Lyndon Johnson won an overwhelming landslide victory in the 1964 election partly because

   a. he repudiated many of the policies of the unpopular Kennedy administration.
   b. he promised to take a tough stand in opposing communist aggression in Vietnam.
   c. Republican candidate Senator Barry Goldwater was seen by many Americans as a "trigger-happy" extremist.
   d. Johnson had achieved considerable personal popularity with the electorate.

___ 8. President Johnson was more successful in pushing economic and civil rights measures through Congress than President Kennedy because

   a. he was better at explaining the purposes of the laws in his speeches.
   b. the Democrats gained overwhelming control of Congress in the landslide of 1964.
   c. Republicans were more willing to cooperate with Johnson than with Kennedy.
   d. Johnson was better able to swing southern Democrats behind his proposals.

___ 9. The Civil Rights Act of 1965 was designed to guarantee

   a. desegregation in interstate transportation.
   b. job opportunities for African-Americans.
   c. desegregation of high schools and colleges.
   d. voting rights for African-Americans.

___ 10. Most of the racial riots of the 1960s occurred in

   a. northern inner-city areas.
   b. southern inner-city areas.
   c. white neighborhoods where black families attempted to move in.
   d. college campuses.

11. Escalation of the aerial bombardment in Vietnam
    a. bolstered the stability of the South Vietnamese government.
    b. forced the Viet Cong and North Vietnamese to turn to conventional warfare.
    c. strengthened the Viet Cong and North Vietnamese will to resist.
    d. enabled the United States to limit the use of ground forces in Vietnam.

12. Opposition to the Vietnam War in Congress was centered in
    a. the House Foreign Affairs Committee.
    b. the Senate Armed Services Committee.
    c. the Republican leadership of the House and Senate.
    d. the Senate Foreign Relations Committee.

13. The antiwar presidential candidates whose political showing forced Johnson to withdraw from the race were
    a. Nelson Rockefeller and Ronald Reagan.
    b. Eugene McCarthy and Robert Kennedy.
    c. J. William Fulbright and George McGovern.
    d. George Wallace and Curtis LeMay.

14. One dominant theme of the 1960s "youth culture" that had deep roots in American history was
    a. conflict between the generations.
    b. distrust and hostility toward authority.
    c. the widespread use of mind-altering drugs.
    d. a positive view of sexual experimentation.

15. The cultural upheavals of the 1960s could largely be attributed to the "three P's" of
    a. pot, promiscuity, and publicity.
    b. presidential failure, political rebellion, and personal authenticity.
    c. poverty, protest, and the "pill."
    d. population bulge, protest against racism, and prosperity.

C. Identification

Supply the correct identification for each numbered description.

1. Kennedy administration program that sent youthful American volunteers to work in underdeveloped countries

2. High barrier between East and West erected during the 1961 Berlin crisis

3. Elite antiguerrilla military units expanded by Kennedy as part of his doctrine of "flexible response"

4. An attempt to provide American aid for democratic reform in Latin America that met with much disappointment and frustration

5. Site where anti-Castro guerrilla forces failed in their U.S.-sponsored invasion

6. Tense confrontation between Kennedy and Khrushchev that nearly led to nuclear war in October 1962

7. New civil rights technique developed in the 1960s to desegregate lunch counters and other public facilities in the South

_____ 8. LBJ's broad program of welfare legislation and social reform that swept through Congress in 1965

_____ 9. The 1964 congressional action that became a "blank check" for the Vietnam War

_____ 10. Law, spurred by Martin Luther King, Jr.'s march from Selma to Montgomery, that guaranteed rights originally given blacks under the Fifteenth Amendment

_____ 11. Racial slogan that signaled a growing challenge to King's non-violent civil rights movement by militant younger blacks

_____ 12. The Vietnamese New Year celebration, during which the communists launched a heavy offensive against the United States in 1968

_____ 13. Student activist protest at the University of California that criticized corporate interests and impersonal university education

_____ 14. Student organization that moved from nonviolent protest to underground terrorism within a few years

_____ 15. Site of an off-duty police raid in 1969 that spurred gay and lesbian activism

D. Matching People, Places, and Events

Match the person, place, or event in the left column with the proper description in the right column by inserting the correct letter on the blank line.

___ 1. John F. Kennedy
___ 2. Robert S. McNamara
___ 3. Nikita Khrushchev
___ 4. Martin Luther King, Jr.
___ 5. Lyndon B. Johnson
___ 6. Barry M. Goldwater
___ 7. James Meredith
___ 8. Malcolm X
___ 9. Mario Savio
___ 10. Eugene J. McCarthy
___ 11. Robert F. Kennedy
___ 12. Richard M. Nixon
___ 13. George C. Wallace
___ 14. Hubert Humphrey
___ 15. Alfred Kinsey

A. First black student admitted to the University of Mississippi, shot during a civil rights march in 1966
B. Cabinet officer who promoted "flexible response" but came to doubt the wisdom of the Vietnam War he had presided over
C. New York senator whose antiwar campaign for the presidency was ended by an assassin's bullet in June 1968
D. Former vice president who staged a remarkable political comeback to win presidential election in 1968
E. Charismatic Black Muslim leader who promoted separatism in the early 1960s
F. Minnesota senator whose antiwar "Children's Crusade" helped force Johnson to alter his Vietnam policies
G. Early student activist and leader of the Free Speech Movement at the University of California
H. Nonviolent black leader whose advocacy of peaceful change came under attack from militants after 1965
I. Vice president whose loyalty to LBJ's Vietnam policies sent him down to defeat in the 1968 presidential election
J. Charismatic president whose brief administration experienced domestic stalemate and foreign confrontations with communism
K. Third-party candidate whose conservative, hawkish 1968 campaign won 9 million votes and carried five states
L. Aggressive Soviet leader whose failed gamble of putting missiles in Cuba cost him his job
M. Controversial Indiana University "sexologist" who documented Americans' changing sexual behavior
N. Conservative Republican whose crushing defeat opened the way for the liberal Great Society programs

Name_____ Section_____ _____ Date_____

        O. Brilliant legislative operator whose domestic achievements in social welfare and civil rights fell under the shadow of his Vietnam disaster

E. Putting Things in Order

Put the following events in correct order by numbering them from 1 to 5.

____ A southern Texas populist replaces a Harvard-educated Irish-American in the White House.

____ An American-sponsored anticommunist invasion of Cuba fails.

____ Kennedy successfully risks nuclear confrontation to thwart Khrushchev's placement of Russian missiles in Cuba.

____ A candidate running on a "peace" platform obtains a congressional "blank check" for subsequent expanded military actions against the Communist Vietnamese.

____ Communist military assaults, political divisions between hawks and doves, and assassinations of national leaders form the backdrop for a turbulent election year.

F. Matching Cause and Effect

Match the historical cause in the left column with the proper effect in the right column by writing the correct letter on the blank line.

Cause

____ 1. Kennedy's unhappiness with the corrupt Diem regime

____ 2. Khrushchev's placement of missiles in Cuba

____ 3. Johnson's landslide victory over Goldwater in 1964

____ 4. The Gulf of Tonkin Resolution

____ 5. Martin Luther King, Jr.'s civil rights marches

____ 6. Angry discontent in northern black ghettos

____ 7. American escalation of the Vietnam War

____ 8. The Communist Vietnamese Tet Offensive in 1968

____ 9. Senator Eugene McCarthy's strong antiwar campaign

____ 10. The deep Democratic party divisions over Vietnam

Effect

A. Pushed Johnson into withdrawing as a presidential candidate in 1968

B. Brought ever-rising American casualties and a strengthened will to resist on the part of the Communist Vietnamese

C. Led to a U.S.-encouraged coup and greater political instability in South Vietnam

D. Helped push through historic civil rights legislation in 1964 and 1965

E. Brought along huge Democratic congressional majorities that passed a fistful of Great Society laws

F. Helped Nixon win a minority victory over his divided opposition

G. Became the questionable legal basis for all of Johnson's further escalation of the Vietnam War

H. Led to a humiliating defeat when Kennedy forced the Soviet Union to back down

I. Sparked urban riots and the growth of the militant "Black Power" movement

J. Led to an American military request for 200,000 more troops as well as growing public discontent with the Vietnam War

G. **Developing Historical Skills**

Interpreting Line Graphs

Read the line graph of *Poverty in the United States* on p. 931 carefully and answer the following questions.

1. In what year did the number of people below the poverty line return to approximately the same level it had been at in 1964?

2. In what two years did the percentage of the American population below the poverty line reach its lowest point since 1960?

3. Between what years did the absolute numbers of people below the poverty line *rise* slightly at the same time those in poverty *declined* slightly as a percentage of the total population? What would explain this difference?

4. The number of people in poverty in 1966 was about the same as the number in poverty in which subsequent year?

H. **Map Mastery**

Map Discrimination

Using the maps and charts in Chapter 39, answer the following questions.

1. *Vietnam and Southeast Asia*: Besides North Vietnam, which two other Southeast Asian countries bordered on South Vietnam?

2. *Presidential Election of 1964*: How many electoral votes did Barry Goldwater win outside the Deep South in 1964?

3. *Presidential Election of 1968*: What four northeastern states did Nixon carry in 1968?

4. *Presidential Election of 1968*: Which five states outside the Northeast did Humphrey carry in 1968? (One of them is not in the continental United States.)

Map Challenge

Using the electoral maps of the five elections of 1952, 1956, 1960, 1964, and 1968 (pp. 889, 902, 906, 928 and 940 (in Chapters 38 and 39), write a brief essay describing the changing fortunes of the Republican and Democratic parties in different regions of the country from 1952 to 1968. Include a discussion of which states and regions remained relatively loyal to a single party, which shifted loyalties, and which were most contested. What are the most plausible explanations for these patterns?

PART III: Applying What You Have Learned

1. What successes and failures did Kennedy's New Frontier experience at home and abroad?
2. How did the civil rights movement progress from difficult beginnings to great successes in 1964–1965 and then encounter increasing opposition from both black militants and "white backlash" after 1965?
3. What were Johnson's major domestic achievements, and why did they come to be overshadowed?
4. Why did the Vietnam War, and the domestic opposition to it, come to dominate American politics in the 1960s?
5. How was the cultural upheaval of the 1960s related to the political and social changes of the decade? Is the "youth rebellion" best seen as a response to immediate events, or as a consequence of such longer-term forces as the population bulge and economic prosperity? What were the long-term results of the "counter-culture" in all its varieties?
6. What led the United States to become so deeply involved in the Vietnam War? (See Chapters 37 and 38 for background on the Cold War, anticolonialism, and earlier events in Vietnam.)

Name_____ Section_____ Date_____

40

The Stalemated Seventies, 1968–1980

PART I: Reviewing the Chapter

A. Checklist of Learning Objectives

After mastering this chapter, you should be able to

1. describe Nixon's policies toward the war in Vietnam and Cambodia.
2. analyze Nixon's domestic policies and his appeal to the "silent majority."
3. describe the American withdrawal from Vietnam, the final communist victory there, and the "new isolationism" represented by the War Powers Act.
4. discuss the Watergate scandals and Nixon's resignation.
5. explain the related economic, energy, and Middle East crises of the 1970s and indicate how Nixon, Ford, and Carter attempted to deal with them.
6. analyze the successes and failures of the détente with Moscow and the opening to Beijing (Peking) pursued by the American administrations of the 1970s.
7. describe the rise of the new feminist movement, and the gains and setbacks for women and minorities in the 1970s.
8. discuss the Iranian crisis and its political consequences for Carter.

B. Glossary

To build your social science vocabulary, familiarize yourself with the following terms.

1. **moratorium** A period in which economic or social activity is suspended, often to achieve certain defined goals. "Antiwar protesters staged a massive national Vietnam moratorium in October 1969. . . ." (p. 948)
2. **Marxism** The doctrines of Karl Marx, advocated or followed by many modern Socialists and communists. "The two great communist powers . . . were clashing bitterly over their rival interpretations of Marxism." (p. 950)
3. **anti-ballistic missile** A defensive missile designed to shoot down or otherwise protect against an offensive missile attack. "The first major achievement was an anti-ballistic missile (ABM) treaty. . . ." (p. 951)
4. **devaluation** In economics, steps taken to reduce the purchasing power of a given unit of currency in relation to foreign currencies. " . . . he next stunned the world by taking the United States off the gold standard and devaluing the dollar." (p. 954)
5. **obstruction of justice** The crime of interfering with police, courts, or other officials to thwart the performance of their legal duties. "Many were involved in a criminal obstruction of justice through tangled cover-ups. . . ." (p. 955)
6. **audit** To examine accounts or records in order to determine their accuracy and legitimacy—a process performed by officials appointed for that purpose. "Even the Internal Revenue Service was called upon by Nixon's aides to audit or otherwise harass political opponents. . . ." (p. 955)

7. **echelon** An ordered subdivision of military troops or of a military or political headquarters. "John Dean III . . . testified glibly . . . as to the involvement of the top echelons in the White House. . . ." (p. 956)
8. **executive privilege** In American government, the claim that certain information known to the president or the executive branch of government should be unavailable to Congress or the courts because of the principle of separation of powers. "He took refuge behind various principles, including separation of powers and executive privilege. . . ." (p. 956)
9. **appropriation** The direct approval, by Congress or other legislative bodies, for the executive to spend money for a specified purpose. (**Authorization** is the prior budgeting of an overall sum for an agency or activity, but does not include permission to spend.) "Finally, with appropriations running short, Nixon agreed to a compromise. . . ." (p. 957)
10. **recession** A moderate and short-term economic downturn, less severe than a depression. (Economists define a recession as two consecutive quarters, i.e., six months, of declining gross domestic product.) "Lines of automobiles at service stations lengthened as tempers shortened and a business recession deepened." (p. 958)
11. **sheik** A traditional Arab clan chieftain or ruler. "The Middle Eastern sheiks [had] approximately quadrupled their price for crude oil. . . ." (p. 958)
12. **illegitimacy** The condition of being contrary to or outside of the law or formal rules. "The sour odor of illegitimacy hung about this president without precedent." (p. 960)
13. **born-again** The Evangelical Christian belief in a spiritual renewal or rebirth, involving a personal experience of conversion and a commitment to moral transformation. ". . . this born-again Baptist touched many people with his down-home sincerity." (p. 967)
14. **balance of payments** The net ratio, expressed as a positive or negative sum, of a nation's exports in relations to its imports. (It may be calculated in relation to one particular foreign nation, or to all foreign states collectively.) "The soaring bill for imported oil plunged America's balance of payments deeply into the red. . . ." (p. 971)
15. **ayatollah** A supreme religious leader in the Shi'ite branch of Islam. "Ayatollah Ruhollah Khomeini, the white-bearded Muslim holy man who inspired the revolutionaries. . . ." (p. 974)

PART II: Checking Your Progress

A. True-False

Where the statement is true, mark **T**. Where it is false, mark **F**, and correct it in the space immediately below.

_____ 1. Nixon's "Vietnamization" policy sought to bring an immediate negotiated end to the Vietnam War.

_____ 2. Nixon's 1970 invasion of Cambodia provoked strong domestic protests and political clashes between "hawks" and "doves."

_____ 3. Nixon and Kissinger's diplomacy attempted to play the Soviet Union and China off against each other for America's benefit.

_____ 4. Nixon attempted to reverse what he saw as the Warren Supreme Court's excessive turn toward "judicial activism."

_____ 5. Nixon consistently opposed the expansion of social security and pro-environmental legislation.

___ 6. The basic issue in the 1972 Nixon-McGovern campaign was inflation and the management of the economy.

___ 7. The 1973 Paris agreement on Vietnam provided for a cease-fire and American withdrawal but did not really end the civil war among the Vietnamese.

___ 8. The strongest charge against Nixon during Watergate was that he had used government agencies to burglarize and harass opponents and cover up the Watergate crimes.

___ 9. The disclosure of the secret bombing of Cambodia led Congress to acknowledge the president's sole authority to take military action in defense of America's national security.

___ 10. The 1973 Arab-Israeli War and OPEC oil embargo added to the inflation that began in the wake of the Vietnam War.

___ 11. Conservative Republicans strenuously opposed Nixon's resignation and urged him to fight to stay in office even after the Watergate tapes were released.

___ 12. President Ford attempted to stop the final communist victory in Vietnam by attacking the captured ship *Mayaguez*.

___ 13. The women's movement achieved success in the 1970s by allying itself with the rising antiwar and black power movements of the decade.

___ 14. The Camp David accords brought an end to the Middle East conflict and the oil crisis and thus substantially eased inflation in the United States.

___ 15. The Iranian revolution against the shah brought the United States into a confrontation with militant Muslim leaders of the country.

B. Multiple Choice

Select the best answer and write the proper letter in the space provided.

___ 1. A primary cause of the economic decline that began in the 1970s was
   a. an international trade war.
   b. a rise in the price of agricultural goods.
   c. the breakup of efficient American companies.
   d. a decline in worker productivity.

___ 2. The severe inflation of the 1970s was largely caused by
   a. Lyndon Johnson's effort to maintain the Vietnam War and the Great Society programs without raising taxes.
   b. Nixon's decision to devalue the dollar and take the U.S. off the gold standard.
   c. the higher prices for scarce natural resources like iron, coal, and lumber.
   d. the strong demands of unionized workers for substantial wage increases.

___ 3. President Nixon's "Vietnamization" policy provided that
   a. the United States would accept a unified but neutral Vietnam.
   b. the United States would escalate the war in Vietnam but withdraw from Cambodia and Laos.
   c. the United States would gradually withdraw ground troops while supporting the South Vietnamese war effort.
   d. the United States would seek a negotiated settlement of the war.

___ 4. The antiwar movement expanded dramatically in 1970 when
   a. the massacre of civilians at My Lai by some U.S. soldiers was revealed.
   b. Nixon ordered further bombing of North Vietnam.
   c. the communist Vietnamese staged their Tet Offensive against American forces.
   d. Nixon ordered an invasion of Cambodia.

___ 5. Nixon attempted to pressure the Soviet Union into making diplomatic deals with the United States by
   a. playing the "China card" by opening U.S. diplomacy and trade with the Soviets' rival communist power.
   b. using American economic aid as an incentive for the Soviets.
   c. threatening to attack Soviet allies such as Cuba and Vietnam.
   d. drastically increasing spending on nuclear weapons and missiles.

___ 6. The Supreme Court came under sharp political attack especially because of its rulings on
   a. antitrust laws and labor rights.
   b. voting rights and election laws.
   c. criminal defendants' rights and prayer in public schools.
   d. environmental laws and immigrants' rights.

___ 7. The most controversial element of Nixon's "Philadelphia Plan" was
   a. its guarantees of women's equal right to employment in the construction trades.
   b. the extension of "affirmative action" to promote the employment of groups of minorities and women.
   c. its insistence that employers and labor provide financial compensation to individuals who had suffered discrimination.
   d. its attempt to get around Supreme Court decisions prohibiting racial and sexual discrimination by business and labor.

___ 8. Some of President Nixon's greatest legislative successes came in the area of
   a. upholding civil rights.
   b. stopping the growth of inflation.
   c. protecting the environment.
   d. maintaining foreign-policy cooperation with Congress.

Name_____ Section_____ _____ Date_____

____ 9. Among the corrupt Nixon administration practices exposed by the Senate Watergate Committee was

   a. payments to foreign agents.
   b. bribes to congressmen and senators.
   c. the illegal use of the Federal Bureau of Investigation and the Central Intelligence Agency.
   d. the illegal use of the Environmental Protection Agency and the Treasury Department.

____ 10. The War Powers Act was passed by Congress in response to

   a. the Watergate scandal.
   b. President Nixon's secret bombing of Cambodia.
   c. the end of the war in Vietnam.
   d. the Arab oil embargo.

____ 11. The Arab oil embargo of 1973–1974 affected the American economy primarily by

   a. causing the successful introduction of alternative energy sources.
   b. leading the United States to open Alaskan and offshore oilfield to exploration.
   c. increasing American investment in the Middle East.
   d. ending the era of cheap energy and fueling severe inflation.

____ 12. Gerald Ford came to be president because

   a. he had been elected as Nixon's vice president in 1972.
   b. he was speaker of the House of Representatives and was next in line after Nixon resigned.
   c. he was elected in a special national election called after Nixon resigned.
   d. he had been appointed vice president by Nixon before Nixon resigned.

____ 13. Despite numerous successes for the women in the 1970s, the feminist movement suffered a severe setback when

   a. the Supreme Court began to oppose the extension of women's rights.
   b. the Equal Rights Amendment failed to achieve ratification by the states.
   c. Congress refused to extend women's right to an equal education to the area of athletics.
   d. the declining economy created a growing gap between men's and women's earning power.

____ 14. President Carter's greatest success in foreign policy was

   a. handling the Arab oil embargo and the energy crisis.
   b. negotiating successful new agreements with the Soviet Union.
   c. negotiating the Camp David peace treaty between Israel and Egypt.
   d. maintaining peace and stability in Central America.

____ 15. President Carter's greatest problem in foreign policy was

   a. the Panama Canal issue.
   b. the Soviet invasion of Afghanistan.
   c. the continuing Arab-Israeli confrontation.
   d. the Iranian seizure of American hostages.

C. Identification

Supply the correct identification for each numbered description.

_____ 1. Nixon's policy of withdrawing American troops from Vietnam while providing aid for the South Vietnamese to fight the war

_____ 2. The Ohio university where four students were killed during protests against the 1970 invasion of Cambodia

_____ 3. Top-secret documents, published by *The New York Times* in 1971, that showed the blunders and deceptions that led the United States into the Vietnam War

_____ 4. The first major achievement of the Nixon-Kissinger détente with the Soviet Union, which led to restrictions on defensive missile systems

_____ 5. Nixon's plan to win reelection by curbing the Supreme Court's judicial activism and soft-pedaling civil rights

_____ 6. Term for the new group affirmative action policy promoted by the Nixon administration

_____ 7. A Washington office complex that became a symbol of the widespread corruption of the Nixon administration

_____ 8. The law, passed in reaction to the secret Cambodia bombing, that restricted presidential use of troops overseas without congressional authorization

_____ 9. Arab-sponsored restriction on energy exports after the 1973 Arab-Israeli war

_____ 10. Nixon-Ford-Kissinger policy of seeking relaxed tensions with the Soviet Union through trade and arms limitation

_____ 11. International agreement of 1975, signed by President Ford, that settled postwar European boundaries and attempted to guarantee human rights in Eastern Europe

_____ 12. Proposed constitutional amendment promoting women's rights that fell short of ratification

_____ 13. Supreme Court decision that declared women's right to choose abortion.

_____ 14. *Two* historic sites seized by American Indian activists in 1970–1972 to draw public attention to Indian grievances

_____

_____ 15. Provision of the 1972 Education Amendments that prohibited gender discrimination and opened sports and other arenas to women

D. Matching People, Places, and Events

Match the person, place, or event in the left column with the proper description in the right column by inserting the correct letter on the blank line.

___ 1. Richard Nixon   A. The Muslim religious leader who dominated the 1979 Iranian revolution

___ 2. Spiro Agnew   B. The first appointed vice president and first appointed president of the United States

___ 3. Rachel Carson   C. Supreme Court justice whose "judicial activism" came under increasing attack by conservatives

Name_____ Section_____ Date_____

    ____ 4. Daniel Ellsberg

    ____ 5. Henry Kissinger

    ____ 6. Earl Warren

    ____ 7. George McGovern

    ____ 8. Sam Ervin

    ____ 9. Gerald Ford

    ____ 10. John Dean

    ____ 11. James Earl Carter

    ____ 12. Anwar Sadat

    ____ 13. Allen Bakke

    ____ 14. Shah of Iran

    ____ 15. Ayatollah Ruhollah Khomeini

D. Nixon's tough-talking conservative vice president, who was forced to resign in 1973 for taking bribes and kickbacks

E. Talented diplomatic negotiator and leading architect of détente with the Soviet Union during the Nixon and Ford administrations

F. Egyptian leader who signed the Camp David accords with Israel

G. California medical school applicant whose case led a divided Supreme Court to uphold limited forms of affirmative action for minorities

H. Environmental writer whose book *Silent Spring* helped encourage laws like the Clean Water Act and the Endangered Species Act

I. South Dakota senator whose antiwar campaign was swamped by Nixon

J. Former Georgia governor whose presidency was plagued by economic difficulties and a crisis in Iran

K. Former Pentagon official who "leaked" the Pentagon Papers

L. Winner of an overwhelming electoral victory who was forced from office by the threat of impeachment

M. White House lawyer whose dramatic charges against Nixon were validated by the Watergate tapes

N. North Carolina senator who conducted the Watergate hearings

O. Repressive pro-Western ruler whose 1979 overthrow precipitated a crisis for the United States

E. Putting Things in Order

Put the following events in correct order by numbering them from 1 to 6.

____ The overthrow of a dictatorial shah leads to an economic and political crisis for President Carter and the United States.

____ An impeachment-threatened president resigns, and his appointed vice president takes over the White House.

____ A U.S. president travels to Beijing (Peking) and Moscow, opening a new era of improved diplomatic relations with the communist powers.

____ The American invasion of a communist stronghold near Vietnam creates domestic turmoil in the United States.

____ The signing of an agreement with North Vietnam leads to the final withdrawal of American troops from Vietnam.

____ A plainspoken former governor becomes president by campaigning against Washington corruption and for honesty in government.

F. Matching Cause and Effect

Match the historical cause in the left column with the proper effect in the right column by writing the correct letter on the blank line.

Cause

___ 1. Nixon's "Vietnamization" policy

___ 2. The U.S. invasion and bombing of Cambodia

___ 3. Nixon's trips to Beijing (Peking) and Moscow

___ 4. The Warren Court's "judicial activism"

___ 5. Pressure on Moscow and renewed bombing of North Vietnam

___ 6. The growing successes of the women's movement in areas of employment and education

___ 7. Nixon's tape-recorded words ordering the Watergate cover-up

___ 8. The communist Vietnamese offensive in 1975

___ 9. The Soviet invasion of Afghanistan

___ 10. The 1979 revolution in Iran

Effect

A. Spawned a powerful "backlash" that halted federal day care efforts and the Equal Rights Amendment

B. Caused Senate defeat of the SALT II treaty and the end of détente with Moscow

C. Brought about gradual U.S. troop withdrawal but extended the Vietnam War for four more years

D. Prompted conservative protests and Nixon's appointment of less activist justices

E. Led to the taking of American hostages and new economic and energy troubles for the United States

F. Brought about a cease-fire and the withdrawal of American troops from Vietnam in 1973

G. Caused protests on U.S. campuses and congressional attempts to restrain presidential war powers

H. Brought an era of relaxed international tensions and new trade agreements

I. Caused the collapse of South Vietnam and the flight of many refugees to the United States

J. Proved the president's guilt and forced him to resign or be impeached

Name_____ Section_____ Date_____

G. Developing Historical Skills

Understanding Political Cartoons

The more controversial a major political figure, the more likely he or she is to be the subject of political cartoons. Richard Nixon was such a controversial figure, and the cartoons in this chapter show several views of him. Answer the following questions.

1. What is the view of Nixon's diplomacy in the cartoon *Balancing Act* on p. 951? What is the significance of his unusual "balance bar?"

2. In the cartoon of *Nixon, the Law and Order Man* on p. 960, what aspect of Nixon's earlier career is satirized? What details suggest the cartoonist's view of Nixon's Watergate strategy?

3. In the cartoon *How Long Will Nixon Haunt the GOP* on p. 960, what is the cartoonist suggesting about Ford's pardon of Nixon? What alleged quality of Nixon's is common to both this cartoon and the previous one on *Nixon, the Law and Order Man*?

4. In the cartoon *Who Lost Vietnam* on p. 962, Nixon is satirized, but less harshly than in the other cartoons. What changes the perspective on him here?

PART III: Applying What You Have Learned

1. What policies did Nixon pursue with Vietnam, the Soviet Union, and China, and what were the consequences of those policies?
2. In what ways did Nixon's domestic policies appeal to Americans' racial and economic fears, and in what ways did he positively address problems like inflation, discrimination, and pollution?
3. How did Nixon fall from the political heights of 1972 to his forced resignation in 1974? What were the political consequences of Watergate?
4. How did the administrations of the 1970s attempt to cope with the interrelated problems of energy, economics, and the Middle East?
5. Why can the 1970s be characterized as a "decade of stalemate?" What caused the apparent inability of the federal government to cope with the new problems of the time?
6. In what ways were the foreign policy and economic issues of the 1970s similar to those of the whole post-World War II era, and in what ways were they different? (See Chapters 37, 38, and 39.)

Name_____ Section_____ Date_____

41

The Resurgence of Conservatism, 1981–1992

PART I: Reviewing the Chapter

A. Checklist of Learning Objectives

After mastering this chapter, you should be able to

1. describe the rise of Reagan and the "new right" in the 1980s, including the controversies over racial and social issues.
2. explain the "Reagan revolution" in economic policy and indicate its immediate and long-term consequences.
3. describe the revival of the Cold War in Reagan's first term.
4. discuss the American entanglement in Central American and Middle Eastern troubles, including the Iran-contra affair.
5. describe the end of the Cold War, and the results for American society abroad and at home.
6. explain America's growing involvement in Middle East conflict, including the Persian Gulf War and its aftermath.
7. explain the Clinton victory in 1992, and Clinton's attempt to navigate between traditional Democratic values and resurgent right in the Republican party.
8. recount the successes and failures of the Clinton administration, and the causes and consequences of his impeachment.

B. Glossary

To build your social science vocabulary, familiarize yourself with the following terms.

1. **neoconservatives (neoconservatism)** Political activists and thinkers, mostly former liberals, who turned to a defense of traditional social and moral values and a strongly anticommunist foreign policy in the 1970s and 1980s. "Though Reagan was no intellectual, he drew on the ideas of a small but influential group of thinkers known as 'neoconservatives.'" (p. 977)
2. **supply side** In economics, the theory that investment incentives such as lowered federal spending and tax cuts will stimulate economic growth and increased employment. "But at first 'supply-side' economics seemed to be a beautiful theory mugged by a gang of brutal facts. . . ." (p. 981)
3. **red ink** Referring to a deficit in a financial account, with expenditures or debts larger than income or assets. "Ironically, this conservative president thereby plunged the government into a red-ink bath of deficit spending. . . ." (p. 981)
4. **oligarchs** A small, elite class of authoritarian rulers. ". . . the aging oligarchs in the Kremlin. . . ." (p. 982)
5. **indictment** In law, a formal statement of charges of legal violations presented by a prosecutor. "Criminal indictments were later brought against several individuals tarred by the Iran-contra scandal. . . ." (p. 986)

6. **welfare state** The political system, typical of modern industrial societies, in which government assumes responsibility for the economic well-being of its citizens by providing social benefits. "They achieved, in short, Reagan's highest political objective: the containment of the welfare state." (p. 987)
7. **leveraged buy-out** The purchase of one company by another using money borrowed on the expectation of selling a portion of assets after the acquisition. "A wave of mergers, acquisitions, and leveraged buy-outs washed over Wall Street. . . ." (p. 990)
8. **logistical (logistics)** Relating to the organization and movement of substantial qualities of people and material in connection with some defined objective. "In a logistical operation of astonishing complexity, the United States spearheaded a massive international military deployment on the sandy Arabian peninsula." (p. 995)
9. **sect** A separatist religious group that claims for itself exclusive knowledge of truth and a superior method of salvation over against all other religious organizations. "That showdown ended in the destruction of the sect's compound and the deaths of many Branch Davidians. . . ." (p. 1001)
10. **paramilitary** Unauthorized or voluntary groups that employ military organization, methods, and equipment outside the official military system of command and organization. "The last two episodes brought to light a lurid and secretive underground of paramilitary private 'militias'. . . ." (p. 1001)
11. **immunity** In law, a guarantee against prosecution for crime granted to a potential defendant in exchange for some benefit to the state. " . . . the tobacco firms would win immunity from further litigation, including at the federal level." (p. 1004)
12. **vouchers** Officially granted certificates for benefits of a particular kind, redeemable by a designated agency or service provider. "Bush championed private-sector initiatives, such as school vouchers. . . ." (p. 1010)

PART II: Checking Your Progress

A. True-False

Where the statement is true, mark **T**. Where it is false, mark **F**, and correct it in the space immediately below.

____ 1. Conservative Christian groups provided an important component of Reagan's "new right" coalition.

____ 2. The Supreme Court's *Bakke* decision upheld the principle of racial quotas in college and medical school admissions.

____ 3. Once in office, Reagan backed away from most of his ideologically conservative election promises and concentrated on practical management of the economy and relations with the Russians.

____ 4. The fact that Reagan's "supply-side" economic proposals bogged down in Congress demonstrated the continuing stalemate between Congress and the executive branch.

____ 5. "Reaganomics" was successful in lowering interest rates and balancing the budget but had difficulty bringing down inflation and creating economic growth.

____ 6. Reagan's revival of the Cold War in the early 1980s caused rising military budgets and growing doubts about American policy in Western Europe.

___ 7. Reagan pursued a tough policy of military intervention and aid in opposition to leftist governments in Central America and the Caribbean.

___ 8. Soviet leader Mikhail Gorbachev's policies of *glasnost* and *perestroika* helped reduce Soviet-American conflict in Reagan's second term.

___ 9. The Iran-contra affair involved the secret exchange of weapons for American hostages and the illegal transfer of funds to Nicaraguan rebels.

___ 10. One of the greatest American concerns during the Persian Gulf War was that Iraq would use its stockpile of chemical and biological weapons.

___ 11. Bill Clinton's presentation of himself as a "new" Democrat was designed to emphasize his commitment to reversing past Democratic party positions on civil rights.

___ 12. Clinton's ambitious reform goals suffered a severe setback when his health-care proposal failed.

___ 13. After victory in the 1994 congressional elections, the militant conservatism of Speaker Newt Gingrich stumbled when it shut down the federal government for a time.

___ 14. Clinton put conservative Republicans on the defensive by fighting hard for traditional Democratic policies like defense of social welfare and support for affirmative action.

___ 15. George W. Bush defeated Albert Gore in the Electoral College but not in the popular vote.

B. Multiple Choice

Select the best answer and write the proper letter in the space provided.

___ 1. In the 1980 national elections,
   a. Edward Kennedy challenged incumbent President Carter for the nomination of the Democratic party.
   b. although Ronald Reagan won the presidency, both houses of Congress still had Democratic party majorities.
   c. third-party candidate John Anderson won three states and seventeen Electoral College votes.
   d. Ronald Reagan won the presidency by the closest margin since the Kennedy-Nixon election of 1960.

___ 2. The "new-right" movement that helped elect Ronald Reagan was spearheaded by
   a. fiscal conservatives.
   b. evangelical Christians.
   c. gold-standard advocates.
   d. midwesterners

3. Many "new-right" activists were most concerned about
   a. cultural and racial issues.
   b. economic questions.
   c. foreign policy.
   d. Medicare and Medicaid programs.

4. Of all the social issues, the most politically explosive for the "new right" was
   a. affirmative action.
   b. the teaching of evolution in public schools.
   c. balancing the federal budget.
   d. sex and violence on television.

5. That preference in the admission policies of institutions of higher education could not be based on ethnic or racial identity alone was the Supreme Court's decision in
   a. *Roe* v. *Wade*.
   b. the *Bakke* case.
   c. *Brown* v. *Board of Education*.
   d. the *Miranda* decision.

6. Ronald Reagan was similar to Franklin D. Roosevelt in that both presidents
   a. disliked big business.
   b. championed the common person against vast impersonal menaces.
   c. were raised in wealthy families.
   d. favored social engineering by the government.

7. Ronald Reagan differed from Franklin D. Roosevelt in that Roosevelt
   a. saw big government as the foe of the common person, and Reagan said the foe was big business.
   b. appealed to the working class and Reagan appealed only to the rich.
   c. advocated a populist political philosophy and Reagan did not.
   d. branded big business as the enemy of the common person, while Reagan branded big government as the foe.

8. Conservative Democrats who helped Ronald Reagan pass his budget and tax-cutting legislation were called
   a. boll weevils.
   b. Sagebrush rebels.
   c. scalawags.
   d. neoconservatives.

9. The Iran-contra scandal reflected a sharp conflict between Congress and President Reagan over
   a. U.S. aid for rebels against the leftist government of Nicaragua.
   b. the American policy of refusing to trade arms for U.S. hostages in the Middle East.
   c. the attitude of American Christian and Jewish leaders toward Iran's Islamic Revolution.
   d. the U.S. economic boycott of Fidel Castro's Cuba.

Name_____ Section_____ Date_____

_____ 10. Two hotly debated cultural issues that embroiled the Supreme Court during the Reagan-Bush administrations were

   a. hairstyles and rock music.
   b. affirmative action and abortion.
   c. child-rearing practices and television.
   d. language teaching and dress in the workplace.

_____ 11. The major American and Allied success in the Persian Gulf War was

   a. the overthrow of Saddam Hussein.
   b. the liberation of Kuwait from Iraqi rule.
   c. the freeing of the Kurds from Iraqi oppression.
   d. the achievement of an enduring peace in the Middle East.

_____ 12. Two areas where the first Clinton administration experienced the most success in domestic affairs was

   a. health care reform and gay rights.
   b. political campaign reform and term limits.
   c. gun control and deficit reduction.
   d. immigration reform and improved race relations.

_____ 13. Clinton worked to promote free trade through his advocacy of

   a. NAFTA, GATT, and the World Trade Organization (WTO)
   b. NATO, the UN, and the PLO.
   c. greater emphasis on human rights as the key factor in U.S.-China relations.
   d. closer ties between the United States and the former Soviet Union and Yugoslavia.

_____ 14. The two charges for which President Clinton was impeached and tried were

   a. violation of the War Powers Act in the bombing of Serbia and excessive use of force in the Branch Davidian assault.
   b. abuse of the power of presidential pardon and the Whitewater scandal.
   c. obstruction of justice and perjury before a grand jury.
   d. adultery and violation of moral norms of the presidency.

_____ 15. The fundamental issue in the presidential election of 2000 was

   a. foreign policy toward China, Russia, and Latin America.
   b. trade policy toward Europe and nations of the Third World.
   c. whether to use projected budget surpluses for tax cuts or for debt reduction and Medicare.
   d. whether to build a unilateral American missile defense system.

C. Identification

Supply the correct identification for each numbered description.

_____ 1. Outspoken conservative movement of the 1980s that emphasized such "social issues" as opposition to abortion, the Equal Rights Amendment, pornography, homosexuality, and affirmative action

_____ 2. Evangelical Christian organization that aroused its members to fervent support of Reagan and the Republican party in the 1980s

_____ 3. The economic theory of "Reaganomics" that emphasized cutting taxes and government spending in order to stimulate investment, productivity, and economic growth by private enterprise

_____ 4. The protest movement, supported by Reagan Interior Secretary Watt, that attempted to reduce federal environmental controls on industrial activities in the West

_____ 5. Conservative southern Democrats who supported Reagan's economic policies in Congress

_____ 6. Polish labor union crushed by the communist-imposed martial-law regime in 1983

_____ 7. The leftist revolutionary rulers of Nicaragua, strongly opposed by the Reagan administration

_____ 8. Popular name for Reagan's proposed space-based nuclear defense system, officially called the Strategic Defense Initiative

_____ 9. Physical symbol of the Cold War and divided Europe that came down in 1989

_____ 10. Nation whose invasion by Iraq in 1990 led to the Persian Gulf War

_____ 11. Conservative campaign platform that led to a sweeping Republican victory in the 1994 mid-term elections

_____ 12. International trade organization that prompted strong protests from anti-global trade forces in Seattle, Washington in 1999

_____ 13. Clinton Arkansas investment deal that spurred a federal special prosecutor and led to widespread investigations of his administration

_____ 14. Colorado high school where a deadly shooting in 1999 stirred a national movement against guns and gun violence

_____ 15. Third party led by environmentalist Ralph Nader that took votes from Democratic presidential nominee Albert Gore in 2000 election

D. Matching People, Places, and Events

Match the person, place, or event in the left column with the proper description in the right column by inserting the correct letter on the blank line.

___ 1. Jimmy Carter   A. Texas billionaire who won many votes as independent candidate in 1992 and 1996
___ 2. Edward Kennedy   B. Son of a former president who narrowly defeated Albert Gore in the disputed 2000 presidential election
___ 3. Ronald Reagan   C. Soviet leader whose summit meetings with Reagan achieved an arms-control breakthrough in 1987
___ 4. Oliver North   D. Supreme Court Justice who was narrowly confirmed despite charges of sexual harassment
___ 5. Sandra Day O'Connor E. Iraqi dictator defeated by the United States and its allies in the Persian Gulf War
___ 6. Mikhail Gorbachev   F. Brilliant legal scholar appointed by Reagan as the first woman justice on the Supreme Court
___ 7. George Bush, Sr.   G. Well-meaning but luckless president whose reelection attempt was swamped by the 1980 Reagan landslide

___ 8. Albert Gore
___ 9. Saddam Hussein
___ 10. George Walker Bush
___ 11. Clarence Thomas
___ 12. William Clinton
___ 13. H. Ross Perot
___ 14. Hillary Rodham Clinton
___ 15. Newt Gingrich

H. Clinton's vice president who won popular vote but lost electoral vote in 2000 presidential election
I. The first baby-boomer president, and the second U.S. president to be impeached and acquitted
J. Prominent child care advocate and health care reformer in Clinton administration; won U.S. Senate seat in 2000
K. Liberal Democratic senator whose opposition to Carter helped divide the Democrats in 1980
L. Long-time Republican political figure who defeated Dukakis for the presidency in 1988
M. Promoter of the "Contract with America" and the first Republican Speaker in 40 years
N. Marine colonel involved in the Iran-contra affair
O. Political darling of Republican conservatives who won landslide election victories in 1980 and 1984

E. Putting Things in Order

Put the following events in correct order by numbering them from 1 to 6.

___ Reagan easily wins reelection by overwhelming divided Democrats.

___ The United States and its allies defeat Iraq in the Persian Gulf War.

___ Republicans win Congress and confront President Clinton on taxes and spending.

___ Reagan's "supply-side" economic programs pass through Congress, cutting taxes and federal spending.

___ George Walker Bush defeats Albert Gore in a razor-close election.

___ President Clinton is impeached on charges of perjury and obstruction of justice and acquitted in a U.S. Senate trial.

F. Matching Cause and Effect

Match the historical cause in the left column with the proper effect in the right column by writing the correct letter on the blank line.

Cause

___ 1. The growth of the "new-right" movement focused on social issues
___ 2. Reagan's crusade against big government and social spending
___ 3. By 1983, Reagan's "supply-side" economic policies
___ 4. The revival of the Cold War in the early eighties
___ 5. Continued political turmoil and war in Lebanon

Effect

A. Led to a breakoff of arms-control talks, U.S. economic sanctions against Poland, and growing anxiety in Western Europe
B. Brought about an overwhelming Republican victory in the 1984 presidential election
C. Resulted in the failure of the American marines' peacekeeping mission in 1983
D. Helped curb affirmative action and limit the right to abortion.
E. Led to sharp cuts in both taxes and federal social programs in 1981
F. Strained relations with America's European allies

_____ 6. Reagan's hostility to leftist governments in Central America and the Caribbean

_____ 7. Reagan's personal popularity and Democratic divisions

_____ 8. Reagan's "Star Wars" plan for defensive missile systems in space

_____ 9. The huge federal budget deficits of the 1980s

_____ 10. Reagan's and Bush's appointments of conservative justices to the Supreme Court

_____ 11. The Reagan administration's frustration with hostages and bans on aid to Nicaraguan rebels

_____ 12. Violent episodes like the Oklahoma City bombing and the Columbine school shootings

_____ 13. The Congressional Republicans' ideological rhetoric and government shutdown of 1995

_____ 14. The Monica Lewinsky affair

_____ 15. The U.S. Supreme Court's intervention in the 2000 election

G. Curbed inflation and spurred economic growth but also caused sky-high deficits and interest rates
H. Prompted Congress to pass the Gramm-Rudman-Hollings Act calling for automatic spending cuts and a balanced budget by 1991
I. Helped fuel Ronald Reagan's successful presidential campaign in 1980
J. Caused the U.S. invasion of Grenada and the CIA-engineered mining of Nicaraguan harbors
K. Encouraged the public and the Clinton administration to press for tougher gun control
L. Enabled Clinton to regain political momentum and defeat Bob Dole in 1996
M. Was a windfall for prosecutor Kenneth Starr and laid the basis for Clinton's impeachment
N. Halted Florida's vote counting and permitted Bush to declare victory over Gore
O. Led to the Iran-contra affair

G. Developing Historical Skills

Using Chronologies

Properly read, chronologies provide handy tools for understanding not only the sequence of events but also their historical relations.

Examine the Chronology for this chapter (p. 1012), and answer the following questions.

1. In which year did a number of events indicate deep Soviet-American tension and a revived Cold War?

2. How many years did it take after the first Reagan-Gorbachev summit to reach agreement on the INF treaty?

Name_____ Section_____ Date_____

3. List three events *prior* to the Persian Gulf War in 1991 that reflect growing American involvement in the Middle East.

3. List three events between the imposition of sanctions against Poland (1981) and the dissolution of the Soviet Union (1991) that show the *progress* in easing Cold War tensions.

5. How many years elapsed between the Persian Gulf War and the U.S.-British air strikes against Iraq under the Clinton administration?

PART III: Applying What You Have Learned

1. What caused the rise of Reagan and the "new right" in the eighties, and how did their conservative movement affect American politics?
2. What were the goals of Reagan's "supply-side" economic policies, and what were their short-term and long-term effects?
3. What led to the revival of the Cold War in the early 1980s and to its decline and disappearance by 1991?
4. Describe the major changes affecting American foreign policy from 1982 to 1992 in Central America, the Middle East, and Eastern Europe. Which of these changes occurred as a result of American policy and which occurred primarily as a result of developments within those regions?
5. What were the successes and failures of the Bush administration? Was Bill Clinton's election a positive mandate for change, or was it primarily a repudiation of the Bush record?
6. How did the antigovernment mood of the 1990s affect both Bill Clinton and his Republican opponents? In what ways did Clinton attempt to uphold traditional Democratic themes, and in what ways did he serve to consolidate the conservative Bush-Reagan era?
7. What new foreign policy challenges did the United States face after the end of the Cold War? What were the principal themes of U.S. relations with the world in the Clinton administration?
8. Some historians have compared the "Reagan revolution" with the New Deal because of the way it seemed to transform radically American economics and politics. Is this a valid comparison? Is it correct to see the "Reagan legacy" as a reversal or overturning of the New Deal and the Great Society of Lyndon Johnson?

Name_____ Section_____ Date_____

42

The American People Face a New Century

PART I: Reviewing the Chapter

A. Checklist of Learning Objectives

After mastering this chapter, you should be able to

1. describe the changing shape of the American economy and work force, and the new challenges facing the United States in an international economy during the "information age."
2. explain the changing roles of women since World War II and the impact of those changes on American society.
3. analyze the difficulties affecting the American family, and explain the new power of the elderly.
4. describe the impact of the newest wave of immigration from Asia and Latin America and the growing voice of minorities in American society.
5. describe the difficulties and challenges facing American cities, including poverty and drug abuse.
6. describe the changing condition of African-Americans in American politics and society.
7. discuss the major developments in American culture and the arts since World War II.

B. Glossary

To build your social science vocabulary, familiarize yourself with the following terms.

1. **biosphere** The earth's entire network of living plants and organisms, conceived as an interconnected whole. ". . . the fragile ecological balance of the wondrous biosphere in which humankind was delicately suspended." (p. 1016)
2. **nuclear family** A parent or parents and their immediate offspring. "The nuclear family, once prized as the foundation of society. . . ." (p. 1020)
3. **undocumented** Lacking official certification of status as a legal immigrant or resident alien. ". . . attempted to choke off illegal entry by penalizing employers of undocumented aliens. . . ." (p. 1023)
4. **amnesty** An official governmental act in which some general category of offenders is declared immune from punishment. ". . . by granting amnesty to many of those already here." (p. 1023)
5. **civil trial** A trial before a judge or jury instigated by a private lawsuit in which one party seeks relief, compensation, or damages from another. A **criminal trial** is instigated by an indictment for criminal law violations brought by a state prosecutor on behalf of the government ("the people"); it may result in fines, imprisonment, or execution. "In a later civil trial, another jury found Simpson liable for the 'wrongful deaths' of his former wife and another victim." (p. 1025)

PART II: Checking Your Progress

A. True-False

Where the statement is true, mark **T**. Where it is false, mark **F**, and correct it in the space immediately below.

____ 1. The communications and genetics revolutions in postwar America created new social and moral dilemmas as well as widespread economic growth.

____ 2. The United States remained the world's richest nation with the highest per capita income in the 1990s.

____ 3. Continuing discrimination as well as different career patterns still caused women to receive lower wages than men in the late 1990s.

____ 4. By the 1990s almost all women without children at home were employed, but a majority of mothers remained outside the workplace.

____ 5. One of the greatest problems caused by the weakening of the family was the growing poverty of America's elderly.

____ 6. One factor that made Hispanic immigration to the U.S. unique was the close proximity of Mexican-Americans to their former homeland across the border.

____ 7. The fastest growing American minority in the 1980s and 1990s was African-Americans.

____ 8. By the late 1990s, a majority of Americans lived in suburbs rather than central cities or rural areas.

____ 9. The large-scale Los Angeles riots of 1992 occurred in reaction to the jury's verdict in the O. J. Simpson murder case.

____ 10. African-Americans attained considerable success in both local and national political leadership positions in the 1980s and 1990s.

____ 11. The rise of a substantial black middle class after the 1980s created a growing division between the well-off and poor within the African-American community.

____ 12. The rise of television and rock music caused a sharp decline in the number of Americans who were consumers of the "high culture" of museums and symphony orchestras.

____ 13. The 1980s and 1990s witnessed the decline of regional themes in American writing and culture.

____ 14. American playwrights and theatre audiences generally turned away from sensitive subjects like the AIDS epidemic.

____ 15. Environmental concerns and disillusionment with wealth caused some late twentieth-century Americans to advocate a "no-growth" economy for the country.

Name_____ Section_____ Date_____

B. **Multiple Choice**

Select the best answer and write the proper letter in the space provided.

____ 1. The "flagship business" of the heavy industrial economy of the *early* twentieth century was
   a. the International Business Machines Company.
   b. the Microsoft Corporation.
   c. the U.S. Steel Corporation.
   d. the General Mills Corporation.

____ 2. The primary engine driving the U.S. economy of the 1990s was
   a. scientific knowledge.
   b. corporate mergers and acquisitions.
   c. labor union activism.
   d. international investment in American companies.

____ 3. The earliest great successes of the "genetic revolution" occurred in
   a. improving the human gene pool.
   b. increasing crop yields and curing genetic diseases.
   c. providing new sources for human organ transplants.
   d. artificial insemination and human cloning.

____ 4. Compared to other countries' median incomes, Americans in the 1990s were
   a. still the wealthiest people in the world.
   b. in the middle third of the world's income levels.
   c. seeing a steady decline in their average incomes.
   d. no longer at the top but still among the world's most affluent people.

____ 5. The most striking development in the American economic structure in the 1980s and 1990s was
   a. the growing inequality between rich and poor.
   b. the slow general decline in the American standard of living.
   c. the growing reliance on investments and real estate rather than jobs for income.
   d. the increasing concentration of wealth in certain regions and affluent suburbs.

____ 6. Which of the following was *not* among the causes of the income gap in the United States?
   a. intensifying global economic competition
   b. the shrinkage in manufacturing jobs for unskilled and semi-skilled labor
   c. the decline of labor unions.
   d. the weakening family structure

____ 7. The most dramatic change in the patterns of women's employment from the 1950s to the 1990s was
   a. the end of "occupational segregation" in certain female job categories.
   b. that the majority of mothers with young children went to work outside the home.
   c. that women were unable to break through into traditional single-sex colleges and universities.
   d. that married women worked at a higher rate than single women.

8. Perhaps the most significant sign of the weakening of the traditional American family was
   a. that television no longer portrayed family situations.
   b. that a majority of children no longer lived with their birth parents.
   c. that families were increasingly slow to form at all.
   d. that the elderly were no longer likely to live with their adult children.

9. The increasingly longer lives of America's senior citizens were often eased by
   a. the ability of the potent elderly lobby to obtain government benefits for seniors.
   b. the willingness of younger generations to provide income support for aged parents.
   c. the large-scale migration of senior citizens to the West Coast.
   d. the more positive portrayals of the elderly in movies and television.

10. The deepest problem caused by federal programs like Social Security and Medicare in the twenty-first century was likely to be
    a. that benefits could not keep up with rising inflation.
    b. that the Social Security and Medicare trust funds would exercise too great a control over the economy.
    c. that the higher taxes necessary to support benefits would create a generational war with younger workers.
    d. that the health care system could no longer meet the rising demand for services to the elderly.

11. The "new immigrants" of the 1980s and 1990s came to the United States primarily because
    a. they wanted jobs and economic opportunities unavailable in their homelands.
    b. they were fleeing religious and political repression.
    c. they admired American cultural and intellectual achievements.
    d. they wanted to strengthen the minority voting bloc to the United States.

12. The largest group of the "new immigrants" came from
    a. East Asia.
    b. Mexico and other Latin American countries.
    c. Africa and the Middle East.
    d. South Asia.

13. The period between 1920 and the mid-1990s will likely be seen as a unique but passing age in American demographic history because
    a. a majority of people lived in the Northeast rather than the South and West.
    b. a majority of people were of European rather than African-Americans or Hispanic ancestry.
    c. a majority of people were the children or grandchildren of immigrants.
    d. a majority of people lived in central cities rather than in rural areas or suburbs.

14. An increasingly important development among African-Americans since the 1960s has been
    a. the growing equality of incomes within the community.
    b. the inability of African-Americans to break through into politics or the arts.
    c. the growing gap between successful affluent African-Americans and those in poverty.
    d. the concentration of nearly all African-Americans in the central cities.

___ 15. The most striking development in American literature in the past two decades has been
   a. the importance of the fantastic literature of absurdism and "black comedy."
   b. the rise of writers from once-marginal regions and ethnic groups.
   c. the focus on themes of nostalgia and lost innocence.
   d. the rise of social realism and attention to working-class stories.

C. Identification

Supply the correct identification for each numbered description.

_____ 1. The computer corporation that symbolized the U.S. economy in the 1990s much as U.S. Steel did in 1900

_____ 2. Health care program for the elderly, enacted in 1965, that created large economic demands on the American economy by the 1990s

_____ 3. Law of 1986 that granted amnesty to past illegal immigrants and penalized employers of future illegal workers

_____ 4. The largest of the "new immigrant" groups

_____ 5. Organization headed by Cesar Chavez that worked to improve conditions for migrant workers

_____ 6. City where major racial disturbance erupted in 1992

_____ 7. American region that saw a particularly rich literary revival in the 1980s and 1990s

_____ 8. Zora Neale Hurston's 1937 novel that received widespread new attention because of interest in feminist and African-American literature

_____ 9. Avant-garde painting movement pioneered by Jackson Pollock and others in the 1940s and 1950s

_____ 10. Oil tanker whose 1989 spill off the coast of Alaska sparked deep concern over oil drilling and transportation on the world's oceans

D. Matching People, Places, and Events

Match the person, place, or event in the left column with the proper description in the right column by inserting the correct letter on the blank line.

___ 1. O. J. Simpson
___ 2. L. Douglas Wilder
___ 3. Carol Mosely-Braun
___ 4. Larry McMurtry
___ 5. Norman MacLean
___ 6. August Wilson
___ 7. Toni Morrison

A. Leading Indian writer, author of *House Made of Dawn*
B. Pioneer artistic creator of "abstract expressionism" in the 1940s and 1950s
C. The first African-American state governor
D. Irish-American writer whose memoir *Angela's Ashes* revived interest in the older European immigrant groups
E. African-American writer of the 1930s whose works were rediscovered and gained popularity in the 1980s and 1990s
F. Playwright who deployed gritty American slang in socially critical dramas like *Glengarry Glen Ross*
G. Former football star whose murder trial became a focus of racial tension
H. Author of *Beloved* and winner of the Nobel Prize for Literature

___ 8. N. Scott Momaday
___ 9. David Mamet
___ 10. Zora Neale Hurston
___ 11. Jackson Pollock
___ 12. Frank McCourt

I. Western writer who portrayed small towns in *Last Picture Show* and the cattle-drive era in *Lonesome Dove*
J. First African-American woman elected to the U.S. Senate
K. African-American playwright who portrayed the psychological costs of the northern migration
L. Former English professor who wrote memorable tales of his Montana boyhood

E. **Putting Things in Order**

Put the following events in correct order by numbering them from 1 to 5.

___ F. Douglas Wilder is elected the first African-American governor.

___ Congress passes the Immigration Reform and Control Act to try to thwart illegal immigration.

___ Jackson Pollock and others pioneer "abstract expressionism" and the leading form of modern American painting.

___ Los Angeles experiences a major riot as the result of a racial incident involving police brutality.

___ California voters approve Proposition 209 in an attempt to overturn affirmative-action policies.

F. **Matching Cause and Effect**

Match the historical cause in the left column with the proper effect in the right column by writing the correct letter on the blank line.

Cause

___ 1. Decline of manufacturing jobs and higher pay for educated workers

___ 2. The computer revolution and the new trend toward "genetic engineering"

___ 3. Expanding economic opportunities for women

___ 4. Rise of the median age of the population since the 1970s

___ 5. Growing numbers and political power for Hispanic Americans

___ 6. The growth of the African-American middle class and their migration to the suburbs

___ 7. Poverty and economic upheavals in Latin America and Asia

Effect

A. Made the American southwest increasingly a "bi-cultural" zone
B. Changed both child-rearing patterns and men's social roles
C. Brought major literary prominence to minority and Western writers
D. Contributed to sharply increased income inequality in the U.S.
E. Made the elderly a powerful political force
F. Further isolated the poverty-stricken lower class in the inner cities
G. Made New York City the art capital of the world
H. Created the highest rates of immigration to the United States since the early 1900s
I. Led California voters to pass measures restricting the use of racial categories
J. Expanded the economy but threatened many traditional jobs while creating new ethical dilemmas for society

___ 8. The resentment against many affirmative action measures

___ 9. The rise of previously "marginal" ethnic groups and regions

___ 10. The success of modernist American art movements since the 1940s

PART III: Applying What You Have Learned

1. What were the consequences of the dramatically changed American economy in the 1990s? What caused the rapidly increasing gap between rich and poor in this period?
2. How did women's new economic opportunities affect American society? What barriers to women's complete economic equality proved most difficult to overcome?
3. How did the "new immigration" and the rise of ethnic minorities transform American society in the 1990s? Were the effects of the new immigration similar to that of earlier waves of immigration, or fundamentally different?
4. How were the changes in American society reflected in literature and the arts in the 1980s and 1990s?
5. What social and moral challenges seem most urgent as America enters a new millennium? How are these challenges rooted in American history, and how does understanding that history contribute to engaging these problems?

Answer Key to the Guidebook

Chapter 22

II. A.

1. True
2. False. White Southerners strongly rejected Northern political domination.
3. True
4. True
5. True
6. False. Johnson had been a poor white who opposed the planter elite.
7. True
8. False. It weakened the moderates and strengthened the radicals.
9. True
10. False. Redistribution of land was opposed by moderates and never became part of reconstruction policy.
11. False. Blacks controlled only one house of one state legislature—South Carolina.
12. True
13. False. The Klan did succeed in intimidating black voters.
14. True
15. False. The moderate plan failed to deal with the deeper economic and social aftermath of slavery.

II. B.

1. c
2. c
3. b
4. b
5. c
6. a
7. a
8. c
9. c
10. b
11. c
12. c
13. a
14. b
15. d

II. C.

1. freedmen
2. Freedmen's Bureau
3. Baptist
4. 10 percent plan
5. Thirteenth Amendment
6. Black Codes
7. Fourteenth Amendment
8. moderates
9. radicals
10. Union League
11. *Ex parte Milligan*
12. scalawags
13. carpetbaggers
14. Fifteenth Amendment
15. Alaska

II. D.

1. H
2. K
3. C
4. M
5. B
6. J
7. O
8. I
9. F
10. G
11. E
12. A
13. L
14. N
15. D

II. E.

4
1
5
3
2

II. F.

1. D
2. E
3. J
4. C
5. I
6. F
7. H
8. B
9. A
10. G

II. G.

1. Eight whites, three blacks; the white woman seated in the center; they are in the rear and partly hidden, suggesting that they might hold subordinate positions on the staff.

2. The shabby clothes of the boy and young woman; the crude log cabin dwelling. The people seem weary but hopeful: at least three of them have partial smiles.

3. The men in the line appear to be working people—perhaps farmers in their best clothes. The voting officials, black and white, appear more affluent and well-dressed. The drawing shows the new voters as somewhat hesitant and uncertain, perhaps being manipulated by the more politically knowledgeable officials.

Chapter 23

II. A.

1. False. Grant's lack of political experience hurt, and he did engage in Republican party politics.
2. True
3. False. The political mistakes of the Liberal Republicans caused them to fail.
4. True
5. False. The parties agreed on national issues; their disagreements were at the local level.
6. True
7. False. The Republicans got the presidency and the Democrats other political and economic concessions.
8. True
9. True
10. True
11. True
12. False. The campaign was based on personal mudslinging rather than issues.
13. True
14. True
15. False. Cleveland remained attached to the gold standard and failed to address the depression.

II. B.

1. c
2. c
3. b
4. b
5. a
6. d
7. c
8. a
9. a
10. b
11. d

12. b
13. b
14. a
15. d

II. C.

1. (waving the) bloody shirt
2. Credit Mobilier
3. Liberal Republican party
4. silver
5. Greenback Labor party
6. Gilded Age
7. Grand Army of the Republic
8. Stalwarts
9. Half-Breeds
10. Compromise of 1877
11. Chinese
12. civil service
13. McKinley Tariff
14. Populists (People's Party)
15. grandfather clause

II. D.

1. D
2. B
3. A
4. N
5. J
6. H
7. I
8. K
9. O
10. C
11. G
12. E
13. L
14. F
15. M

II. E.

4
1
5
3
2

II. F.

1. G
2. E
3. C
4. I
5. A
6. J
7. B
8. F
9. D
10. H

II. G.

1. The fundamental difference was in their ethnic and religious composition. The Republicans were based on morally-oriented groups with Puritan backgrounds; the Democrats on immigrant ethnic groups of Catholic or Lutheran background.
2. Most of the controversial issues existed at the state or local level.
3. The two parties each had well-mobilized machines that got out the vote no matter who the candidates were.
4. Winning elections was crucial for patronage—passing out jobs to party supporters.

II. H.

1. none
2. Connecticut, New Jersey, New York, and Indiana
3. four
4. Texas

5. none

Chapter 24

II. A.

1. False. The railroads received subsidies and land grants to build the rail lines.
2. True
3. True
4. False. Railroads were often unfair and corrupt in their dealings with shippers, the government, and the public.
5. True
6. False. The description applies to Carnegie's technique of "vertical integration." Rockefeller's "horizontal integration" meant consolidating with competitors in the same market.
7. True
8. True
9. False. The South remained poor and dependent, despite the "new South."
10. True
11. False. Industrialization gave the wage earner less control and status.
12. True
13. True
14. True
15. False. The AFL did not even attempt to organize these categories of workers.

II. B.

1. b
2. d
3. b
4. d
5. c
6. c
7. c
8. d
9. d
10. b
11. b
12. d
13. a
14. c
15. b

II. C.

1. land grants
2. Union Pacific Railroad
3. Central Pacific Railroad
4. Great Northern Railroad
5. stock watering
6. *Wabash* case
7. Interstate Commerce Commission
8. telephone
9. Standard Oil Company
10. United States Steel Corporation
11. New South
12. Colored National Labor Union
13. Knights of Labor
14. craft unions
15. American Federation of Labor (or AF of L)

II. D.

1. J
2. H
3. M
4. G
5. F
6. O
7. A
8. I
9. E
10. B
11. D
12. L
13. N

14. C
15. K

II. E.
5
4
3
2
1

II. F.
1. I
2. D
3. E
4. H
5. A
6. B
7. J
8. F
9. G
10. C

II. G.
1. The family of "pieceworkers" are in their own home; each concentrates on their own single tasks, but they are able to relate to one another and perhaps offer advice and assistance around the table. The black textile workers are at separate posts, but the women and children can also probably converse and assist one another. In both these two cases the children and adult workers are mingled and performing the same tasks. By contrast, the adult male Westinghouse workers are dwarfed by their industrial machinery and serve its demands. In the final photo, the child textile workers are by themselves and almost encased by the machines. They are evidently without adult assistance or supervision, and plainly in danger of industrial accident.

2. The scene takes place in front of the owner's house. The men have evidently come directly from the factory. There appears to have been some conflict over wages or working conditions.

3. The owner and the woman—evidently his wife—are very well dressed. The workers, and worker's family on the left, are shabbily dressed. The painting illustrates the considerable class difference between the owner and his immigrant work force.

4. The workers are conversing with the owner and his wife, and also with one another. The first conversation is probably about the grievance. The second may be about what the workers should do next—whether to strike or resort to violence (as the one worker seems about to do).

5. The presence of women and children points out that factory conditions affected families as well as employees. The woman at the center is probably the owner's wife. Her fine dress and vigorous manner is contrasted with the poverty and passive condition of the worker's wife.

Chapter 25

II. A.
1. True
2. False. They came from southern and eastern Europe.
3. False. Most were originally peasants driven from the countryside.
4. True
5. True
6. True
7. False. Darwinian science weakened the churches and religious belief.
8. False. Secondary education was increasingly carried out in public schools.
9. False. Washington advocated economic equality but not social equality.
10. True
11. True

12. False. They favored social realism in their fiction.
13. True
14. True
15. True

II. B.

1. c
2. c
3. c
4. c
5. a
6. b
7. d
8. d
9. c
10. b
11. d
12. b
13. a
14. a
15. d

II. C.

1. dumbbell tenement
2. New Immigration
3. birds of passage
4. social gospel
5. Hull House
6. social work
7. American Protective Association
8. Roman Catholicism
9. Tuskegee Institute
10. National Association for the Advancement of Colored People (or NAACP) (Niagara Movement less preferable but OK)
11. *Progress and Poverty*
12. Comstock Law
13. *Women and Economics*
14. National American Women's Suffrage Association (or NAWSA)
15. Women's Christian Temperance Union (or WCTU)

II. D.

1. M
2. E
3. J
4. N
5. D
6. F
7. L
8. G
9. A
10. O
11. B
12. H
13. K
14. I
15. C

II. E.

4
2
3
5
1

II. F.

1. G
2. B
3. E
4. I
5. H
6. C
7. F
8. A

9. J
10. D

II. G.

1. five peaks: end of Civil War, anti-Jewish pogroms, early twentieth-century prosperity, the end of World War I, and the end of World War II and the quota system

    four valleys: Panic of 1873, Panic of 1893, World War I, and the introduction of quotas

2. Each major period lasted 15–20 years. The most recent growth period has lasted for 40 years.
3. sharpest rise: 1900–1905; sharpest decline: 1915–1920
4. 800,000: approximately 1882, 1910, 1923

    200,000: about 1867, 1875, 1880, 1898–99, 1917, 1932, 1948–49
5. about a million fewer (1.2 million to 200,000)

    about 350,000 to 400,000 more (about 225,000 to 600,000)

Chapter 26

II. A.

1. True
2. False. The Indians were defeated only slowly and with difficulty.
3. True
4. False. Humanitarian reformers did not respect the Indians' culture and tried to destroy their tribal way of life.
5. True
6. True
7. False. More families acquired land from the states and private owners than from the federal government under the Homestead Act.
8. True
9. True
10. False. The greatest problem was declining prices for their crops.
11. True
12. True
13. False. Hanna had no difficulty raising large sums of money for McKinley's campaign.
14. True
15. True

II. B.

1. d
2. c
3. a
4. c
5. b
6. b
7. d
8. c
9. c
10. b
11. d
12. b
13. a
14. a
15. b

II. C.

1. Sioux
2. Apaches
3. reservations
4. Ghost Dance
5. Dawes Severalty Act
6. Comstock Lode
7. long drive
8. Homestead Act
9. barbed wire
10. Oklahoma
11. Populists (People's Party)
12. Coin's Financial School
13. Pullman strike

14. Cross of Gold speech
15. "goldbugs"

II. D.
1. H
2. J
3. E
4. B
5. G
6. I
7. F
8. C
9. K
10. D
11. L
12. A

II. E.
3
5
2
1
4

II. F.
1. J
2. E
3. I
4. D
5. H
6. C
7. G
8. B
9. A
10. F

II. G.
1. All six (Kansas, Nebraska, Colorado, Wyoming, Nevada, Idaho) were carried by Bryan.
2. Any six of the following: New Jersey, Delaware, Maryland, Pennsylvania, West Virginia, Kentucky, Ohio, Indiana, Illinois, Wisconsin, California. Most were in the Midwest or Middle Atlantic region.
3. Republican: any five of the following: Maine, Vermont, New Hampshire, Connecticut, New York, Michigan, Iowa, Minnesota, South Dakota, North Dakota, Washington.

   Democratic: any five of the southern states, plus Missouri.
4. Three went Republican (North Dakota, South Dakota, and Oregon); six went Democratic (Nebraska, Kansas, Colorado, Idaho, Wyoming, Nevada).

II. H.
1. Montana, Washington, and California
2. Texas, North Carolina, Oklahoma, and Georgia
3. Thirty-seven
4. none

Chapter 27

II. A.
1. False. America was unconcerned and isolated from international affairs.
2. False. He argued that control of the sea was the key to history.
3. False. It nearly resulted in war with Britain.
4. False. It was resolved when Britain backed down because of its conflict with Germany.
5. True
6. True

7. False. The Hearst press promoted war with Spain.
8. False. Business and Wall Street opposed war; the pressure came from the public and the press.
9. True
10. True
11. False. It was inefficient but cost few battlefield casualties.
12. True
13. False. It was approved by a narrow margin—one vote.
14. False. It ruled that these constitutional rights did not apply.
15. True

II. B.

1. b
2. c
3. d
4. a
5. c
6. c
7. b
8. b
9. b
10. d
11. a
12. b
13. c
14. a
15. d

II. C.

1. *Our Country*
2. Samoan Islands
3. Chile
4. Monroe Doctrine
5. Pearl Harbor

6. yellow press or yellow journalism
7. *Maine*
8. Teller Amendment
9. Manila Bay
10. Rough Riders
11. Puerto Rico
12. Anti-Imperialist League
13. insular cases
14. Platt Amendment
15. yellow fever

II. D.

1. J
2. F
3. K
4. D
5. N
6. C
7. H
8. L
9. G
10. A
11. O
12. E
13. B
14. M
15. I

II. E.

1
3
2
5
4

II. F.

1. F
2. C

3. E
4. G
5. B
6. D
7. A
8. I
9. J
10. H

II. G.

1. Great Britain
2. (a) Pago Pago Harbor; (b) Pearl Harbor
3. Luzon
4. San Juan Hill
5. Puerto Rico

Chapter 28

II. A.

1. True
2. False. Foreign intervention in China continued, and the notes were not the reason partition was prevented.
3. True
4. False. Roosevelt believed in active international involvements for the United States and the presidency.
5. True
6. False. A canal could have been built through Nicaragua.
7. True
8. False. It earned the hostility of both Russia and Japan.
9. True
10. True

II. B.

1. c
2. c
3. b
4. d
5. a
6. c
7. b
8. b
9. d
10. b
11. c
12. b
13. c
14. b
15. b

II. C.

1. Open Door
2. Boxer Rebellion
3. big stick
4. Hay-Pauncefote Treaty
5. Colombia
6. Hay-Bunau-Varilla Treaty
7. Roosevelt Corollary (to the Monroe Doctrine)
8. Russo-Japanese War
9. "Gentlemen's Agreement"
10. Great White Fleet

II. D.

1. G
2. D
3. J
4. H
5. F
6. I
7. A
8. E
9. C
10. B

II. E.

4
1
2
5
3

II. F.

1. E
2. A
3. H
4. C
5. F
6. I
7. G
8. J
9. D
10. B

II. G.

Any three of the details in each section acceptable:

1. *Little Brown Brothers*: The Filipinos revolted against American rule; the war turned into a brutal guerrilla conflict; water torture and concentration camps were used; the Filipinos continued to resent American control. (other answers possible)

2. *TR*: Roosevelt published books by age twenty-four; he was athletic and could shake thousands of hands and ride horseback many miles; he loved people and mingled with all ranks; he was a showman who was always front-page copy; he condemned the courts and law as too slow. (other answers possible)

3. *Uncle Sam*: American naval forces prevented Colombia from putting down the uprising; Roosevelt recognized Panama three days after the revolt; Washington immediately signed a Canal treaty with Panama; the conspirators knew of Roosevelt's sympathies and counted on his support. (other answers possible)

4. *Monroe Doctrine*: The U.S. intervened in the Dominican customs collection in 1905; the Corollary led to repeated landing of American marines; Latin Americans came to curse the Monroe Doctrine; the U.S. intervened in Cuba in 1906. (other answers possible)

5. *Roosevelt on World Stage*: Japanese officials asked Roosevelt to end the war; both sides presented outrageous demands; Roosevelt blustered them both into a compromise; Roosevelt received the Nobel Prize; Russia accused Roosevelt of robbing them of military victory; Japan felt robbed of its indemnity. (other answers possible)

Chapter 29

II. A.

1. False. Progressives favored the growth of government power over the economy and society.
2. True
3. False. The progressives arose mostly from the middle class.
4. True
5. False. He threatened the owners with federal intervention, saying he would seize their mines.
6. True
7. False. He believed that there were "good trusts" and "bad trusts," and that only the bad trusts should be broken up.
8. False. It was intended to focus attention on the plight of the meat-packing workers.
9. True
10. True
11. True
12. False. Dollar diplomacy failed and resulted in little American business investment.
13. False. Progressives grew angry over his tariff and conservation policies
14. True
15. True

II. B.

1. c
2. a
3. c
4. c
5. d
6. b
7. a
8. c
9. b
10. a
11. d
12. a
13. a
14. c
15. c

II. C.

1. progressivism
2. muckrakers
3. initiative
4. recall
5. Square Deal
6. Hepburn Act
7. Triangle Shirtwaist Fire
8. *The Jungle*
9. Women's Christian Temperance Union
10. Roosevelt panic (Panic of 1907)
11. dollar diplomacy
12. Standard Oil Company

II. D.

1. E
2. I
3. F
4. K
5. D
6. C
7. H
8. J
9. B
10. A
11. L
12. G

II. E.

5
1
4
2
3

II. F.

1. I
2. B
3. G
4. C
5. J
6. D
7. A
8. F
9. H
10. E

II. G.

1. D
2. B
3. A
4. B
5. A
6. C
7. C
8. A
9. B
10. B
11. D

12. B

Chapter 30

II. A.

1. True
2. False. Wilson's "New Freedom" favored small enterprise and antitrust activities; Roosevelt's "New Nationalism" favored federal regulation and social activism.
3. True
4. True
5. False. Wilson's policies were unfavorable to blacks.
6. True
7. False. Wilson sent troops to Haiti and Santo Domingo.
8. True
9. True
10. False. It was sent in response to Villa's raids into New Mexico and the killing of United States citizens.
11. False. Most Americans sympathized with Britain from the beginning.
12. True
13. False. The East was ready to go to war; the Midwest and West favored attempts at negotiation.
14. True
15. True

II. B.

1. c
2. b
3. c
4. b
5. d
6. a
7. b
8. c
9. b
10. a
11. c
12. d
13. c
14. d
15. d

II. C.

1. bull moose
2. Socialist Party
3. New Freedom
4. Federal Reserve Board
5. Federal Trade Commission
6. Clayton Anti-Trust Act
7. Railway Labor Act
8. Haiti
9. ABC Powers
10. Central Powers
11. Allies
12. submarine
13. *Lusitania*
14. *Sussex* pledge
15. California

II. D.

1. H
2. K
3. L
4. I
5. D
6. O
7. M
8. C
9. B
10. G
11. F
12. A
13. N
14. J
15. E

Answer Key to the Guidebook   A 15

II. E.

5
2
1
4
3

II. F.

1. D
2. B
3. I
4. E
5. J
6. G
7. H
8. A
9. F
10. C

II. G.

1. German policy was that they would not *try* to sink neutral shipping, but they warned that mistakes might occur.
2. America was an important neutral, and Germany had no reason to want American civilians to be killed. The warning could be used to take the burden of responsibility off Germany and put it on those passengers who chose to travel anyway.
3. Germany knew that the *Lusitania* was in fact carrying 4200 cases of ammunition.
4. America claimed a complete right of neutral and unarmed civilian travel on the high seas. Issuing a warning did nothing to affect that.

Chapter 31

II. A.

1. False. Germany responded by resuming unrestricted submarine warfare.
2. True
3. True
4. True
5. False. The primary targets were antiwar Socialists and members of the Industrial Workers of the World (IWWs).
6. True
7. True
8. True
9. False. It signaled political suffrage but not economic advance.
10. True
11. True
12. False. His poor handling of the Republican opposition weakened his hand in Paris.
13. True
14. True
15. False. Cox supported the League, while Harding tried to evade the issue.

II. B.

1. b
2. c
3. c
4. b
5. d
6. a
7. a
8. b
9. a
10. b
11. c
12. a
13. b
14. d
15. b

II. C.

1. "peace without victory"
2. Zimmerman note
3. Fourteen Points

4. Committee on Public Information (CPI)
5. Industrial Workers of the World (IWWs)
6. War Industries Board
7. Nineteenth Amendment (Women's Suffrage Amendment OK)
8. Liberty Loans
9. Big Four
10. League of Nations
11. Treaty of Versailles
12. Foreign Relations Committee
13. irreconcilables
14. Lodge reservations
15. "solemn referendum"

II. D.

1. E
2. O
3. N
4. H
5. K
6. I
7. C
8. G
9. A
10. M
11. D
12. B
13. J
14. L
15. F

II. E.

2
5
1
3
4

II. F.

1. E
2. H
3. G
4. J
5. A
6. C
7. F
8. I
9. D
10. B

II. G.

1. The message to "Remember Belgium" is reinforced by the cruel, mustached German soldier dragging away a young girl, who is a kind of personification of Belgium and Belgians; he may even be intending to assault her. In general, the image of Germany as a militaristic violator of the innocent reinforces that America is fighting a righteous war to restore virtue, justice, and liberty (hence "liberty loans") where they have been violated.

2. The German brute is charging directly at the viewer and trampling on America. The way to "destroy this mad brute" is to "Enlist" in the Army. The fight is for civilization against violence and barbarism.

3. It portrays the garden vegetables going "over the top," just as soldiers did; the caption suggests that food will produce not only an Allied victory but peace as well.

4. The point is that all American young men must back the war either by working in military industries or by being drafted into the army. Both are necessary, but Uncle Sam is plainly demanding that young men do one or the other. The draft is a tough necessity, something the nation (Uncle Sam) has to thrust on its youth.

Chapter 32

II. A.

1. False. It resulted in attacks on alleged communists and radicals inside the United States.
2. True
3. False. It was strongest in the Midwest and South.
4. True
5. True
6. False. Scopes was found guilty, and the law was upheld.
7. True
8. True
9. True
10. False. They emphasized entertainment and commercial advertising from the beginning.
11. False. The decade saw a further loosening of sexual behavior, especially by women.
12. True
13. False. It was Harlem, New York.
14. False. They attacked small-town values and reflected the most critical values of the cities.
15. True

II. B.

1. c
2. a
3. b
4. d
5. a
6. c
7. c
8. d
9. b
10. a
11. b
12. d
13. b
14. a
15. d

II. C.

1. red scare
2. Ku Klux Klan
3. Immigration Act of 1924
4. Eighteenth Amendment (Prohibition or Prohibition Amendment OK)
5. Bible Belt
6. Scopes trial ("monkey trial")
7. advertising (credit or installment buying OK)
8. Model T
9. airplane
10. radio
11. birth control
12. jazz
13. Universal Negro Improvement Association (UNIA)
14. *American Mercury*
15. stock market

II. D.

1. E
2. C
3. G
4. L
5. H
6. D
7. J
8. A
9. M
10. O
11. K
12. F
13. N
14. B
15. I

II. E.

4
1
5
2
3

II. F.

1. C
2. A
3. J
4. E
5. F
6. I
7. B
8. H
9. D
10. G

II. G.

1. Hollywood's movies, like Henry Ford's cars, were mass-produced consumer products created by industry.
2. New products helped free women from the home and from their traditional roles.
3. Fitzgerald's novel idealized the moral and sexual liberation of youth from the past, and suggested that personal freedom and pleasure were goals of the new affluent American society.
4. These writers all endorsed new moral and social values at odds with those of the American past. Before the 1920s most Americans lived on farms or in small towns, and such values were widely shared. Now there was an audience ready to hear what such writers were saying.

Chapter 33

II. A.

1. False. The corrupt cabinet officers were the secretary of the interior and the attorney general (Fall and Doherty).
2. False. The antitrust laws were generally not enforced.
3. False. They pursued disarmament policies and reduced military spending.
4. True
5. True
6. True
7. False. The main source of La Follette's support was farmers.
8. True
9. True
10. True
11. False. The Hawley-Smoot Tariff represented a policy of economic isolationism and helped undercut international trade.
12. True
13. True
14. False. He modified his policies somewhat and provided some federal funds for relief and recovery.
15. True

II. B.

1. d
2. a
3. b
4. c
5. c
6. d
7. b
8. b
9. b
10. a
11. a
12. d

13. a
14. c
15. c

II. C.

1. Ohio Gang
2. *Adkins* v. *Children's Hospital*
3. American Legion
4. Five-Power Naval Treaty
5. Kellogg-Briand Pact
6. Teapot Dome
7. McNary-Haugen Bill
8. Dawes plan
9. Hoovercrats
10. Hawley-Smoot Tariff
11. Black Tuesday
12. Hoovervilles
13. Reconstruction Finance Corporation
14. Bonus Army (Bonus Expeditionary Force)
15. Manchuria

II. D.

1. I
2. G
3. H
4. M
5. E
6. D
7. F
8. O
9. L
10. K
11. C
12. A
13. B
14. N
15. J

II. E.

5
2
1
4
3

II. F.

1. B
2. E
3. I
4. F
5. D
6. J
7. A
8. C
9. G
10. H

II. G.

1. Americans were private investors in Germany. America also collected allied war debts from France and Britain.
2. France and Britain collected war reparations from Germany.
3. Britain and France both owed war debts to the U.S.
4. Credit from U.S. bankers was the only thing that enabled the whole international financial system to function. When Wall Street collapsed in 1929, Europe and the whole financial system collapsed with it.

Chapter 34

II. A.

1. True
2. False. The economy was turning downward.
3. True

4. False. FDR took the United States off the gold standard and devalued the dollar.
5. False. They were designed for relief.
6. True
7. False. It was excessive farm production, causing falling prices.
8. True
9. False. It was also designed to provide jobs, electricity, and low-income housing to residents of the area.
10. True
11. True
12. False. The Supreme Court "switched" and began approving New Deal measures.
13. True
14. True
15. False. Unemployment remained high despite the New Deal.

II. B.

1. c
2. a
3. b
4. b
5. d
6. a
7. d
8. c
9. b
10. a
11. d
12. b
13. d
14. a
15. c

II. C.

1. New Deal
2. brain(s) trust
3. Hundred Days
4. Civilian Conservation Corps
5. Works Progress Administration (WPA)
6. blue eagle
7. Agricultural Adjustment Administration (AAA)
8. Dust Bowl
9. Tennessee Valley Authority (TVA)
10. Social Security
11. Committee for Industrial Organization (CIO) (Congress of Industrial Organizations OK)
12. Securities and Exchange Commission (SEC)
13. American Liberty League
14. court packing plan
15. Hatch Act

II. D.

1. G
2. E
3. L
4. J
5. B
6. F
7. N
8. K
9. C
10. O
11. H
12. A
13. I
14. M
15. D

II. E.

2
1
4
5

3

II. F.

1. E
2. I
3. G
4. A
5. F
6. B
7. J
8. H
9. C
10. D

II. G.

1. National Recovery Administration (NRA)
2. FDR closes banks, Emergency Banking Relief Act.
   FDR orders gold surrender and abandons gold standard.
   Gold-payment clause repealed. (any three)
3. Securities Exchange Commission, Social Security Act, Public Utilities Holding Company Act
4. National Housing Act creating the FHA.
5. Second Agricultural Adjustment Act
6. The Hundred Days was aimed primarily at recovery, the later New Deal at relief and reform. The most continuity was seen in measures aimed at relief.

II. H.

1. Tennessee, Alabama, North Carolina, Virginia
2. (a) five (b) three
3. 1920
4. 8 million

Chapter 35

II. A.

1. False. It showed that he put domestic recovery ahead of establishing a stable international economic order.
2. True
3. True
4. True
5. False. The United States adhered to its neutrality laws and refused to help the Loyalist government.
6. False. The United States reacted mildly to the Japanese attack.
7. False. The United States did not object to the appeasement policy, and in effect endorsed it.
8. True
9. False. It strengthened the movement to give aid to Britain.
10. True
11. False. Willkie agreed with Roosevelt's pro-British stance and did not attack him on foreign policy.
12. True
13. False. It was an agreement between Britain and the United States only.
14. True
15. False. The point of conflict was Japan's refusal to withdraw from China.

II. B.

1. a
2. c
3. b
4. d
5. b
6. d
7. c
8. d
9. a

10. b
11. d
12. b
13. a
14. c
15. c

II. C.

1. London Conference
2. Philippines
3. Good Neighbor policy
4. Neutrality Acts
5. Spanish Civil War
6. Quarantine Speech
7. Munich
8. appeasement
9. Committee to Defend America by Aiding the Allies
10. America First
11. lend-lease
12. Soviet Union
13. Atlantic Charter
14. *Reuben James*
15. Pearl Harbor

II. D.

1. L
2. E
3. K
4. F
5. O
6. C
7. J
8. N
9. G
10. B
11. D
12. A

13. M
14. I
15. H

II. E.

1
2
5
4
3

II. F.

1. G
2. C
3. I
4. H
5. B
6. F
7. D
8. J
9. E
10. A

II. G.

Order	Context
4	4
6	7
1	2
2	3
7	1
5	5
3	6

II. H

1. 41
2. 41
3. Europe
4. Soviet Union

Chapter 36

II. A.

1. False. The decision was to fight Hitler first and then Japan.
2. False. Americans nearly all supported World War II.
3. True
4. True
5. True
6. False. Most women left the labor force after the war.
7. False. Americans enjoyed economic prosperity during World War II.
8. False. The battles of the Coral Sea and Midway enabled the United States to block Japanese domination of the Pacific sea-lanes.
9. False. The plan was to "island-hop" directly toward Japan.
10. False. The Soviet Union bore the heaviest burden of the ground fighting.
11. True
12. True
13. False. It was conservative Democrats who dumped Wallace for Truman.
14. False. He died a few weeks before Germany surrendered, but four months before Japan's surrender.
15. True

II. B.

1. c
2. b
3. a
4. c
5. a
6. a
7. d
8. c
9. d
10. d
11. c
12. b
13. b
14. d
15. a

II. C.

1. Japanese-Americans
2. War Production Board
3. WAACS and WAVES
4. *braceros*
5. "Rosie the Riveter"
6. Fair Employment Practices Commission (FEPC)
7. Philippines
8. Battle of Midway
9. Unconditional Surrender
10. Casablanca
11. Teheran
12. D-Day
13. Battle of the Bulge
14. Iwo Jima and Okinawa
15. atomic bomb

II. D.

1. F
2. I
3. N
4. E
5. O
6. G
7. J
8. A
9. K
10. D
11. M
12. C
13. H
14. L

15. B

II. E.

3
4
1
2

II. F.

1. I
2. H
3. C
4. E
5. G
6. B
7. D
8. A
9. F
10. J

II. G.

1. (a) Russians: Leningrad and Stalingrad
   (b) Americans and British: Tunisia, North Africa
2. driving the Germans out of Russia
3. in Poland
4. about ten months (July 1944 to May 1945)
5. southern Germany (Austria). The British and Americans were coming from Italy and France, the Russians from Hungary.

II. H.

1. 116,000
2. 7
3. Detroit and New York
4. India and Australia
5. Tunisia
6. Poland, Hungary, and Romania

7. France, Netherlands, and Belgium
8. Elbe

Chapter 37

II. A.

1. False. The economy struggled from 1945 to 1950, and only began to grow dramatically after 1950.
2. True
3. False. Unions declined by the 1950s.
4. False. The Sunbelt relied more than the North on federal spending.
5. True
6. True
7. False. Truman had little experience or confidence.
8. False. The Soviets and Americans had a common enemy, but little mutual trust.
9. False. The reverse is true; the Western Allies wanted a united Germany, while the Soviets endorsed a separate East Germany.
10. False. The threat was to Greece and Turkey.
11. False. It was developed in response to the economic weakness and threat of domestic communism in Western Europe.
12. False. The fundamental purpose of NATO was to defend Europe against the Soviets.
13. True
14. False. Truman defeated Dewey despite splits in his own Democratic party.
15. True

II. B.

1. a
2. d
3. b
4. d
5. d
6. a

7. c
8. b
9. b
10. d
11. a
12. c
13. a
14. d
15. d

II. C.

1. GI Bill of Rights
2. Sunbelt
3. Levittown
4. baby boom
5. Yalta
6. Cold War
7. Bretton Woods
8. United Nations
9. iron curtain
10. Marshall Plan
11. North Atlantic Treaty Organization (NATO)
12. Nationalists
13. NSC-68
14. House Un-American Activities Committee
15. 38th parallel

II. D.

1. B
2. A
3. K
4. M
5. D
6. O
7. L
8. E
9. J
10. H
11. C
12. I
13. G
14. N
15. F

II. E.

2
4
1
3
5

II. F.

1. A
2. E
3. B
4. H
5. J
6. G
7. C
8. D
9. I
10. F

II. G.

1. 1970
2. 1980
   1980–1990
3. 1950–1960: +20%
   1970–1980: –20%
   1980–1990: +5%
   1990–1999: –10%

II. H.

1. France
2. British
3. Austria and Czechoslovakia

4. below
5. U.S.S.R.
6. South Korea

Chapter 38

II. A.

1. False. He presented himself as a nonpartisan president above narrow political battles.
2. True
3. True
4. False. It held that segregation was inherently unequal, overturning the old "separate but equal" doctrine of *Plessy* v. *Ferguson*.
5. False. Eisenhower refrained from using his personal or presidential influence on behalf of the civil rights movement.
6. False. Eisenhower controlled military spending by reliance on nuclear forces.
7. False. Eisenhower did not try to repeal the New Deal laws, even though he disliked many of them.
8. True
9. False. Eisenhower refused to send American troops to aid the French in 1954.
10. True
11. True
12. True
13. True
14. False. It was aimed primarily at suburban middle class women not working outside the home.
15. True

II. B.

1. b
2. a
3. d
4. d
5. c
6. a
7. b
8. d
9. a
10. b
11. c
12. b
13. c
14. c
15. b

II. C.

1. McCarthyism
2. *Brown* v. *Board of Education*
3. massive retaliation
4. SEATO or Southeast Asia Treaty Organization
5. Suez Canal
6. *Sputnik*
7. International Business Machines (IBM)
8. U-2
9. Cuba
10. *The Feminine Mystique*

II. D.

1. G
2. K
3. O
4. F
5. L
6. B
7. M
8. A
9. H
10. N
11. D
12. J
13. C

14. E
15. I

II. E.

3
5
1
4
2

II. F.

1. F
2. A
3. G
4. E
5. C
6. J
7. B
8. H
9. D
10. I

II. G.

1. Missouri
2. Virginia, Florida, Tennessee
3. Texas and Louisiana
4. ten: Nevada: 3, Hawaii: 3, New Mexico: 4
5. 60

Chapter 39

II. A.

1. True
2. False. It was applied mostly to struggles with communism in the underdeveloped world—Asia and Latin America.
3. False. The coup brought military dictatorships and political instability.
4. True
5. True
6. False. It was the civil rights movement that encouraged Kennedy to become more outspoken.
7. False. Johnson won in every part of the country except the traditionally Democratic Deep South.
8. False. The Gulf of Tonkin Resolution gave the president a blank check for the whole war in Vietnam.
9. False. The Great Society authorized deficit spending and gave more power to the federal government.
10. True
11. False. Most of the riots were in the North, which showed that race was a national and not just a southern problem.
12. True
13. True
14. False. The Catholic Church also underwent major change and upheaval.
15. True

II. B.

1. c
2. c
3. a
4. b
5. c
6. a
7. c
8. b
9. d
10. a
11. c
12. d
13. b
14. b
15. d

II. C.
1. Peace Corps
2. Berlin Wall
3. Special Forces or Green Berets
4. Alliance for Progress
5. Bay of Pigs
6. Cuban missile crisis
7. sit-in
8. Great Society
9. Gulf of Tonkin Resolution
10. Voting Rights Act of 1965
11. Black Power
12. Tet
13. Free Speech Movement
14. Students for a Democratic Society (SDS)
15. Stonewall Inn raid

II. D.
1. J
2. B
3. L
4. H
5. O
6. N
7. A
8. E
9. G
10. F
11. C
12. D
13. K
14. I
15. M

II. E.
3
1
2
4
5

II. F.
1. C
2. H
3. E
4. G
5. D
6. I
7. B
8. J
9. A
10. F

II. G.
1. 1974 (1973 or 1975 are acceptable answers)
2. 1973, 1978
3. From about 1974 to 1976. The difference would be explained by a rise in the total U.S. population.
4. 1980

II. H.
1. Laos and Cambodia
2. five
3. Vermont, New Hampshire, New Jersey, and Delaware
4. Michigan, Minnesota, Washington, Texas, and Hawaii

Chapter 40

II. A.
1. False. It sought to transfer the burden of the war to the South Vietnamese while Americans withdrew.
2. True
3. True
4. True
5. False. He supported new social security and environmental laws.
6. False. The basic issue was Vietnam.

Answer Key to the Guidebook   A 29

7. True
8. True
9. False. It led to the War Powers Act, which put congressional restraints on presidential authority to take military action.
10. True
11. False. Conservative Republicans joined in calling for Nixon's resignation.
12. False. The attack on the *Mayaguez* came after the Communist victory in Vietnam, which the United States did not attempt to stop.
13. True
14. False. The Camp David agreement brought peace between Egypt and Israel but did nothing to alleviate American energy and economic difficulties.
15. True

II. B.

1. d
2. a
3. c
4. d
5. a
6. c
7. b
8. c
9. c
10. b
11. b
12. d
13. d
14. c
15. d

II. C.

1. Vietnamization
2. Kent State
3. Pentagon Papers
4. ABM (Anti–Ballistic Missile) Treaty
5. southern strategy
6. Philadelphia Plan
7. Watergate
8. War Powers Act
9. oil embargo
10. detente
11. Helsinki accords
12. Equal Rights Amendment (ERA)
13. *Roe* v. *Wade*
14. Alcatraz (Island) and Wounded Knee (South Dakota)
15. Title IX

II. D.

1. L
2. D
3. H
4. K
5. E
6. C
7. I
8. N
9. B
10. M
11. J
12. F
13. G
14. O
15. A

II. E.

6
4
2
1
3
5

II. F.

1. C
2. G
3. H
4. D
5. F
6. A
7. J
8. I
9. B
10. E

II. G.

1. Nixon's diplomacy involved a delicate and dangerous effort to deal with both the communist powers. His balance bar is a head of wheat—showing his use of American grain sales as a key to his diplomatic effort.
2. Nixon's career as a tough "law and order" anti-crime politician is satirized. The attempt to "cover up" the Watergate crimes is not very successful, since the burglar's tools and tapes are plainly visible.
3. The cartoon suggests that Nixon was really behind the "Ford mask." Both cartoons portray Nixon as deceptive.
4. Nixon is portrayed as only one of the long line of presidents involved in Vietnam.

Chapter 41

II. A.

1. True
2. False. *Bakke* outlawed quotas, but permitted race to be considered as one factor in admissions.
3. False. Reagan kept his conservative promises.
4. False. Reagan's supply-side economic policies did not bog down, and actually broke the stalemate in Congress.
5. False. The reverse is true: Reaganomics lowered inflation and created economic growth but raised interest rates and caused budget deficits.
6. True
7. True
8. True
9. True
10. True
11. False. Clinton sought to reverse past Democratic positions on economic policy, not civil rights.
12. True
13. True
14. False. Clinton largely offered more moderate versions of those same policies..
15. True

II. B.

1. a
2. b
3. a
4. a
5. b
6. b
7. d
8. a
9. a
10. b
11. b
12. c
13. a
14. c
15. c

II. C.

1. new right
2. Moral Majority
3. supply-side economics

4. Sagebrush Rebellion
5. boll weevils
6. Solidarity
7. Sandinistas
8. Star Wars
9. Berlin Wall
10. Kuwait
11. Contract with America
12. World Trade Organization (WTO)
13. Whitewater (Land Corporation)
14. Columbine High School
15. Green Party

II. D.
1. G
2. K
3. O
4. N
5. F
6. C
7. L
8. H
9. E
10. B
11. D
12. I
13. A
14. J
15. M

II. E.
1
3
6
2
5
4

II. F.
1. I
2. E
3. G
4. A
5. C
6. J
7. B
8. F
9. H
10. D
11. O
12. K
13. L
14. M
15. N

II. G.
1. 1983
2. two years (1985 to 1987)
3. any three of the following:
   - 1981 Iran releases American hostages
   - 1983 U.S. marines killed in Lebanon
   - 1986 U.S. bombing raid on Libya
     Iran-contra scandal revealed
   - 1987 U.S. naval escorts begin in Persian Gulf
4. any three of the following:
   - 1985 U.S.-Soviet arms-control talks resume
     Mikhail Gorbachev comes to power in the Soviet Union
     First Reagan-Gorbachev summit meeting, in Geneva
   - 1986 Second Reagan-Gorbachev summit meeting, in Reykjavik, Iceland
   - 1987 Third Reagan-Gorbachev summit meeting in Washington, D.C.; INF Treaty signed
   - 1988 Fourth Reagan-Gorbachev summit meeting, in Moscow
   - 1989 Eastern Europe throws off communist regimes
5. seven

Chapter 42

II. A.

1. True
2. False. The U.S. fell behind several other nations in per capita income.
3. True
4. False. A majority of mothers worked outside the home.
5. False. The elderly improved their relative economic condition through programs like Social Security and Medicare.
6. True
7. False. The fastest-growing minority was Asian-Americans.
8. True
9. False. They were in reaction to an earlier police beating of a suspect.
10. True
11. True
12. False. Both popular culture and "high culture" enjoyed expanded audiences
13. False. Regionalism enjoyed a strong revival in the period.
14. False. Drama often treated sensitive subjects like AIDS.
15. True

II. B.

1. c
2. a
3. b
4. d
5. a
6. d
7. b
8. c
9. a
10. c
11. a
12. b
13. d
14. c
15. b

II. C.

1. Microsoft Corporation
2. Medicare
3. Immigration Reform and Control Act
4. Hispanics (Latin Americans or Mexican Americans OK)
5. United Farm Workers
6. Los Angeles
7. the West (Northwest or Pacific Northwest OK)
8. *Their Eyes Were Watching God*
9. Abstract expressionism
10. *Exxon Valdez*

II. D.

1. G
2. C
3. J
4. I
5. L
6. K
7. H
8. A
9. F
10. E
11. B
12. D

II. E.

2
3
1
4
5

II. F.

1. D
2. J
3. B
4. E
5. A
6. F
7. H
8. I
9. C
10. G